Praise for Kenneth R. Timmerman's
Dark Forces: The Truth About What Happened in Benghazi

"As the father of Navy SEAL Ty Woods, who died while defending the U.S. compounds in Benghazi on September 11, 2012, I highly recommend this book."
— **Charles Woods**

"Benghazi will go down as the greatest government cover-up in history - bigger than the Pentagon Papers, Iran-Contra, and Watergate. Ken Timmerman's investigation exposes the dark underbelly of this scandal."
— **Senator Jim Inhofe (R, OK)**

"Ken Timmerman's suberbly researched *Dark Forces* is a brilliant expose of what actually happened in Benghazi..."
— **Colonel Richard F. ("Dic") Brauer Jr., USAF (Ret.)**; founder, Special Operations Speaks

"Ken Timmerman provides new intelligence on who was behind the attack on the Benghazi Special Mission Compound, as well as why the massive cover-up by the Obama Administration."
— **James A. Lyons, Jr., Admiral, USN (Ret.)**, President and CEO LION Associates, LLC, member of the Citizens Commission on Benghazi

"This book is an excellent read. In fascinating detail, it explores avenues and answers questions that have not previously been pursued."
— **Lieutenant Colonel Denni**
Special Operatio

DECEPTION

THE MAKING OF THE YOUTUBE VIDEO HILLARY & OBAMA BLAMED FOR BENGHAZI

KENNETH R. TIMMERMAN

A POST HILL PRESS BOOK
ISBN: 978-1-68261-192-0
ISBN (eBook): 978-1-68261-193-7

DECEPTION
The Making of the YouTube Video Hillary
and Obama Blamed for Benghazi

Cover Design by Quincy Alivio
Pete Souza, White House Photograph, September 14, 2012

Post Hill Press
275 Madison Avenue, 14th Floor
New York, NY 10016
posthillpress.com

CONTENTS

Also by Kenneth R. Timmerman

Nonfiction

Dark Forces: The Truth About What Happened in Benghazi
*Shadow Warriors: Traitors, Saboteurs, and
the Party of Surrender*
*Countdown to Crisis: the Coming Nuclear Showdown
with Iran*
The French Betrayal of America
Preachers of Hate: Islam and the War on America
Shakedown: Exposing the Real Jesse Jackson
The Death Lobby: How the West Armed Iraq

Fiction

St. Peter's Bones
Honor Killing
The Wren Hunt

www.kentimmerman.com

This book is dedicated to those who remain innocent:

*"And ye shall know the truth,
and the truth shall make you free."*

- John 8:32, KJV

"Once you eliminate the impossible, whatever remains, no matter how improbable, must be the truth."

- Arthur Conan Doyle

INTRODUCTION

As news of the September 11, 2012 attacks in Benghazi reached the United States, Hillary Clinton's State Department went into overdrive.

But contrary to the story we've been told, they weren't pulling out all the stops to rescue the diplomats, intelligence officers, and security staff holed up in the "secret" CIA Annex after the storming and burning of our diplomatic compound. Instead, they were doing their best to shut down a rescue effort – to get the gung-ho pilots and special operations troops to step down from their aircraft – and to put out a cover story many Americans now believe was cooked well before the attacks even began.

It was all because of an "inflammatory" video on the Internet. Benghazi was a protest gone wild that had been provoked by "hateful" right-wing Christians in America who wanted to insult Muslims. After Hillary Clinton phoned President Obama at about 10 PM that night, here is the statement issued in her name by the State Department.

"Some have sought to justify this vicious behavior as a response to inflammatory material posted on the Internet. The United States deplores any intentional effort to denigrate the religious beliefs of others. Our commitment to religious tolerance goes back to the very beginning of our nation. But let me be clear: There is never any justification for violent acts of this kind."

The news media rushed to fill in the blanks, spoon fed by their sources at the State Department, the White House, and the Department of Justice. By the next morning, Americans woke up to scenes from the "hateful" video they were told unequivocally had "caused" the death of Ambassador Chris Stevens, communications officer Sean Smith, and two as yet-unnamed CIA security contractors.

In Bakersfield, California, Cindy Lee Garcia, one of the actresses in the YouTube video, *Innocence of Muslims,* woke up to see her face all over the morning television shows, being blamed by the president of the United States for the murder of four fellow citizens.

She started trembling uncontrollably as she drank her coffee. She couldn't believe what she was seeing. She vaguely recalled the bit-acting part she had taken some fifteen months earlier, but it didn't have anything to do with Muslims or Islam. Here she was being accused of slandering the religion of more than a billion people. *That isn't me!* she wanted to scream at the TV. *I am a pastor, a grandmother, a patriotic American! I would never do anything like this!*

This is Cindy Lee Garcia's story. For the first time, she gives the full, inside account of the making of *Innocence of Muslims,* which she had been told was an adventure film called *Desert Warrior*.

Through her eyes we will experience the universe of hate unleashed by the movie, including a dramatic attempt on her life while she was staying at a New York hotel in between national television appearances. We will examine how the president of the United States and his secretary of state actively promoted the video throughout the Muslim world with the help of witting members of the news media. Without this massive assist from Hillary and Obama, no one would have paid any attention to the "hateful" video.

Like the Fast and Furious scandal in the early days of the Obama administration, the Benghazi Deception was a provocation whose ultimate goal was to advance a political agenda and deflect attention from the very real secrets of Benghazi.

But Mrs. Clinton knew the truth, even as she was blaming the video. At 4:06 PM, an operations alert went out across the State Department. "Mission under attack, armed men, shots fired, explosions heard," it said. It made no mention of a video or a protest.

As the afternoon wore on, reports flooded in about the attackers. Just two hours before Mrs. Clinton issued her statement, she spoke with deputy chief of mission Greg Hicks in Tripoli, who was preparing to evacuate the Tripoli embassy because of intelligence reports that terrorists were preparing to attack there as well. Hicks never mentioned a protest, nor did Ambassador Stevens when the two spoke briefly before he died.

Just one hour after Mrs. Clinton issued her statement she exchanged messages with her daughter via her private email server. Her daughter used the pseudonym "Diane Reynolds" to make it more difficult for a Freedom of Information search to find their correspondence. "Two of our officers were killed in Benghazi by an Al Qaeda-like group," Mrs. Clinton wrote. To her family, she told the truth. To the American people, she flat-out lied.

Later that same evening, she had a conversation with the president of Libya. "Ansar al-Sharia is claiming responsibility" for the Benghazi attacks, she said. The following day, she had a conversation with the Egyptian prime minister. "We know the attack in Libya had nothing to do with the film. It was a planned attack, not a protest."

Hillary Clinton knew the truth. The State Department knew the truth. The CIA and the White House knew the truth. And yet, Mrs. Clinton led the charge is spreading a baseless lie, blaming the attacks on a YouTube video that no one had seen.

+++

Like most Americans, Cindy Lee Garcia knew nothing about Islam or the beliefs of the people who started calling and emailing her the day after the Benghazi attacks, threatening to kill her and rape her children. She had never heard of a "fatwa" until an Egyptian cleric issued one against her, inviting good Muslims to murder her. But once she learned the truth, she was determined to expose how it was exploited by those who were promoting *Innocence of Muslims,* turning a 14-minute YouTube video into a killing machine and a convenient cover for their failed policies.

In preparing this book, I spoke at length with the filmmaker, Egyptian-American Nakoula Basseley Nakoula, who has never before told the story of how he became the first victim of Islamic blasphemy laws in the United States. I will reveal how federal prosecutors broke the law by releasing sealed documents to the media, endangering his life by exposing him as a federal informant.

I also conducted extensive interviews with Cindy's legal

team, who shared never-before seen documents that reveal the extent to which Internet giant Google became an accomplice of the U.S. government in keeping *Innocence of Muslims* online. Google threw every legal trick in the book against Cindy and her legal team, who fought a David versus Goliath battle to get Google to take down the video. Cindy's historic court case against Google will be studied by legal scholars for years to come for its impact on the First Amendment and on copyright laws in the post-Gutenberg Internet era.

Finally, thanks to new information obtained by the Benghazi Select Committee and by Judicial Watch, I have been able to expose the role that Clinton consigliore Sidney Blumenthal played in promoting the false narrative of the YouTube video, where he was helped by a former CIA operative who was a known intelligence fabricator.

This is the story of an ugly lie, a dangerous lie that cost the lives of four Americans and only narrowly averted taking the lives of countless others. It is also the story of a well-orchestrated cover-up, aimed at diverting the attention of the media, the voting public, and Congress from the gun-running and secret intelligence operations in Benghazi, operations that went badly awry.

This is a story that Hillary Clinton doesn't want you to read.

CHAPTER 1
SHATTERED LIVES

Acting had been a form of therapy for her, a new life after decades of struggling to make ends meet. Sexually abused as a child, Cindy had descended into a hell of drugs and violence as a teenager and young adult, only pulling out of it when she came to know the Lord at the age of 26. Life had not treated her gently, but the Lord was good. Even when her husband fell from a narrow filtration tower at the Pastoria Power Plant in 2009 and was nearly killed, the Lord had shown his hand, nudging her to begin an acting career.

But never in her wildest dreams had she ever thought it would come to this. There she was, as clear as day, and she was being blamed by Secretary of State Hillary Clinton and President Obama and everyone in the news media for the deaths of the U.S. ambassador in Libya and three other Americans because she was a hater and religious bigot.

When they rolled tape from the "hateful" video, as it was being called, her face flashed across the screen, saying words that were unfamiliar to her.

"Is your Mohammad a child molester?" the woman's voice said. *Who is Mohammad?* Cindy wondered. *I never made a movie about someone named Mohammad.*

She tried to think back to the set in the summer of 2011, where she had played the mother of a young girl. In the film, her name was Om Roman. It was a short dramatic role, perfectly innocent, or so she had thought. The main character, she recalled, was named "Master George" – not Mohammad. The film was called *Desert Warrior*, not *Innocence of Muslims*. What was going on?

Cindy was thankful that no one else was yet up in the house to see those horrible images of her and the hateful words the TV announcers and the president were saying about her. The President was talking about a 14-minute video that was being shown in Libya, and that had caused the deaths of Ambassador Christopher Stevens, communications officer Sean Smith, and U.S. Navy Seals Tyrone Woods and Glen Doherty in Benghazi. Her heart was pounding so much she could hardly breathe as she flipped the channels, and there it was again: the "hateful" video. *That isn't me*, she wanted to scream. *It can't be!*

She couldn't remember saying anything that would hurt others. She couldn't remember using words that would anger anyone. But what exactly had she said?

She found the binder where she kept the scripts from the parts she had played, along with monologues she'd been given during other auditions. She started tearing through it, searching for her part.

There it was, or what was left of it: just three and a half pages of lines from one of the scenes she had been in. Instinctively, she started running the lines in her head.

Her husband in the movie was named Kero. The scene started with Kero welcoming the main character, Master George, into their home, so he can marry their 13-year-old daughter. "Thank you, Master," Kero says. "You bless me by coming into my humble home."

Master George replies: "You are a good man and a good follower of me, Kero. You will be a good father-in-law and you shall indeed have your place in God's paradise."

"Praise be to God... Praise be to God," Kero says.

Cindy, playing Kero's wife, joins the men at this point, bringing her daughter, Hillary, in from the playground where she has been on the swing. Om Roman takes her over to Master George and puts the girl's hand in George's hand. "Hillary, this is Master George. He is going to be your husband," she says.

And then she caught it: she hadn't paid attention to it before, because it just seemed to be a stage prompt. The next lines read, "George looks at her with that look that only a man can give a woman as he rubs the back of her hand."

That's odd, Cindy thought. *What did that mean? Come to think of it, the whole atmosphere surrounding the making of the film was a bit strange. How could that scene get people so angry they would go out and murder Americans?*

She turned down the television and ran through the rest of the lines.

Hillary, her daughter, is obviously upset. As Master George picks her up to carry the thirteen-year-old away, she looks over her shoulder at her mother and reaches out a hand. "She calls out, nearly in tears," the stage directions read. "Mother, Mother, I'm hungry," Hillary says.

"It's okay, Hillary. Everything will be alright," Om Roman replies. But the stage directions tell a different story: "It is obvious she doesn't believe her own words. A single tear runs down her cheek."

For Cindy Lee Garcia, on the morning of September 12, 2012, that's as far as it went. She had scored a small part in a strange desert drama, and played in a scene about a husband and wife giving away their thirteen-year-old daughter to a much older man who obviously exercised some kind of power over them. Later, she would remember the filmmaker whispering to her on the set, telling her to say that the girl was just seven years old, and his director waving him away. "Don't listen to him," the director said. "Say thirteen. Say, 'our daughter has not yet reached her thirteenth year.'" And that's what she said. She remembered very well thinking how odd it was for someone to give away their daughter at such an age.

In the 14-minute trailer posted to YouTube, Master George was now called Mohammad. Someone apparently had dubbed their voices, and that is where the trouble began. For the scene she had just played was a re-enactment – and a remarkably faithful re-enactment, at that – of a famous moment in Islamic hagiography where the Prophet Mohammad marries the young girl, Aisha, who becomes the favorite of his many wives. In the YouTube version – *Cindy's version* – Mohammad is being called a child molester. And that, of course, is one of the many things in the video that angered Muslims.

+++

The telephone started ringing, only adding to Cindy's confusion. All the calls were from journalists, and they all said more or less the same thing. Are you the Cindy Garcia who was in the film *Innocence of Muslims*? CNN called first, she thinks, then NBC, and virtually every local station in her area. She also got calls that morning from reporters in Israel, Egypt, France, and beyond. Was she the face of *Innocence of Muslims*?

I am an honest person, Cindy remembers thinking. *It is always easier for me to tell the truth than to tell a lie, so I will tell them the truth: this is not the film that we were in.* Instead, she found herself hanging up on the phone, or mumbling something about not accepting any interviews at this time. *How in the world did all these people get my number?* It suddenly hit her: *I am not ready for this.*

Before she could talk to the journalists, she had to call Sam Bacile, the producer.

CHAPTER 2

"TELL THEM
I AM FROM ISRAEL"

She had his cell phone number logged into her phone. She had called him or the assistant director from time to time since the shoot in the summer of 2011 to see what was happening with the movie. Up until this morning, the day after the Benghazi murders, she had thought it was a "swords and sandals" desert drama, maybe something of a cross between *Conan the Barbarian* and *Ben Hur*.

He picked up after a couple of rings. *He must have recognized my number,* she thought.

"Sam, what have you done? Why did you do this to us?" she wailed.

"Cindy," he said. "Tell the world you are innocent. Tell them that the producer of the film did this because he is tired of radical Muslims killing innocent people."

And then, Cindy recalls, he added this: "Oh, and tell them that I am from Israel." Then he hung up the phone.

Now she was more confused than ever. She had thought he was from Egypt. *Was he really from Israel? What was going on?* She didn't understand the content of the video or the reason someone would do something like this that would cause people to get so angry they would storm a U.S. diplomatic facility and murder our Ambassador. She didn't understand Islam or Muslims. She just knew that she felt horrible. And that she wanted to tell the world that she was innocent.

All day she saw television reports quoting Sam as saying exactly the same words she was certain he had spoken to her on the phone about being Israeli. One widely quoted report, from the Associated Press, claimed that Sam had told them he was an Israeli-American and that he had made the movie because "Islam was a cancer." The AP claimed that he told them he had made the film as a "provocative political statement condemning the religion." A *Wall Street Journal* report claimed that Bacile told them that he had "raised $5 million from 100 Jewish donors to make the film."[1]

"Sam" insisted to me repeatedly that none of those statements were true, and that he never spoke with any reporter at that point – not with the AP, not with the *Wall Street Journal*, "not with anybody."

Why wasn't he speaking to the media? "I was afraid for my life," he told me. He also insisted he never told Cindy that he was Israeli, and that she most likely came to that conclusion after hearing the media reports. I will reveal later in this book exactly who spoke to those reporters, pretending that the filmmaker behind *Innocence of Muslims* was an Israeli-American *(see chapter 12).*

At the time, Cindy knew nothing about the extraordinary game being played by the United States government and an

---

[1]   Shaya Tayefe Mohajer, "Sam Bacile, Anti-Islam Filmmaker, in Hiding After Protests," Associated Press, Sept. 12, 2012: 12:29 AM ET; Matt Bradley and Dion Nissenbaum, "U.S. Missions Stormed in Libya, Egypt," *Wall Str\\eet Journal*, Sept. 11, 2012. The version of the WSJ story most readily available on the Internet, via the Huffington Post, has this title: "U.S. missions stormed in Libya, Egypt, in reaction to anti-Islam film funded by 100 Jewish donors."

activist media to influence public opinion. She didn't know that Hillary's office manager, Nora Toiv, was in touch with top Google and YouTube executives, to ensure that the movie stayed up on YouTube so the government would have an excuse to prosecute Nakoula for the alleged crime of blasphemy against Islam.[2] Nor could she know that the U.S. Embassy in Tripoli, Libya had emailed Washington to emphatically deny any relationship whatsoever between the video and the Benghazi attacks, exposing the story repeated by Obama and Hillary Clinton as an utter fiction.[3] She just knew that all of these references to the Middle East were making her head spin. She felt herself sucked into a spiral of events she simply didn't understand.

The New York Times claimed that the video "gained international attention when a Gainesville, Florida pastor began promoting it along with his own proclamation of September 11 as "International Judge Muhammad Day." The pastor, Terry Jones, had long been on the radar screen of Hillary Clinton, who regularly trotted him out for condemnation and ridicule as a right-wing bugaboo. The Times claimed Jones had issued a statement calling the film "an American production, not designed to attack Muslims but to show the destructive ideology of Islam," and that it "further reveals in a satirical fashion the life of Muhammad."[4]

Muslims "have no tolerance for anything outside of Muhammad," the Times quoted Jones as saying. Islam was "a total deception," he added. He originally had planned to screen the film on September 11 in Florida as part of his "International Judge Muhammad Day," according to a separate piece from

---

[2]   See Chapter 14.
[3]   Email released by the Benghazi Select Committee in April 2016, available here: http://kentimmerman.com/IOMdocs/2012_09_14-Tripoli-email.pdf.
[4]   David. D. Kirkpatrick, "Anger Over a Film Fuels Anti-American Attacks in Libya and Egypt," New York Times, Sept. 11, 2012.

the Associated Press.[5]

The *Times* went on to claim that Jones "inspired deadly riots in Afghanistan in 2010 and 2011 by first threatening to burn copies of the Koran and then burning one in his church." Hillary Clinton condemned him publicly at the time in a speech before the Council on Foreign Relations. "It's regrettable that a pastor in Gainesville, Florida, with a church of no more than fifty people can make this outrageous and distressful, disgraceful plan and get, you know, the world's attention," she said then.[6]

Both she and President Obama were hoping that liberal reporters would fall for that fiction once again, and would blame an Internet video, made with $5 million raised by a "right-wing" pastor in Florida from Jewish donors, for the Benghazi attacks.

How convenient that would be, especially since the real story of what the U.S. was doing in Benghazi, where CIA personnel were tracking surface to air missiles flowing to jihadi groups in Syria, and where several teams of undercover former special operations troops were working as private U.S. government contractors on top secret projects tracking terrorists, was a secret Mrs. Clinton and President Obama were intent on keeping from the American public.

Look over here, they were saying. Watch this horrific YouTube video, made by bigots and Islamophobes. Don't watch what my hands (and your tax dollars) are really doing, funneling guns to rebels in Syria and assassinating terrorists.

Oh, and if there really were people influenced by the video (and there were), don't think for an instant to blame our complacent policies that enabled the Muslim Brotherhood and radical Islamic groups around the world, or that empowered a

5   "American killed in Libya attack; filmmaker in hiding, " Associated Press, Sept. 12, 2012, 08:43 AM ET.
6   Lucy Madison, "Hillary Clinton, Joe Lieberman Denounce Florida Pastor's Planned Quran Burning Event," CBS News, Sept. 8, 2010.

vision of Islam that could explode into extraordinary violence because of a cartoon or a video.

As I wrote in my earlier book, *Dark Forces: the Truth about What Happened in Benghazi:*

> For Hillary, it was a twofer. Not only would the [YouTube video] story take the heat off the administration for what had been going on in Benghazi, but if Republicans didn't condemn the video as self-righteously as she did, she would tar them as bigots as well. Heck, she'd even accuse them of being responsible for [Ambassador] Chris Stevens' death, since they had the temerity to "slash" the State Department budget. [p335]

The State Department was actively promoting the film. In fact, as I will reveal in chapter 11 of this book, it was largely because of U.S. State Department Twitter feeds and related YouTube channels that the movie ultimately went viral across the Middle East.

But what was astonishing in the early hours after the September 11, 2012 attacks in Benghazi, was how quickly the liberal media was able to focus attention on the YouTube video as the cause of the violence spreading across the Middle East, rather than Obama administration policies or Islamic ideology.

+++

Max Fisher, a self-appointed watchdog of "Islamophobia," appears to have been the first to report on the impact of the video on the morning of September 11, 2012 – several hours *before* the attacks in Benghazi began.

In a screed that appeared in the online version of the once-venerable *Atlantic* magazine, Fisher breathlessly described protests in Cairo that he claimed were sparked by the video.

> "Right now, protesters in Cairo are gathered at the U.S. Embassy compound, where some have scaled the walls and pulled down the American flag, with which they've replaced a black flag bearing the prayer, 'There is no god but Allah and Mohammad is his messenger.'"[7]

Fisher failed to inform his audience that the black flag was the flag of al Qaeda (today, ISIS), and that the demonstration in front of the U.S. Embassy in Cairo had been planned several days ahead of time to protest the continued detention in the U.S. of Sheikh Omar Abdul Rahman, the "Blind Sheikh" convicted by a U.S. District court for plotting in 1994 to blow up the Holland and Lincoln tunnels in New York.

Fisher also failed to report that the Cairo protesters, led by the son of the Blind Sheikh and by Mohammad al-Zawahri, the brother of al Qaeda leader Ayman al-Zawahri, had been calling on jihadi groups to storm the U.S. Embassy for several *days*, not because of the video but because of the alleged assassination of al Qaeda leader Abu Yahya al Libi in a U.S. drone strike. So insistent and so prominent were these threats that U.S. Ambassador to Egypt, Anne Paterson, ordered embassy personnel to stay home that day, just in case the planned protests got out of hand. Completely ignoring all of this, Fisher claimed that the Cairo demonstrators were "protesting an American film that insults [the] Prophet Mohammad," when none of the protesters or the organizers had mentioned the

---

7   Max Fisher, "The Movie So Offensive That Egyptians Just Stormed the U.S. Embassy Over It," The Atlantic, Sept. 11, 2012.

film in interviews they had given to CNN and other international media in front of the U.S. Embassy complex.[8]

Fisher went on to post a now-dead link to the YouTube video.[9] "If you've never heard of it," he said, "that's because most of the few clips circulating online are dubbed in Arabic." He claimed that the link he posted was one of the only ones in English. "That's also because it's associated with Florida Pastor Terry Jones (yes, the asshole who burnt the Koran despite Defense Secretary Robert M. Gates' pleas)," Fisher added.[10]

Fisher apparently hadn't been able to see the YouTube video himself, even though the version he linked to was in English. Was it too obscure for him to find on the YouTube server? "It's still not clear [what the film says], but it appears to compare Mohammed to a donkey and Muslims, according to one translation, to 'child-lovers,'" he wrote.

So he linked to several tweets from *New York Times* reporter Liam Stack, who had recently returned from Cairo. "4 minutes in and I don't think they've said the title yet, but the opening scene is a doozy," Stack tweeted. Fisher continued: "The man in the scene says of his donkey, 'This is the first Muslim animal.' He asks the donkey if he likes girls; when it doesn't answer, he bursts into laughter and says, 'He doesn't like girls,' according to Stack."[11]

---

8   Nic Robertson, "Exclusive: Al Qaeda leader's brother offers peace plan," CNN, Sept. 11, 2012; updated 1:34 PM ET.

9   https://www.youtube.com/watch?v=4sQPRtS2h7k

10   I will return to this particular YouTube version of the film in chapter 12. An archived version is titled, "The Coptic Abroad insulting the prophet in doing Movie Trailer," and as of September 11, 2012 had received just 405 views.

11   Liam Stack actually tweeted, "he then asks if the goat likes girls..." The animal in the movie was clearly a donkey and not a goat, so this raises questions as to whether Stack was actually watching the movie, or having it described to him by another source. The date stamp on his tweets is 2:17 and 2:18 PM ET.

Does that sound like a put-up job to you? Fisher is quoting second and possibly third-hand accounts of a YouTube video he hasn't been able to view himself, because he has been unable to locate it on the YouTube server. Why has he been unable to locate it? Because no one has been viewing it, making it hard to locate on the Google search engine. Indeed, the archived version from the day that Fisher wrote about it, September 11, shows that it had gotten just 405 views.

But unnamed U.S. government sources told him that the movie, "like Terry Jones himself and his earlier Koran-burning stunt, have received attention far beyond their reach" and were "producing real-world damage."

How much damage exactly? As of early evening September 11, 2012 Cairo-time, when his column first appeared, he admitted: "That damage is apparently limited to one American flag" at the U.S. Embassy in Cairo.

Hello? And just why is the damage to one American flag at a U.S. Embassy a big deal? Why would *The Atlantic* even bother to publish an article about it? Unless, of course, Fisher's Internet article was meant to lay the table for a much greater set of falsehoods to come.

+++

From emails sent to Secretary of State Hillary Clinton's private server released thanks to Freedom of Information Act requests from Judicial Watch and from multiple media organizations, it has now become clear that a key proponent of blaming the attacks on the YouTube video *Innocence of Muslims* was Hillary Clinton consigliore, Sid Blumenthal.

In a memo sent to Secretary Clinton that is date-stamped 12:50 AM on September 12, Washington time, Blumenthal doubled-down on the blame-the-YouTube video narrative that Hillary had adopted in her first public statement, issued at 10:08 PM Washington time the night of the attacks (see the Introduction). In a detailed report from "sources with direct access to the Libyan National Transitional Council, as well as the highest levels of European Governments, and Western Intelligence and security services," Blumenthal blamed the video for the Benghazi attacks.

This extraordinary report, which has gotten little to no publicity, provided grist for Secretary Clinton's mill. And she used that grist abundantly in addressing the media in reports that Cindy Lee Garcia felt in her innocence were aimed directly at her.

Sid Blumenthal's "report," which we now know was copied and pasted from emails he had received from former CIA official Tyler Drumheller, was a tissue of lies from start to finish. Here is the original email header, as released by the State Department:

From: Sidney Blumenthal [email address redacted]
Sent: Wednesday, September 12, 2012 12:50 AM
To: H:
Subject: Magariaf on attack on U.S. in Libya. Sid
Attachments: hrc memo magariaf, attack on U.S. in Libya 091212.docx

"During the afternoon of September 11, 2012, new interim President of Libya Mohammed Yussef al Magariaf spoke in private with senior advisors, including members of the Libyan Muslim Brotherhood, to discuss the attacks by demonstrators on U.S. missions in Tripoli and Benghazi," the report claimed.

That would be a bombshell, if only it were true.

The attacks against the U.S. diplomatic compound in

Benghazi began at 9:42 PM local time, well after sundown, so it was impossible for Magariaf to be discussing them "during the afternoon" of the same day. Greg Hicks, the Deputy Chief of Mission at the U.S. Embassy in Tripoli, ordered the evacuation of the embassy at around 2 AM on September 12 – not because any attacks were then underway, but as a precaution based on intelligence information. (The attacks on the embassy in Tripoli began later that night).

There were never any demonstrations in front of *either* U.S. diplomatic facility in Libya. Ever. That was just a full-throated lie, invented whole cloth by Sid Blumenthal and his ghost-whisperer, Tyler Drumheller, who had a checkered record at the Central Intelligence Agency. Drumheller had been outed publicly by his former boss, CIA Director George Tenet, for lying to the president of the United States about Weapons of Mass Destruction in Iraq.[12]

The Drumheller/Blumenthal memo gets better. "According to a sensitive source, el Magariaf was shaken by the attacks, and gave permission to commanders on the ground for security forces to open fire over the heads of the crowds in an effort to break up mobs attacking the missions."

That is just another fantasy, invented out of whole cloth. There were never any Libyan security forces around the U.S. diplomatic compound in Benghazi on the afternoon of September 11, let alone at the U.S. Embassy in Tripoli. Nor did any Libyan security forces come to the rescue of the beleaguered Benghazi compounds (diplomatic or CIA) until around 5:30 AM *the next day*. Nor were there ever crowds

---

[12]   Tenet rebuked Drumheller in his 2007 memoir, *At The Center of the Storm*. See, Kenneth R. Timmerman, "Why was Sid Blumenthal advising Hillary Clinton on Libya," Accuracy in Media, March 11, 2015. http://www.aim.org/aim-column/why-was-sid-blumenthal-advising-hillary-clinton-on-libya/

of demonstrators in front of either the Benghazi diplomatic compound or the Tripoli embassy. A organized band of armed jihadis attacked in Benghazi starting at 9:42 PM and within twenty minutes set fire to the ambassador's residence, causing the Ambassador and Sean Smith to die by smoke inhalation.

But why should Blumenthal – or his patron, Hillary Clinton – worry about the facts, when they had a good story to spin that would besmirch their political opponents?

The memo went on to claim that "a senior security officer told el Magariaf that the attacks on that day [remember, they didn't occur until that evening] were inspired by what many devout Libyan[s] viewed as a *sacrilegious internet video* [emphasis mine] on the prophet Mohammed originating in America."

A thorough search of social media posts by a State Department Arabic language media team found *one tweet* blaming the attacks on the video. The linguists also reported that "some Twitter users in Libya and Egypt are spreading reports that the attacks in Libya may not be related to the infamous film but to the killing of Al Qaeda's second in command, who is Libyan." Why were they looking for reports mentioning the "infamous film?" Because that's what Hillary and her top staff had tasked them to find. Political hack Sid Blumenthal saw a huge political opportunity for his patron, Hillary Clinton, to blame the video for the death of a U.S. ambassador and other U.S. personnel.[13]

Just 12 hours later, at 1 PM Washington time on September 12, Blumenthal emailed to Mrs. Clinton another spin story, this

---

[13]   See, Kenneth R. Timmerman, "The Clinton Record on Libya," Accuracy in Media, June 9, 2015. Judicial Watch obtained the reports from the State Department linguists and posted them here: http://www.judicialwatch.org/wp-content/uploads/2015/05/Pgs.-67-68-from-2690-05112015.pdf

time penned by his son, notorious left-wing pseudo-journalist, Max Blumenthal. .

Here is the email header as it has now been released by the State Department – more than three years after Congress initially demanded that the State Department produce all communications relating to the Benghazi attacks:

> **From:** H <hrod17@clintonemail.com>
> **Sent:** Wednesday, September 12, 2012 2:11 PM
> **To:** 'Russorv@state.gov'
> **Subject:** Fw: Meet The Right-Wing Extremist Behind Anti-Muslim Film That Sparked Deadly Riots
>
> Pls print.
>
> **From:** sbwhoeop mailto:sbwhoeop
> **Sent:** Wednesday, September 12, 2012 01:00 PM
> **To:** H
> **Subject:** Meet The Right-Wing Extremist Behind Anti-Muslim Film That Sparked Deadly Riots
>
> http://maxblumenthal.com/2012/09/meet-the-right-wing-extremist-behind-anti-muslim-film-that-sparked-deadly-riots/

In the top part of the header, hrod17@clintonemail.com is Hillary Clinton's email address, one of several she created for official State Department communications on her family's private email server. Blumenthal tried to simulate his former White House email address (his initials coupled to the abbreviation of White House-Executive Office of the President) for his communications with the secretary of state.

The initial version of the story, published on Max Blumenthal's blog, picked up the AP and *Wall Street Journal* false allegations that filmmaker Sam Bacile was an Israeli-American and had financed the film with $5 million raised from "100 Jewish donors."[14] But Max was just warming up. He then tied the film to a vast conspiracy led by Steve Klein, "a known anti-Muslim activist with ties to the extreme Christian right and the militia movement."

Cindy wouldn't have recognized Klein or his name because he had nothing to do with making the movie and never appeared on the set or in post-production. But hey, we're not talking about reality here. We're talking about how the Obama White House and Hillary Clinton's State Department created a phony story out of whole cloth and sold it to the American people, at least until the 2012 presidential election was in the bag.

+++

Max Blumenthal was no slouch at inventing a "vast right-wing conspiracy." After all, he learned from the best: his father was the author of Hillary's mid-1990s fantasy about an earlier vast right-wing conspiracy that aimed to defeat her husband in the 1996 presidential election (a fiction I was proud to be part of, through my work at the American Spectator).

The younger Blumenthal asserted that Klein, who claims to have led a 'hunter-killer team' in Vietnam, "is a right-wing extremist who emerged from the same axis of Islamophobia that produced Anders Behring Breivik [the notorious anti-Muslim nutcase who murdered scores of schoolchildren in Norway] and which takes inspiration from the writings of Robert Spencer, Pamela Geller, and Daniel Pipes." How did Blumenthal figure that out? Not because he spoke with Klein

---

14   http://maxblumenthal.com/2012/09/meet-the-right-wing-extremist-behind-anti-muslim-film-that-sparked-deadly-riots/

(although, as we shall see, Klein was starting to speak to the media on behalf of the terrified filmmaker, who was holed up in his home in Cerritos, California). Blumenthal knew all about Klein because he had become "an enthusiastic commenter on Geller's website, Atlas Shrugged."

Wow. That makes anyone who comments on your Facebook page an active member of whatever conspiracy a left-wing hack like Max Blumenthal dregs out of the fever swamps.

Klein was everything the Blumenthals and Hillary Clinton loved to hate. As Max painted him, he was involved in "organizing resentment against all the usual targets – Muslims, homosexuals, feminists, and even Mormons. He is a board member and founder of a group called Courageous Christians United, which promotes anti-Mormon, anti-Catholic and anti-Muslim literature (including the work of Robert Spencer) on its website."

Are you hyperventilating yet? Max Blumenthal certainly was.

But it gets better. "Klein has been closely affiliated with the Church at Kaweah, an extreme evangelical church located 70 miles southeast of Fresno that serves as a nexus of neo-Confederate, Christian Reconstructionist, and militia movement elements. The Southern Poverty Law Center produced a report on Kaweah this spring that noted Klein's long record of activism against Muslims."

If you are not an ardent leftist, you might not realize that to Hillary Clinton, a report by the Southern Poverty Law Center condemning someone as a bigot and a hater is like the Good Housekeeping seal of approval. To the rest of thinking humanity, it's a political hatchet job.

Blumenthal also tied Klein to the National American Coptic Assembly, "a radical Islamophobic group headed by Morris Sadek," whom Blumenthal credited with discovering *Innocence of Muslims* and promoting it online.

Hillary asked her aides to print out the initial Max

Blumenthal screed. When Sid Blumenthal emailed her a link to a more elaborate version that appeared the next day as an opinion column on the Guardian website in Britain, she replied, "Your Max is a mitzvah!"

The elder Blumenthal didn't mind her mangled use of Hebrew, if he had even noticed it.[15] "Max knows how to do this and is fearless," he fired back. "Hope it's useful and gets around, especially in the Middle East."

The Blame-the-YouTube-made-by-Anti-Muslim-Bigots narrative got picked up everywhere. *The New York Times* led with the story in their coverage of the Benghazi attacks.[16] So did the *Washington Post* and other national media. There was Obama in his press conference that morning in the Rose Garden up on his high horse, rejecting "all efforts to denigrate the religious beliefs of others." And in Cairo, a separate *New York Times* story quoted a spokesman for Muslim Brotherhood president Mohammad Morsi calling on the U.S. government to "prosecute the 'madmen' behind the video."[17]

Such was the landscape Cindy watched unfold before her eyes that morning on the national media, where everyone involved in the movie was painted in bright colors as anti-Muslim bigots, haters, racists, right-wing Christian extremists. Each time she saw her face in the b-roll on the screen, she wanted to scream, *"That isn't me!"*

---

[15]   A *mitzvah* in colloquial usage generally means a good deed or a blessing. What Hillary probably meant was that Max was a *mensch*, meaning, a great guy. I suppose she felt that since Sid Blumenthal had a Jewish name, she had to use the only Jewish-sounding word that came to mind.

[16]   Robert Mackey and Liam Stack, "Obscure Film Mocking Muslim Prophet Sparks Anti-U.S. Protests in Egypt and Libya," *New York Times*, Sept. 11, 2012, 7:25 PM ET.

[17]   David D. Kirkpatrick, "Anger Over a Film Fuels Anti-American Attacks in Libya and Egypt," *New York Times*, Sept. 11, 2012.

Cindy had always been a patriot in her heart, from childhood up until that morning. She grew up saying the pledge of allegiance every morning in school and singing the national anthem and all the great songs about America that filled her heart with pride and a deep sense of honor. When she heard the roar of fighter jets overhead, her heart swelled. *I love America, I have the utmost respect for our country. I have always respected the office of the president with great reverence toward the men in office. Until now!* she thought.

What Obama and Hillary and the media were saying about her was so wrong. It was hateful and she knew in her heart it wasn't true.

That day began a spiral of events that changed her life forever. *The world has become darker and more sinister than I have ever dreamed,* she thought. *My eyes have been closed to what is really going on. I was lost behind a veil of ignorance. But no more. I am not the same person I once was, who lived life with closed eyes. I will never be that person again.*

She worried that the unconditional love Jesus had filled her heart with for so many years had somehow been changed, and that hatred had taken its place. Did that mean she wasn't a good Christian?

She was angry. She wanted to get her story out. She prayed that what now seemed like a nightmare from Hell would one day help others. *That's how the Lord has always worked his way in the past,* she thought. *I know you won't abandon me now!*

In the midst of all the confusion she got a call from an entertainment lawyer named Cris Armenta, who sketched out ways that people in the past had dealt with similar situations. Cindy didn't have to be all alone, Armenta said. She could find people who were on her side, and who could help her to defend her good name.

Perhaps, just perhaps, Cindy thought, *help was the on the way.*

+++

Sam Bacile, whose real name was Nakoula Basseley Nakoula, also underwent a life-changing experience as a result of all the attention the Obama administration and a compliant media had showered on the 14-minute trailer from his feature-length movie, *Innocence of Muslims*.

It didn't take long after the first media reports identifying him as the person behind YouTube video for reporters to find him. By Wednesday, September 12, 2012, dozens of television crews had pulled their vans up in front of his modest residence in the Los Angeles suburb of Cerritos, California. They knocked on his door repeatedly, day and night. CNN reporter Miguel Marquez, who later interviewed Cindy, seemed to get a big kick out of pounding on the door as people made noises inside. At one point that evening, Nakoula phoned the Los Angeles County Sheriff's Department to report a disturbance and ask for police protection. Instead of offering him that protection, an LAPD spokesman, Steve Whitmore, revealed his phone call, his request, and quite probably his address, to the media.[18]

CNN then phoned the U.S. Attorney's office in Los Angeles to inquire if Nakoula had a criminal past. In response, federal prosecutors obligingly sent them documents showing that Nakoula had been convicted for credit card and bank fraud in 2009, and had spent two years in jail on separate convictions.

The media circus had begun. And life would become hell for Cindy, Nakoula, and everyone else publicly identified with the movie.

---

[18] Moni Basu, "New details emerge of anti-Islam film's mystery producer," CNN, Sept. 14, 2012.

CHAPTER 3
BESIEGED BY THE MEDIA

Cindy gave an initial telephone interview to Gawker, a Hollywood tip sheet, where she talked in some detail about the lines she had been given to read on set and the words that eventually got dubbed over her voice. "I had nothing to do really with anything," she told the reporter. "Now we have people dead because of a movie I was in. It makes me sick... I'm going to sue his butt off," she added.[1]

That was her gut reaction. Everybody seemed to sue everybody in California.

Cindy joined approximately 80 members of the cast and crew in a statement they sent to CNN and other news outlets, denouncing the film and claiming they had been misled by the producer.[2] So when CNN called the next day, Thursday, September 13, Cindy wasn't surprised. She agreed to meet Miguel Marquez in the lobby of a hotel near her home in Bakersfield, CA.

---

[1]   http://gawker.com/5942748/it-makes-me-sick-actress-in-muhammed-movie-says-she-was-deceived-had-no-idea-it-was-about-islam

[2]   See http://www.cnn.com/2012/09/12/world/anti-islam-film/, and https://www.washingtonpost.com/blogs/blogpost/post/innocence-of-muslims-cast-disavows-movie/2012/09/13/5c4d0a52-fdaf-11e1-a31e-804fccb658f9_blog.html

"She is horrified at what happened," Marquez said, oozing sympathy to on-air host Erin Burnett. "The only reason she went on camera is because she was horrified at what happened." Cindy told him she was angry with the filmmaker and believed she and other cast members had been misled. "There was no discussion of Mohammad during the film," he said. "She made a small, low-budget film and finds herself now at the center of an international nightmare."

To prove her point, Cindy took a copy of the few pages of script she had been able to locate. They all identified the main character as "George," "Master George," but never "Mohammad." She had wanted to show those pages during the interview so everyone in America could see she was innocent and had not spoken the lines attributed to her, but CNN never broadcasted that part of the interview, only a 15-second clip of her denouncing the filmmaker and appearing to make an abject apology to Muslims.

"I would never been involved in a film that would bring harm to anyone," she said. "It makes me sick to my stomach to think I was involved in that movie that brought death to those people. I think it's very unfair. I am very sorry for that man and his family and everybody else who was hurt." She appeared to be sobbing by the end of the segment.

Initially, Cindy had intended to do just that one TV interview. But instead of calming the storm, the CNN piece had just the opposite effect. Within hours, television news trucks blocked the street outside her house in Bakersfield and reporters were pounding on the door. She agreed to meet with a reporter from the Bakersfield *Californian*, which posted a brief video of the interview online. Cindy repeated what she had told CNN. "It's not me stating those words" about Mohammad, the founder of Islam. She had been misled. "Everything else in that YouTube, I never saw," she insisted.[3] But clearly, she was beginning to have second thoughts, and volunteered that the producer had called her back on March 2, 2012 to overdub her voice, because it hadn't come out right in the initial shoot.

Cindy became so exhausted with all the media attention she just wanted to shut it all out. At one point, she collapsed on the sofa and her husband went to the door and told the reporters to leave her alone. When several of them got angry, because they had traveled quite far to stake out the house, he told them to go rent a room and come back the next day, which they did. This went on for days.

Angry Muslim men started calling her at home and said vulgar things about her and her family, threatening to kill them because they had insulted Islam. *Who are these people?* she thought. *How can they say such horrible things?* One of them threatened to rape her. Another described how he intended to sodomize her. Yet another said he would cut her head off and put it on a pole. Men called up saying they would rape her children and anybody who worked with her. Another man suggested that she murder the producer if she wanted to save her own life.

Then the threats started coming in over her personal Facebook page and pages she operated for her Christian ministry, from users with screen names like "Assasin Junglee," "Ali Abdulrehman," "LionZaid Hamid," "Ahmad Masanawa," "Ahmed Batni," "Hani Reda," "Xaadi Mian," and many others. Cindy, perhaps mistakenly, tried to respond to them, using reason and the love of Christ she felt in her heart. They only responded with more hatred, and with a sexual vulgarity I will not reproduce here.

A few days later, she got a call from a producer at an Arabic-

---

[3]   https://www.youtube.com/watch?v=e7YIU-4KIIM

language TV station, who said their network was widely viewed in Egypt. Because Sam had told her he had wanted to show the movie in Egypt, Cindy felt she owed them an answer to what had really happened with the film, so she agreed to come to their studio. As she drove the freeway over the Grapevine, the mountain range separating Bakersfield from Los Angeles to the south, she thought of all the threats against her and took her .38 Special from the glove compartment and tucked it into her pants. *Thank God for concealed carry,* she thought.

Along the way, she prayed, asking the Lord for wisdom. *I do not know these people or what they are about. Lord, please help me to understand their hearts.* And as she drove along, she felt a powerful recollection, as if the breath of the Holy Spirit had come over her, reminding her of the story of Abraham and his two sons, the first with an Egyptian slave woman, Hagar, because his wife Sarai had been unable able to conceive; and then, late in life, through God's miracle, a second son with his lawful wife.

It was that second son, Isaac, who received Abraham's blessing and became the father of Israel. But the first-born, Ishmael, became an outcast. As the angel of the Lord warned Sarai,

> He will be a wild donkey of a man;
> His hand will be against everyone
> And everyone's hand be against him,
> And he will live in hostility
> Toward all his brothers. [Genesis 16:11-12]

Cindy knew those verses well and had preached on them at her church. As she drove down to Los Angeles over the Grapevine, they repeated them over and over again. *Why?* She wondered. *Why am I thinking of this now?*

And then it hit her. This was the story of the Middle East today, an unending war between two brothers from the same father and different mothers, and she started to weep uncontrollably.[4] *I have two children from two different fathers, but that does not mean that I love one more than the other,* she thought. She felt her heart was bursting with unfamiliar emotions, and it frightened her. And then, almost in comic relief, she thought, *get a grip on yourself, or you're going to have to pull over and you'll be late for the interview.*

The interview with Middle East Broadcasting in Los Angeles went well. A female assistant producer escorted her into a private room and placed her in front of a microphone and a camera and seemed to connect her to the Middle East, where a female interpreter was translating her words in real time so the audience could understand what she was saying. She felt they treated her with dignity and respect, the first time in fact she had felt that in the interviews she had given. Something of the peace of Christ had come down upon her while she was driving, and she managed to hold onto it during the interview.

She repeated what she had been saying all along. The producer had deceived her and the other members of the cast. "I never mentioned the name of Mohammed, I never heard the name of Mohammed except when I saw the clip, trailer, and I never understood what they were trying to do. None of it made sense to me," she said.[5]

She also mentioned that the producer "said that he was from Israel." It was the type of statement that fed into the deep-

---

[4]   While Cindy was not familiar with Hal Lindsey's definitive work, *The Everlasting Hatred: The Roots of Jihad,* the concept that Ishmael and his rejection by Abraham had led to centuries of Muslim resentment against Jews is a theme that modern Biblical scholars have written about with increasing frequency.

[5]   http://english.alarabiya.net/articles/2012/09/17/238618.html

held belief among Muslims of a world-wide Jewish conspiracy. But Cindy was too wrapped up in trying to keep her world from collapsing around her to realize the impact of what she was saying, even though she now knew it wasn't true and had told Gawker earlier in the week that Sam had told her on set that he was Egyptian. She felt that by apologizing to the people who were getting hurt she could put an end to the negative media attention. She thought she could wash away the tremendous burden of guilt she felt for the deaths in Benghazi. And she was confused. The death threats were scaring her.

She decided to shut down her church, as well as the small modeling company she had set up a few years before. She even decided to move into another house, so nobody close to her would get hurt by these strange Muslim men. She felt they were watching her, stalking her, everywhere she went. No matter how much love she tried to show from her heart, they kept on pouring out hate against her.

CHAPTER 4
THE LAWYER

President Obama and Secretary Clinton continued to talk about the movie. Cindy couldn't turn on the television, or so it seemed, without them rubbing more salt in her wounds, blaming her for the death of four innocents in Benghazi. Mrs. Clinton was now blaming the video for violent protests that had erupted all across the Middle East and beyond.

> "Let me state very clearly and I hope it is obvious that the United States government has absolutely nothing to do with this video. We absolutely reject its content and its message. To me personally, this video is disgusting and reprehensible. It appears to have a deeply cynical purpose – to denigrate a great religion and to provoke rage."[1]

---

[1]   See, Mary Lu Carnevale, "Hillary Clinton Denounces the video and the Violence," *Wall Street Journal*, Sept. 13, 2012 11:34 AM ET. This statement went way beyond what she had said earlier in public, even though her own State Department and the CIA were reporting to her that the video had not been the cause of the Benghazi attacks. Her five minute remarks at the opening of the U.S.-Morocco Dialogue at the State Department, can be seen at https://www.youtube.com/watch?v=qXYdb57P7T4

Secretary Clinton repeated that claim when she appeared along with the president at the ramp ceremony at Andrews Air Force base that Friday to welcome home the bodies of the four Americans killed in Benghazi. "We've seen rage and violence directed at American embassies over an awful Internet video that we had nothing to do with. It is hard for the American people to make sense of that, because it is senseless. And it is totally unacceptable."[2]

The appearance of U.S. ambassador to the United Nations Susan Rice on the Sunday talk shows that week, blaming the Benghazi attacks on the video despite all evidence to the contrary then available to the administration, was perhaps the worst. It was impossible not to see her, or hear her accusations, as she went on and on about the "hateful video," "this heinous and offensive video." She seemed to be on every channel that Sunday, blaming Cindy.

One thing was certain, however: the Middle East was on fire, with everyone talking about the movie and using it as a pretext for mass protests and killing sprees against the United States and against Christians. Of the 85 violent attacks that occurred throughout the world in the coming weeks, 83 of them were clearly provoked by Muslim anger over the video. Benghazi was not one of them.

Cris Armenta and her law partner, Jason Armstrong, began calling Cindy more frequently to discuss strategies for getting YouTube to take down the video so it couldn't do any more harm. The lawyers also had intense exchanges with their families and with local law enforcement in their respective hometowns. Armenta was divorced and had two small children and was worried that something might happen to them on the

---

[2] Video of the ramp ceremony is here: https://www.youtube.com/watch?v=QSooz2wXpes

way to school or at home in her absence. She wanted to make sure they would be alright. That was her first duty.

They decided to reach out to YouTube directly. They start by asking them to take down the video, with the hook that they would be filing suit on Cindy's behalf if they did not. She and Jason were initially thinking of a right of publicity case, since Google had violated Cindy's right to control the commercial use of her name and image.

When YouTube didn't respond, they drew up legal papers and arranged to meet up with Cindy in Los Angeles on Thursday, September 20, to file an injunction in Los Angeles County Superior Court against Google, YouTube's parent company.

By the time they got there, the violence had taken a dramatic turn for the worse, spreading across the Middle East and beyond.

Nobody knew if Los Angeles would be next.

+++

Cindy and her husband had come down to Los Angeles the night before for the premiere of *Broken Roads*, a family drama written and produced by Justin Chambers that went on to win the Best Picture Award at the 2012 Indie Fest. Cindy had scored a bit part in the film. To celebrate, her husband picked out a long red dress for her to wear as they made their first walk down a Hollywood red carpet. She was thrilled. She felt a new world was opening up to her.

Early the next morning, Armenta picked her up at her motel in south Hollywood to drive her downtown to the courthouse. Cindy was surprised at how *small* she was. But she exuded confidence and seemed to know what to do.

"We phoned ahead to the LAPD and to courthouse security," Armenta told her.

"What for?" Cindy asked.

"We're doing everything we can to keep you safe," Armenta said.

"I want everybody to know I didn't say those words."

"We'll have a press conference after the hearing. "

"I want the world to know I didn't say those words."

Armenta was thinking about the troubling conversations she had had with her ex-husband, and with the sheriff's office at the LA Courthouse. They had given Armenta a special number to call when she was en route so they could coordinate her arrival. They told her that she and Cindy would only be offered protection at the courthouse itself. Once outside, they were on their own.

"We've arranged for our own armed security for the press conference," she said.

"Why?" Cindy said. "I brought my gun."

She opened her purse and showed Armenta her .38 Special.

Armenta sighed. Many of her friends and family owned firearms, and she was comfortable around guns. Just not at Court. Her ex-husband was an avid hunter, and lived on 20 acres in Montana. With the threats pouring in, it gave her comfort knowing her kids were safe, protected by an excellent marksman.

"It's not our job, Cindy. We need to stay focused."

Armenta asked her to go through the death threats she had received. She planned to lay it squarely before the judge, citing them in all their hatefulness and vulgarity. Surely the actual danger Cindy was in ought to weigh in their favor to get the court to order Google to take down the *Innocence of Muslims* trailers.

She was wrong.

+++

Armenta was directed by telephone to a building separate from the civil courthouse. The deputies were waiting for them, and waved them down a ramp that plunged into an underground garage. Armed deputies seemed to be everywhere, urging them forward. They directed Armenta to a secure entrance for high-profile cases, and told her to park in the midst of the police vehicles. There wasn't another "civilian" car in sight.

Cindy was confused by the sight of the uniformed sheriff's deputies, many carrying shotguns. *What's all the fuss?* she thought. She was used to having her own back and felt sure she could handle anything on her own. Despite what Armenta had been telling her on the way over, it hadn't sunk in that she actually might have become a target.

"You need to leave your .38 in the glove compartment," Armenta said. "Courthouse rules."

The officers escorted the two women down a long underground corridor linking the criminal building, where they had parked, to the civil courthouse, a block away. Armenta hadn't known the underground tunnel even existed and was bummed out because she was in high heels. *I should have brought walking shoes*, she thought.

When they reached the public area the deputies formed a phalanx around them, six in front, six behind, and rushed them into the elevator and took them up to the sheriff's conference room on the seventh floor to await the hearing. The deputies told them they would remain right outside the door, armed and ready.

"We're here to protect you, ma'am," the one in charge said to Cindy.

"Thank you," she said. "You make me feel safe."

"You're the only one who does," Armenta whispered under her breath. *Feel safe,* she meant.

Armenta went out to the clerk's window to file papers, with an armed deputy in tow. The rest of them stayed outside the door. It was a mob scene out in front of the courtroom. *Every reporter in LA must be here,* she thought.

As Cindy sat there waiting for their case to be called, she felt confident that the judge would understand her and agree to order Google to take down the video. By this point, her lawyer had told her, everyone knew that she and the other actors and even the producer had been subjected to death threats. Surely the judge would want to protect innocent American citizens. *This is America. I have a right to protection,* Cindy thought.

She was smiling by the time the deputies escorted her and Armenta to the courtroom. She beamed at the judge, *an American judge*, she thought.

+++

Armenta took in the scene as the deputies cleared a path for them, leading them to the table set aside for attorneys and clients. There wasn't an empty seat in the courtroom. Journalists crowded up to the railing and called to Armenta, trying to get a comment, but she turned to face the front of the courtroom, waiting for the judge to take the bench.

A tall, older man in a grey suit approached and asked to speak with her. Focused on the upcoming hearing, Armenta just assumed it was another reporter.

One of the deputies gave her a meaningful nod, indicating that she should speak with the man.

"Don't worry, we've got you covered," the deputy said.

It turned out the older man was the chief of security. So she accompanied him out into the hallway. He had a grandfatherly way about him, she thought, and spoke softly so they couldn't be overheard.

"Young lady, do you know what you're getting into? The people you are dealing with are very patient. They have long memories. If they want to hurt you, they could do it tomorrow or they could do it ten years from now when you are not paying attention. What you are now undertaking is something that will stay with you for the rest of your life."

Armenta explained that she had already discussed the security issues with her family and her legal team, and they had all agreed with her decision to take precautions but move ahead.

It turned out the head of security was a retired Superior Court judge. He gave her his card, and wrote his home phone number on the back. "If you ever step foot in one of my courthouses again, you call me first," he said. "I am responsible for the safety of everyone that walks through that door. We want to know when you are here."

Armenta told him that she and Cindy planned to hold a press conference in front of the courthouse after the hearing, where she knew a mob of reporters would be waiting. "I'll make sure my deputies take care of you," he said.

Normally that wasn't the case, Armenta knew, which is why she had made her own arrangements. More security couldn't hurt.

"Thank you," she said.

+++

The minute her lawyer started to address the court, Cindy lost the feeling of goodness and safety that had come over her. She felt the judge looking down at her as if *she* were the one behind the film, as if *she* was the guilty one.

"I became so angry, I wanted to jump up and speak for myself," she recalls. "I raised my hand, but the bailiff came up to me and tapped me on the shoulder and said, 'Ma'am, you cannot speak right now.'"

But as she calmed down and started to listen to Armenta, she realized that her lawyer was saying everything that she felt. It was as if she were able to reach inside her heart. She was amazing, Cindy thought.

After the judge denied the injunction, the deputies ushered them to the public elevator, once again forming a phalanx around them. Cindy hadn't realized how nervous everybody was until later when she saw pictures from the press conference on the Internet. "I suddenly realized that the media people were standing a great distance away from us, so that if something happened, maybe they would be safe. The sheriff's deputies who didn't have shotguns all had their hands on their holsters."

She and Armenta let rip.

Armenta told the media that Cindy "did not sign on to be a bigot" when she agreed to play in the film, and pledged to be back in federal court shortly. Cindy vented her anger. She was furious at the court, furious at the producer, furious at the way her own government was blaming her. She told reporters she had been threatened "at least eight times" and had "called the FBI" but never heard back.[3]

Later, back in Armenta's office, Cindy saw a photo of herself from the press conference they pulled off of the Internet, and started to laugh. She towered over Armenta like a giant scarecrow.

"I look completely crazy," she said.

"Yeah, we both look really angry," Armenta said. "Scary bitches."

The laughter helped take away the anger Cindy still felt, outraged at the way the judge just seemed to blame her for the

3   Greg Risling, "Cindy Lee Garcia & 'Innocence of Muslims': Actress Wants Judge to Block Anti-Muslim Film, Request Denied," Sept. 20, 2012, 12:15 PM ET.

deaths in Benghazi and didn't give a crap what was happening to her life because of this film.

Where are the other actors, she wondered? *Why haven't any of them come forward in public?*

+++

One person who watched the sidewalk press conference that afternoon was Saudi billionaire Prince al-Waleed bin Talal, who owned a 6.6% interest in the parent company of FoxNews. Armenta learned this the next day when his U.S. attorney, Khalid al-Mansour, phoned Armenta and offered to help finance the lawsuit. Armenta had taken the call from an unfamiliar 215 number in Texas not knowing what to expect.

"Waleed thinks you two are the bravest women he has ever seen," al-Mansour said. "He was impressed because both of you are women, and he wants to support professional women. He also wants to help take the video down."

Although Armenta didn't realize it at the time, this was the same Khalid al-Mansour, formerly known as Donald Warden, who helped found the Black Panthers in Oakland, California, in the early 1960s. Many years later, al-Mansour was identified by former Manhattan Borough chairman Percy Sutton as having contacted him on behalf of his boss, al-Waleed bin Talal, to help a young black community organizer named Barack Obama get into Harvard Law School.

"I was introduced to [Obama] by a friend who was raising money for him," Sutton said in a video-taped interview during the 2008 presidential campaign. "The friend's name was Dr. Khalid al-Mansour, from Texas. He is the principle advisor to one of the world's richest men. He told me about Obama."

In the interview, which can be viewed at YouTube, Sutton goes on to say that al-Mansour asked him to write a letter in support of Obama's application to Harvard Law School. "I wrote a letter of support of him to my friends at Harvard saying to them I thought there was a genius that was going to be available and I surely hoped they would treat him kindly."

I spoke to al-Mansour after the Percy Sutton revelations, and while he was quite open about his relationship to the Saudi prince, he cautiously protected his ties to Obama, having pledged to Obama that he would not become another Reverend Jeremiah Wright by publicly embarrassing him.[4]

Armenta turned down his offer of money, but the two stayed in touch and communicated by email. Months later, when the lawsuit dragged on and Armenta realized that the money would come in handy, she tried reaching out to al-Mansour again. "He pretended he didn't know who I was," Armenta told me. "So I said, look, I'll forward you the emails you sent me."

Despite that, nothing came of it. Because by that time, the YouTube video, and Armenta's lawsuit on behalf of Cindy Lee Garcia, had served their intended purpose.

---

4   Ken Timmerman, "Obama Had Close Ties to Top Saudi Adviser at Early Age," Newsmax, Sept. 3, 2008

CHAPTER 5
A NOVEL THEORY

Another person who watched the sidewalk press conference was David Hardy, the president of Massachusetts-based DMCA Solutions LLC, a company that provided anti-piracy services to Internet content owners. Hardy had been a practicing attorney for 25 years, specializing in technology and intellectual property law. His wife had won some acting roles, so he had an inherent sympathy for Cindy's plight. As he listened to Armenta describe the case, he became convinced that Cindy had a copyright interest in her performance in *Innocence of Muslims* that gave her standing to go after Google and YouTube directly.

His business partner, Eric Bulock, wandered into his office and the two began discussing Cindy's situation. "This poor woman has had death threats against her, for something she had nothing to do with," David said.

They argued back and forth whether there was a legitimate free speech factor in keeping the video up on YouTube. "How can someone dub words in your mouth and make you their mouthpiece for speech?" Eric said. "Cindy Lee Garcia is the victim here. We can help her!"

"I bet she never signed a release," Hardy said. "If she never signed a release then we argue that she has a right to her performance and retains a copyright. But do we really want to get involved in this? Won't we be putting ourselves and our families at risk?"

"I can just see it...insulting the Prophet (*Peace Be Upon Him*)," Bulock said. He could feel they were going to do this, and wanted to start insulating himself against attacks from Islamic radicals by using the standard Muslim reference to their Prophet.

"We would be perceived as the good guys, right, not opponents of free speech?" Hardy said. "Removing this film that is perceived by so many to be hateful?"

"Let's do it," Eric agreed.

The following morning, a Saturday, Hardy found Cris Armenta's email address on the Internet and together they drafted a memo explaining their copyright strategy. To their surprise, five minutes after he pressed "Send" his cell phone rang. It was Armenta. "Talk to me," she said.

Hardy and Bulock explained how big Internet service providers (ISPs) such as Google and YouTube operated. Because they did not produce content but hosted content that was uploaded by users, they had huge potential liability problems stemming from content piracy and copyright infringement. In essence, anybody wanting to make money with a YouTube "host" account could lift copyrighted material from another website, a movie, or another source, and post it without permission.

In the early days of the Internet, Hollywood and the music industry were intent on protecting their property from digital theft. They wanted to hold the ISPs liable for any content that violated their copyright interests, as much as the users who uploaded it. But the ISPs argued that was like suing General Motors if somebody carried out a hit-and-run with a Corvette.

It meant that the ISPs would be responsible for policing the actions of their users, an arduous if not impossible task.

So in 1998, Congress crafted a compromise intended to protect content owners as well as the Internet service providers, the Digital Millennium Copyright Act, commonly known as the DMCA. "Hence the name of our company, DMCA Solutions," Hardy said.

Under the new rules, ISPs could obtain "safe harbor" from liability for copyright infringement if they promptly removed infringing content upon receiving a "takedown notice" from the content owner or agent. "So let's say Madonna is miffed because somebody uses one of her songs as the sound track for a video about devil worshippers," Hardy said. "She sends a DMCA-compliant takedown notice to YouTube, and after they review it, they take down the offending video. When you click on it after that, you get one of those notices, 'This video has been removed due to copyright infringement,' or words to that effect."

The DMCA contains procedures allowing the user accused of a copyright violation to dispute it. And it explicitly determines that ISPs and "Web 2.0" companies that rely on users uploading massive amounts of content to their sites be considered as platforms for content, not publishers. "That means they are not responsible for self-policing the content posted to their websites and linked by their search engines," Hardy explained.

"And here's the kicker," he added. "If YouTube fails to remove copyright-infringing content after receiving a DMCA-compliant takedown notice and following all the counter-notification requirements, then it loses its safe harbor."

"And gets sued," Armenta concluded.

"So we need to have Cindy assert a copyright interest in the Mohammad video trailer," Hardy said.

"And then if YouTube refuses to take it down, we sue them," Bulock added.

Hardy and Bulock believed that Cindy could assert a copyright interest because the producer of the video had committed fraud to obtain her performance, by never telling her that the movie was about Mohammad and Islam. Normally in the film industry, the producer owns the copyright because each actor signs a release.

Then Hardy popped the delicate question. "Did Cindy ever sign a release?"

"Not that I know of," Armenta said.

"I'm not surprised. This whole thing seems so terribly amateurish. This guy is no film producer, he's just a hack."

Without a release assigning her performance to the producer, coupled to the underlying fraud of the movie itself, he felt they had a terrific copyright infringement claim against the producer and against anyone re-posting the trailer on YouTube.

It had been Google's policy to remove content within 24 to 48 hours once they received "takedown" notices under the DMCA. If Cindy filed such a notice as the "owner" of the YouTube video, Hardy and Bulock expected that Google would promptly agree to remove the Mohammad movie trailer.

"We found nearly *900* separate postings of the trailer on YouTube," Bulock added. "That gives us 900 potential lawsuits should they fail to comply."

It was a novel legal theory. The more Armenta listened, the more excited she became. And the more the call turned into a brainstorming session.

They were going to make legal history.

+++

Over the weekend Armenta's legal team, now with Hardy and his DMCA Solutions partner Eric Bulock on board, developed a plan of action. Armenta and her entertainment lawyers would prepare a revised complaint, including a claim for copyright infringement against Google and YouTube, for filing in the federal district court in Los Angeles the following week. Hardy and Bulock would prepare DMCA takedown notices and file them with Google and YouTube on Monday, citing all 900 YouTube channels they had identified that were posting the Mohammad movie trailer in one form or another.

They all felt Google would comply. After all, in the high-profile copyright infringement lawsuit brought by Viacom against Google over pirated copies of MTV videos appearing on YouTube, Google testified that its policy was *always* to comply with DMCA-compliant takedown notices, usually within 24 hours, and not their responsibility to determine the results of each infringement claim.

24 hours went by. Then 48. And then more.

Hardy and Bulock were baffled by Google's lack of response.

"They get something like ten *million* requests for piracy removal every week," Bulock told Armenta on one of their conference calls.

Here was a case that was on the front pages of all the newspapers. It was being discussed publicly by the president of the United States, the secretary of state, and other top U.S. officials, and yet Google not only wouldn't take down the movie; it wouldn't even acknowledge the takedown requests.

Could they actually want the slaughter of innocents to continue?

What was going on?

CHAPTER 6
NEW YORK

While Cris Armenta was plotting the next legal steps to take on Cindy's behalf and whether she could afford to take on such a potentially huge case on a *pro bono* basis, Cindy continued to be besieged by calls from the media. But now it was the national media, based in New York. The *Today Show*. *The View*. *Day Break*. And many more. They wanted to bring her to New York so she could tell her story on national television. For several days, she told them she would think about it. Everything seemed to be spinning out of control.

She continued to get ugly emails full of violent and lewd comments, but she was also starting to get letters from Muslims who told her that they appreciated her apology and believed she was a good person who had just been duped. That made her feel a bit better. But the negative stories about her and the movie continued. And they hurt.

Now family members and friends had started calling, asking what in the world was going on. She didn't have time to sit down and explain everything to them, but at least she could tell them she was alright. That wasn't enough when it came to her great-grandchildren. They were just babies, 11 months apart, and she had been taking care of them since birth while their mother worked. It broke her heart when her grandson wrote her a letter, demanding that his two children and his wife leave Cindy's house for fear that Cindy's notoriety would get them murdered. That was the cruelest blow of all.

One day three of her best friends showed up at her house, offering her a place to stay if she needed to get away. She hugged them and thanked them. *Having people that love you is amazing,* she thought.

+++

Finally, on Friday she made up her mind. She had been wanting to go to New York for some time for her small consulting company, Sugar & Spice, to meet a lady in the fashion industry. With the *Today Show* offering to pay all her expenses, it would be a great way of getting there. She'd pretend to herself that she was going on business.

"I'm going to need security," she told the producer. "I've had death threats. The LA Sheriff's office freaked out during our court hearing."

NBC scoured about and found that a former Rome bureau chief lived in Southern California, so they had him pick her up that Sunday morning, drive her to the airport, and fly with her all the way to New York. "Steven was a delightful man who said he had flown with the Pope for six years," Cindy said. "That touched my heart. I felt blessed to be protected by such a person."

The NBC producers had a car waiting for them at the airport in New York that drove them directly to her midtown hotel. Steven got her checked in and introduced her to the retired NYPD police officer NBC had hired to take over as her bodyguard in New York.

"Don't worry, Cindy. I'll be with you at all times," the retired officer said. He escorted her up to her room, where she found a note from Armenta. The lawyer had arrived earlier on a separate flight from her office in Bozeman, Montana, along with a friend. "Join us for drinks when you get in," it said. "We're right next door."

When Cindy and her bodyguard joined them, she was feeling so overwhelmed by the trip, the fancy hotel, and all the attention from the NBC producers that she asked them to pray with her, to ask God to bless their meetings and to keep them safe and help them to speak the truth.

The next day, Monday, September 24, 2012, was her big day.

+++

Armenta was on the plane from Bozeman, surfing the Internet to see if any new threats had turned up, when she saw the news. Some whack-job Islamic cleric in Egypt had put out a fatwa on Cindy. Here is the *LA Times* headline she found:

POLICE PROBE THREATS, FATWA AGAINST 'INNOCENCE OF MUSLIMS' ACTORS

Was it serious, or just a bluff? She sent off a flurry of emails – *thank God for in-flight WiFi*, she thought – to get a better picture of what it meant. She contacted Khaled al-Mansour, the lawyer for the Saudi prince, and asked him to comment on safety issues. After all, the cleric was in Egypt and they were in the United States. Should they really be worrying about this? Just in case, she also sent it to her contacts with local law enforcement in Bozeman, and the LAPD. *Why didn't they send it to me directly?* she wondered. "We weren't getting anything from law enforcement," Armenta told me. "That's what was so weird. We were never warned about anything."

Al-Mansour got back to her almost immediately. Oh yeah, he said. She should take it very seriously. The fatwa was like a court ruling to these people, and it authorized Muslims, including Muslims living in the United States, to kill anybody involved in the movie. *Including you,* he added. The guy who issued it was a well-known Salafist named Ahmad Fouad Ashoush. He'd published the fatwa on the Internet, where it had been picked up by thousands of jihadi websites around the world. It read as follows:

"Those bastards who did this film are belligerent disbelievers. I issue a fatwa and call on the Muslim youth in America and Europe to do this duty, which is to kill the director, the producer, and the actors and everyone who helped and promoted the film. So hurry, hurry. O Muslim youth in America and Europe, and teach those filthy lowly ones a lesson that all the monkeys and pigs in America and Europe will understand! May Allah guide."[1]

She got another email form her office and saw that Salman Rushdie had given an interview after the news of the fatwa hit, describing the living hell he was still living some 23 *years* after the Iranian ayatollah had put out a fatwa on him. *Holy crap!* And all this for a case they had taken on *pro bono* because they wanted to help a woman who seemed completely out of her league.

Armenta immediately took down her social media pages, anything that disclosed where she lived, and urged her law partners to do the same. She also contacted various organizations where she sat on the board and asked them to take down all

---

[1]   Armenta asked UCLA Islamic scholar Dr. Khaled Abou El Fadl, whom she retained as an expert witness, to translate the text of the fatwa and include it and his analysis of what it meant in a sworn statement they could use in court. *Garcia et al v. Google Inc., et al,* 2:12-cv-08315-MWF-VBK, United States District Court for the Central District of California, Declaration of Dr. Khaled Abou El Fadl, Docket 14.

references to her. And she emailed the NBC producers to let them know they would be needing extra security.

+++

As soon as Cindy got settled into her room, Armenta told her the news.

"Cindy, there's been a fatwa put out on you."

"What's that?" Cindy asked.

"It's a ruling by a Muslim cleric. They issue them all the time. It's something like a court ruling here in the U.S."

"So they agreed to take down the movie?" Cindy asked. She didn't see what Cris was getting at.

"No. The ruling invites Muslims, including Muslims here in the U.S., to kill anybody involved in the movie. Including you. Probably including me, too."

Cindy went into shock as the news sank in. Her lips started trembling, as if she was going to cry.

"Don't worry," Armenta said. "I've told the hotel and NBC. They've put on extra security."

"I'm not worried," Cindy said, shaking it off. "It's just, how can these people have so much hate in their heart?"

Armenta began to realize how little any of them knew about Islam. After the court appearance in Los Angeles, the fact that they could be facing very real danger had begun to sink in with her. She wasn't sure that Cindy yet realized that Islam was an ideology, and that a fatwa issued by a respected cleric was a call to action – that could have potentially deadly results.

+++

The *Today Show* came and went in a whirlwind. The producers sent her a car at some ungodly hour, and then she and Armenta were whisked into the green room for makeup and coffee and then she was on the set and it seemed the hosts just kept talking and talking. Reporter Mike Taibi had done a set-up piece showing where the movie had been filmed and clips from the press conference she and Armenta had given in front of the LA courthouse the week before.

But then, *bang*, he brought on a man claiming to be a first amendment lawyer who said she didn't stand a chance to get Google to take down the video. What's worse, he said that her own actions in coming forward had made her "potentially much more of a target." Savannah Guthrie drilled down on her safety as soon as she brought the two of them on live.

"Aren't you worried that coming forward in this public way, you'll make yourself even more recognizable?" she asked.

"No," Cindy said. "I'm coming forward to clear my name."

She went on to recite what by now had become her script, that she had been duped, the film never mentioned Mohammad or Muslims, and was just "an adventure film" about desert life 2,000 years ago. She had never uttered the words she appeared to speak in the movie.

"To be clear," Guthrie said, eager for the "apology" moment, "this does not reflect your views of the Muslim faith."

"Absolutely not," Cindy said. "I would not do that."

And then, as Guthrie asked her about the filmmaker, they showed b-roll for the third time of Nakoula Basseley Nakoula being escorted from his home on September 15 by LA County sheriff's deputies, a white scarf wrapped around his face, hiding him from the cameras and the reporters shouting questions at him, as if he were being taken on a perp walk. He looked small and frightened and guilty as hell.

Questioned about her chances of succeeding in the lawsuit, Armenta agreed that Congress had passed a law that immunized Google. But then she pivoted in a way she hoped would win them the sympathies of millions of Americans as well as the Obama administration, which continued to blame the movie for the murders in Benghazi and the anti-American protests sweeping across the Muslim world.

"They say in their own terms and guidelines that 'hate speech' is not allowed. How can this not be hate speech? How can this not be wrong, morally, intellectually, legally?" she said.

After the show, YouTube issued a statement that NBC put up on their website that left Armenta baffled.

"We are pleased with the Judge's decision [to dismiss the case]. YouTube is and will remain a platform for free expression."[2]

Armenta couldn't believe that Google was going to fight a free speech battle over this. Wary and suspicious, she suspected something else must be going on.

Their SUV was waiting for them after the show. As they drove back to the hotel, Cindy started to get a bad feeling about the driver. He looked like he was from the Middle East. Armenta and her friend were talking away, and suddenly her friend burst out talking about their room numbers, and both Cindy and the NBC bodyguard told her to be quiet. The two of them exchanged a glance, and Cindy knew that the bodyguard understood.

She had been raised by her stepfather, and one of the things he had taught her was not to trust anyone. Especially now. She never went to a public place unless she was facing the door, and was always careful to pay attention to her surroundings. She would not run wearing a headset, so she could hear what was going on. And she always slept with her

---

[2]   See: http://www.today.com/id/49146658/ns/today-today_news/t/
actress-anti-islam-film-i-was-duped/#.VrpWwzZxv8s

loaded .38 and a double-barrel 12-gauge shotgun in the room. "Not that I am paranoid," Cindy said. "But you never know when you will get unwelcome visitors. Lord knows, I have had them in the past, long before this."

+++

Later, Cindy and Armenta's friend decided to take the car and driver for a tour of New York City, leaving Armenta back at the hotel to work on the legal filings. Cindy wanted to see Ground Zero and Fifth Avenue and so many other things. She began thinking of the SUV driver, and realized she was so innocent of Islam. She didn't understand how a religion could motivate people to violence. She had never spoken to a Muslim before. She didn't even know what a Muslim was! She had so many questions. *Here's my chance*, she thought. *If this guy is a Muslim, I can ask him.*

"Where would you ladies like to go?" he asked politely.

"Are you a Muslim?" Cindy asked him, point blank.

"Yes," he said. "And I know who you are."

"I have so many questions for you," she said.

So she began asking him about his faith, and they spoke about God and prayer and submission to God's will and to his Prophet.

"So why has all this violence broken out in the Middle East after the release of this stupid film?" she asked.

The driver looked at her in the mirror. "If I know that someone has insulted the Prophet, peace be upon him, I will kill him," the driver said. He said it so calmly that Cindy wasn't afraid. It was just a fact, stunning, but in her heart she knew it was true.

"I never insulted your Prophet," she said.

"I know that you say this."

"But it's true. I am innocent."

They drove down to Ground Zero and at one point the driver asked if he could take a picture with them to post to his Facebook page. He said he wanted to tell his friends that she was innocent. Cindy agreed.

+++

The emotional tug of Ground Zero exhausted her. So many people dead, all because of 19 terrorists – and she had never before realized they were Muslims, that's how much her government had kept from her. Cindy wanted to get back to the hotel and get some rest before the next round of interviews the next day. But as she lay down, she started thinking about the SUV driver and the photo and she couldn't sleep. *What if someone didn't believe that I was telling the truth?* she thought. *What if they put pressure on him to tell them where I am?*

She started getting spooked, and went to see her Armenta next door and explained the photo.

"I think we should change hotels, just to be safe," Cindy said.

Armenta called down to the hotel security, and asked them to make sure no one could come up to their room.

"We'll be fine," Armenta said. "Get some rest."

When she finally fell asleep back in her room, Cindy had a dream that someone was trying to break down the door to her room. In her dream, she jumped up to close it, but someone outside was pushing very hard, and it was a heavy metal door and it seemed to press steadily into her, driving her into the wall.

She woke up in a panic. But then a scripture came to her about the Lord opening doors that no man can close and closing doors that no man can open, and she realized that the dream was from the Lord and that He was opening the door to the Muslim world for her. *God has a plan for each one of our lives*, she thought. *It's all starting to make sense.*

She thought again how the Lord had sent her to Hollywood in the first place, after her husband's horrible accident, and then how she had felt God's love for Muslims when she was driving across the Grapevine to meet the journalists who would broadcast her words into Egypt. She began thinking how Isaac and Ishmael were half-brothers, and that God loved both of them equally. *What does He want from me?* she wondered. And then she fell asleep again.

When she woke up the next time, a man was knocking at the door. "Room service," he said. She thought he had a Middle Eastern accent, and her heart started beating so fast she could hardly breath.

"Room service! Open the door!" he hissed.

Cindy realized she had nowhere to go. She was too high up to go out the window, and the door to Armenta's adjoining room was locked.

"I didn't order room service," she called through the door.

Just then, the phone at her bed rang. It was Armenta, and she was breathing as heavily as Cindy was.

"Cindy, whatever you do, *do not* open your door. There is a man in a disheveled hotel uniform just outside your door and he does not look like he should be there," Armenta said. "I saw him just as I was getting on the elevator."

"Where's the bodyguard?"

"He went home, remember? Look, I'm going downstairs to get help. You call 911. AND STAY PUT!"

The elevator was packed. Armenta remembers somebody asking her if everything was alright, and that's when she lost it. "Fuck no, everything is not alright. Somebody is trying to kill my client," she said.

When they got down to the lobby she found the hotel security chief and explained that the "room service" man had brought nothing with him; no tray, no cart, no nothing.

"He was probably just picking up the dirty plates," the security man said.

That sent Armenta off on a rant. "You've got to be fucking kidding me. You know as well as I do that they don't send somebody to pick up plates unless you call. And we never called." She demanded to see the duty roster, but the security chief drew the line. When she got back upstairs with a hotel security guard, the man who had been in front of Cindy's door was gone.

They demanded to change rooms after that and checked in under pseudonyms just to play safe.

Armenta was convinced that Cindy had narrowly escaped an attempt on her life.

+++

The next morning, it was *The View*.

President Obama had just spoken at the United Nations in New York, once again blaming the "crude and disgusting" video for the Benghazi attacks and the anti-American unrest sweeping across the Middle East. "We understand why people take offense to this video because millions of our citizens are among them," he said. "The future must not belong to those who slander the prophet of Islam."[3]

It was one heck of a lead in. Cindy's segment was hot.

Co-host Chris Cuomo kicked off by stating that the film was responsible for the deaths of 40 people in protests after the Benghazi attacks. "Did you know it was going to be anti-Muslim?" he asked.

---

[3] Toby Harden, "Obama tells United Nations it is 'time to heed the words of Gandhi', condemns 'digusting' anti-Islam video...." *Daily Mail*, Sept. 25, 2012

"No," Cindy said. "It was based on an adventure film 2,000 years ago in the desert."

One of the hosts then mentioned that many of the actors in the film "have been getting death threats, including you. You've had to go into hiding. They've gone into hiding."

"No, I haven't went [sic] into hiding," Cindy said.

"She's right here," Cuomo added, and the audience laughed.

They asked her why she was coming out publicly. "I don't want the Muslim world to think that America is behind this. I don't want them to think that I am behind it," she said. "I am a pastor of a church. I've been a pastor for over 15 years. And my congregation knows me, that I love Christ, that I've never taught them to hate other religions or other people's beliefs."

Whoopi Goldberg asked if she had spoken to imams, so they could spread the word to their congregations. Cindy wasn't familiar with the word "imam," but she was in the groove. "I have spoken to the Middle East at least four times," she said. "And I've gotten good response from so many Muslims. They say, 'we believe you. We can tell from your heart, when you were speaking, that you are truthful and honest.' It was beautiful to me to get that response."

Then they all piled on Sam Bacile, aka Nakoula Basseley Nakoula, the filmmaker. A larger than life clip from the famous b-roll of him being bundled into a sheriff's patrol car loomed over the set. Co-host Joy Behar waxed indignant. "47 people at least have been killed in those riots. Maybe more. I mean, he is responsible for part of that."

In the last minute of the segment they called on Armenta, who had been miked and placed down in the audience, to comment on the legal approach they planned to take. "There is a first amendment right to say what you think. But there's also a first amendment right not to be forced to say that which you don't think," she said, carefully. "And that is exactly what happened here. Someone put words in Cindy Lee Garcia's mouth, to make her look like a religious bigot. And she isn't."

It was a wrap. Everyone on the set was pleased with how it had gone. And Cindy got to schmooze with Dwight Yokem and his band out in the green room before they left. She felt vindicated. It never occurred to her to object when ABC News posted the segment with her appearance with the title, "Anti-Muslim Film Actress Talks with *The View*."[4]

+++

They had checked out of the hotel and brought their luggage with them to the studio at 320 West 66th street, and now they were down on the street, piling in a cab to head out to LaGuardia airport to catch their flights home. Cindy was exhausted. Exhausted, but satisfied. She had wanted to go the United Nations the day before to try to speak to President Obama, to tell him that the movie was an evil lie, but Armenta had told her to not even try.

When they pulled into the taxi drop-off area in front of the terminal, several police officers were waiting.

"Are you Ms. Garcia?" one of them asked, politely.

"Why, yes!" Cindy said. She was thrilled that someone recognized her. *Maybe he saw me on* The View, she thought.

"Ma'am, please come with us," the officer said. "It's for your own safety. We'd like to keep you in a private lounge until your flight is called."

The 'private lounge' turned out to be the airport police station. But they offered her coffee and treated her with

---

4   http://abcnews.go.com/US/video/anti-muslim-film-actress-cindy-lee-garcia-talks-view-17329329

respect. When it was time to board, they drove her directly out onto the tarmac in a police vehicle before the other passengers were allowed to board, and actually searched the plane with dogs before they would let her get on board. She had on a big coat to keep her warm and wore a hat and sunglasses, so it would be harder to recognize her.

It was a long ride home to Bakersfield. She had to change planes in Chicago and Phoenix. But once she got off the first flight, no one was paying any attention to her any more. She just wanted all of this to be behind her, but clearly that wasn't going to happen. She was marked. She knew that God had a plan for her, just as He did for each and every person. But right now, that plan seemed to be leading her in a very difficult, even dangerous direction.

Her life as she had known it up to then was over.

CHAPTER 7

THE INNOCENCE OF CINDY LEE GARCIA

Cindy grew up one of six children in a blue-collar family outside of Los Angeles. She never knew her natural father because he left when she was a child. Her mother was the backbone of the family, working to support her children in a variety of jobs. And her mother was strong. She worked doing a man's job at the lumber mill in Johnsondale, California, up near Ponderosa, and taught her children to be strong, too. "My siblings and I learned to ride horses, cook, and do chores," Cindy said.

When her mother remarried, her new stepfather taught her to fight. "He taught me to fight like a man, to fight for my life, and that meant if someone was going to try to rape me or kill me, I would take their life instead," Cindy said. Because of that, she found herself throughout life defending women and children who could not protect themselves as well as she could. "The things he taught me were bittersweet."

When she was a toddler Cindy was sexually abused by someone she should have been able to trust. "I was too young to tell my mother," she said. For many years, she blocked the memory and went on with her life, "a very troubled life filled with wrong choices that brought only brokenness." All the while, she carried the tragic secret locked up inside her, suppressing it for years.

Nakoula remembers Cindy telling her later that she had been molested as a child, and that was why she had empathized so strongly with her character in the movie, a mother being forced to give up her seven-year-old child to a horny 53-year-old man. She still kicks herself for telling him that. She so felt that he was using her.

When Cindy was 14, home had become hell. Her parents were always fighting, and finally her mom threw her stepdad out for good. Cindy dropped out of high school and ran away to San Diego with an older boy, thinking to give her mother one less mouth to feed. At 15, pregnant with her first child, she learned that her 22-year-old boyfriend was cheating on her and walked out. Pregnant and alone, she worked as a waitress and at any odd job she could find to support her baby, just as her mother had done. It was a rough road.

Anger and violence filled her heart and she became involved with a string of troubled men who were both abusive and drug users. "By the time I was 18, I had my next child, and I'll be damned if the same thing didn't happen again. I was a lousy judge of character," she admits. "I was unlucky in my choice of men, already at that age." She had two daughters with two different men.

For years she desperately sought a new beginning for her daughters and for herself, but never managed to go back to school because she always had to work to feed her family. She built walls around her heart until it became cold and calloused. She was determined that no one would be able to hurt her again. She was in control, or so she thought.

But as time went by, she began to realize that the anger she carried in her heart had taken over.

She began to think that she would never be able to love someone again. Her heart had become hard. "I could recall the love of my mother and grandparents as if it were in a very distant place. I felt I was going to be one of those people that would never find their way back to tenderness," she said.

The trigger was Doyle. He was a very large man, much bigger than she was (and Cindy was 5'9"). They fought worse than cats and dogs, both of them so high on drugs they hardly felt the pain they inflicted. Often, he drew blood, smashing her head into hard objects until the blood poured out of her nose. She remembers a song that was popular at the time. It was titled "Maybe It's a Lunatic You're Looking For." She felt it pretty much summed up her life.

+++

One night, Doyle had her by the throat and had lifted her in a rage up onto the sink. She realized that if she didn't do something quickly, he was going to smash her head through the window. They had begun their fight in the bathroom, which by now was smeared with her blood. But that hadn't seemed to bother him.

Cindy managed to pull her legs into her chest, and with all her might she kicked him in the face to get him off. She remembers him putting up his hand to try to stop the blow, but instead it just got in the way and her feet smashed into him so hard that she drew blood. She figures she must have struck an artery in his hand or something because blood began to squirt out of his wrist in pulsating streams. To her surprise, Doyle just walked away, and left her alone for the night.

From that time on, she carried a loaded gun on her at all times, until finally she stole Doyle's truck and got away from him for good.

+++

Shortly after her escape, she remembers sitting in her chair one night and having a talk with God. "Lord, if you are real, please help me. I cannot live like this any more," she said. And that was it. No answer, no voice, no nothing. Or so she thought.

A few days later, her sister came by with a bottle of wine and a photo of Jesus and invited her to go to church. Cindy's heart leapt, and she said yes, immediately. There were about 200 people in the church. She sat in the back row feeling ashamed of her life and all her mistakes. She remembers thinking, "Lord, let this man give an altar call, I am so sorry, Lord, for the sinful life that I have lived."

To her surprise, at the end of the service the pastor called people to the altar that wanted to give their lives to Christ. "I jumped out of my chair and I ran as fast as I could to the altar. I felt like I couldn't get there quick enough," Cindy says. "I remember feeling that God had heard my heart crying out to him, and he told that preacher to give that call just for me. I fell on my knees on that altar and whispered, 'Lord, I am so sorry.'" She burst into tears and the freedom of it seemed to wash away the burden of her sins, the violence, the heavy drug use, the wasted years.

Gradually, as she started to attend church and to read God's word and to pray, she found the most wonderful change taking place inside of her. "I began to love others, but it was different than anything I had ever known," she said. "The hardness was leaving me. I began to find hope and purpose, even a sense of destiny."

One day, she was invited to a revival service at a small church packed with people. Just as she walked through the front door, the guest speaker walked in through the back. He was a small, African man Cindy had never met before. From opposite sides of the room their eyes met, and they made their way through the crowd as if they had known each other forever. Cindy felt they knew each other in the spirit, that they knew each other in some deep and profound way through Christ. When they reached each other they hugged, and then he went up front to the speaker's platform and Cindy went to find a seat in the back.

Not long into his sermon he stopped preaching and called her up to the front of the congregation. "Sister," he said. "I feel that the Lord wants me to give you this word. One day, God will give you a worldwide platform. I don't know what it is. Maybe you don't know what it is, either. But one day, you will."

Cindy didn't know what to say. It seemed like such a tall order, and her life was such a mess. But that was when things began to turn around.

+++

When Cindy decided to turn her life over to God and accept Jesus as her Savior at the age of 26, the healing of the many broken pieces of her soul began. She felt his unconditional love and it taught her to forgive all the people who had hurt her, including the one who abused her as a child. "That was a secret I kept to myself out of fear and shame, one I had shoved so deep down inside my soul because of the ugly truth of it all that I didn't want to remember it," she said. "But when I became a Christian and read the Bible, I learned that God commands us to forgive and that he gives us the grace to forgive. I had to let it go! And I did."

And then, in 1995, she was working on a construction site and a man came into the room she was painting and introduced himself. "Hello, my name is Mark, and I love Jesus," he said. Soon, Mark Garcia asked her to marry him. They've been together ever since.

+++

In October 1998, she was driving with her sister, Jerrie, and felt an empty place inside of her. *Lord, what more do you want from me?* She felt that he wanted her to start a church. Where was she going to get the money for that?

The next day, she felt drawn to visit a small wedding chapel on Brundage Lane in Bakersfield. The owners said they would sublet the building for $200 a month, and so by November 1, she founded a ministry called Flame of Fire Outreach and held her first service. Within a year, they outgrew the building and needed something bigger.

This time, Cindy encountered a pastor who was moving out of his 200-seat church into a bigger one and wanted to sell the building. She asked him to pray about renting it to them instead, and so for a year they paid him $1,200 a month for the premises. By now, he really wanted to sell the church and asked her if they were ready to buy it, so Cindy took it to her elders. They said yes, as long as they could qualify for a loan. She went to a local bank, and they qualified for the loan, but the bank officer asked her for a down payment of $13,258, that she needed to deposit the next day.

"I said, okay, I don't have that kind of money and no one in our church has that kind of money. So I prayed and said, 'Lord, you told me to start this church and I did, you led us this far and now we have the chance to buy it. So, Lord, you need $13,258 and you need it tomorrow.' I threw it right back at him."

Cindy is proud when she tells this story, proud and in awe of the power of prayer.

The next day, a woman from her church came up to her and placed $13,000 in cash in her hand. Cindy said they would pay her back in a year. And they did.

+++

Through the church and her ministry, Cindy felt alive. As she immersed herself in Scripture to prepare her sermons, she felt that she was doing what she had always been called to do, despite her previously violent life. She raised enough money through her ministry to open a recovery home for addicts and the homeless and kids who had been sexually abused. She put them in cabins at an old motel, ten miles out of Bakersfield. "Every person who sought refuge with us had a tragic story to tell," she recalls. "My mission was to help those folks to see that a turn in the road is always possible, especially with Jesus Christ on their side. And to do that, I always shared my own story."

Her Mom had also found Jesus and became the head cook at the shelter, eventually taking over a ministry she called the Lord's Table to feed the hungry. She was so beautiful and so strong, Cindy thought. She had remained single since she divorced Cindy's stepdad.

On February 23, 2009, tragedy struck again. Her husband, Mark, was working as a foreman at the Pastoria Power Plant in Grapevine, California. While changing filters in a narrow filtration unit tower, Mark fell twenty feet and got stuck on an internal walkway, suspended sixty feet in the air. Firefighters managed to hoist him out, but his injuries were severe. Cindy was at her mother's making breakfast when the phone rang. "They told me only that Mark had fallen off a ladder and had a cut on his head," she recalls. Not thinking much of it, she went to the hospital a bit later to visit him. "When they wouldn't let me see him, I got worried," she says.

All day long she waited at the hospital, the dread just digging a hole in her gut. It was well past midnight when the doctors finally allowed her in. "His head was swollen and enlarged. He had undergone multiple surgeries. They said that his face had been 'degloved,' meaning that most of the skin had been torn off and turned inside out, like a tight-fitting glove."

Thanks to the EMT medics, who had stapled his face back in place on the way to the hospital, the surgeons had been able to reconstruct his face. But it took multiple surgeries. His shoulder was crushed, and a bone fragment pierced his eye. In the end, he lapsed into a coma and was breathing heavily when she saw him.

Over the next two weeks, Cindy prayed constantly. Her family and friends and a very attentive and skilled medical team at the Kern County hospital kept her together. Finally Mark woke up. But over the next 18 months, he required extensive care.

+++

In 2011, she felt like she was finally coming up for air from a string of family tragedies (her Mom died of cancer just weeks after Mark's accident), and decided to try to build a new career in modeling and acting.

As a child, she had participated in plays in school and at church, and even taken parts as an extra in Hollywood Westerns filmed in a ghost town not far from her house. Now, 30 years later, she took a professional modeling course and found a new pride in standing tall and walking in front of others. Performance modeling gave her the inspiration to try to find paid work as an actor. She'd never been shy; God had given her the strength to speak in front of other people. Maybe this was what she had always been meant to do.

She took her modeling photographs and placed them on talent websites, and was thrilled when she got called for three jobs in the first year. "I felt strong and alive. It was as much about 'me' as it was about my life's work. I believed that I could use acting as a tool to communicate my newfound strength and my passionate beliefs," she said.

How could she have known that the film that would later be called *Innocence of Muslims* would offend not only her religious beliefs and convictions, but also the confidence and strength she had cultivated over so many years? That was why she felt so betrayed by Sam Bacile and his duplicity. She had been duped. She had been betrayed. She had been used.

"I took it personal," she said.

And the anger returned. But this time, it was a righteous anger, a justified anger, an anger that she felt served a higher purpose.

CHAPTER 8
CASTING CALL

On July 19, 2011, Cindy saw a casting call for a desert adventure film called *Desert Warrior*. Here is how the producers pitched the movie on Craigslist:

NOW CASTING: SAG and SAG ACTORS for "DESERT WARRIOR." Director Alan Roberts. Historical desert drama set in Middle East. Indie Feature film shoots from 18 days in L.A. in August. Studio and backlot locations.

Male roles: DR. MATTHEW (Lead): Middle Eastern Pharmacist, 40-50, intelligent, family man; GEORGE (Lead): 40-50, Middle Eastern warrior leader, romantic, charismatic; YOUNG GEORGE (featured), 18-22; PRIEST (featured): 60-70, bearded; ABDO (featured): 60-70, Elder tribe leader; ISRAELI MEN 30-50 (featured); WARRIORS (featured) 18-50, Various Middle Eastern types, bearded.

Female Roles: CONDALISA (featured): 40, attractive, successful, strong willed; HILLARY (featured): 18 but must look younger, petite, innocent; YOUSTINA (featured) 16-18, Daughter of doctor;

MIDDLE EASTERN WOMEN (Various Featured Roles) 18-40, attractive, exotic; OLDER WOMAN (featured) 60-70, feisty.
Please place Role desired in SUBJECT line of email.

Cindy was excited. She loved the idea of a desert drama. Maybe they would have sword fighting and hand-to-hand combat? She thought she'd be good at that. At the very least, it would be fun to watch. Looking back now, she saw there was no mention of Mohammad, Muslims, or the religion of Islam.

She circled the role "Condalisa," and thought: *attractive, strong-willed: that's me.* But when she emailed the director, Alan Roberts, she said that she wanted to play the part of a warrior. "I know the call is only for men in this role. But this is my character," she wrote. She included photographs of her posing with her .38 Special and with her shotgun, as well more traditional modeling photographs. It all seemed so official, so real. The director even had a special email address just for the movie: *desertwarrior2011@yahoo.com.* The casting call said it was an Indie film, but that didn't necessarily mean it was low budget or amateurish. *Maybe they'd go to the Oscars like Ben Hur!*

Roberts emailed back, inviting her to audition for the movie. So on July 25, she drove down from Bakersfield to an address off North La Cienega Blvd in West Hollywood that turned out to be a run-down former restaurant that Roberts and his on-again, off-again partner, Jimmy Israel, had rented for the occasion. A broken sign for the "Spires" restaurant chain hung outside. She was greeted by a middle-aged woman of Middle Eastern descent, the producer's wife. It was her first contact with the family of Sam Bacile, aka Nakoula Basseley Nakoula, the man behind the film.

Cindy again asked if she could play one of the desert warriors. "I like sword fighting," she said. "And I'm good at it. I even have my own two-edged sword!"

Alan, the director, shook his head and handed her sides for the part she had signed up for. "Women didn't fight in those days," he said. She remembers reading the lines several times to herself to get a feel for the character. Then Alan called her into the room where they had the camera crew, the casting director and another, quiet man who seemed to observing everything without saying anything. (Later, she realized that was Nakoula). She ran through the lines, giving them her best shot. And then she was gone.

Tim Dax, who left New York because his heavily-tattooed body was attracting stares, liked to walk around with a sleek black helmet covering most of his skull. It made him look like a desert warrior in real life. An aspiring actor, like most of the others who applied to the casting call, Dax thought he would be perfect for a role in the movie, maybe "a character like the one Arnold Schwarzenegger played in *Conan the Barbarian*... How perfect would I be for something like that?"

But when he showed up at the dingy building in West Hollywood, his hopes sank. "It couldn't be anybody important, since this is a shithole," he told a reporter from *Vanity Fair*. Still, he read for a part and remembers meeting the producer, who seemed to like him. As Dax was leaving that day, Nakoula called after him: "Are you SAG?" – that is, a member of the Screen Actors Guild. Dax said he was not, so Nakoula smiled. "You will be!" At least, that got his hopes up.[1]

+++

Jimmy Israel, a book-keeper and sometime film producer, first met Nakoula in 2010 through a mutual acquaintance,

---

[1]   Michael Joseph Gross, "Disaster Movie," *Vanity Fair*, Dec. 27, 2012.

Robert "Bobby" Brownell, aka Alan Roberts. At the time, Jimmy had wanted to audition for a role in the film, *Desert Warrior*, which Brownell said he was getting ready to direct and produce. After reading some lines, he got to talking with Nakoula. "I told him that I was not only a performer, but that I had been a producer-writer of fine films in Europe in the early '80s for a short time and was now in the real estate business."[2]

Israel didn't get a part. But awhile later, Brownell called him to say that Nakoula was getting treated for cancer and so the film had been put off, at least for now. Nakoula had confided "that he wished to make a political film before he passed" and that he was working with Brownell to improve the screenplay.

As the months went by with no word from Nakoula, both Brownell and Israel began to suspect something was afoot. "My thought was that something had happened in the Coptic Christian community that caused [Nakoula] to back off for awhile. My guess is that the money to make the film was coming from them and couldn't be delivered at the time," Israel wrote.

Then in June 2011, Brownell called him and said that Nakoula had recovered and wanted to shoot the film. Because Brownell was engaged on another project, he asked Nakoula to hold off for several months. Instead, Nakoula called Israel, and asked him to produce and direct the film, and offered to pay him $10,000 for the work.

Brownell didn't take offense, and sent Jimmy Israel his copy of the 111-page screenplay for *Desert Warrior*. "The screenplay showed that [Nakoula] and whoever else may have helped him write the film is both a radical Coptic Christian and anti-Muslim,"

---

[2]   Jimmy Israel has given multiple, often conflicting accounts of his involvement in the movie. This passage follows the version he wrote for Vice.com that appeared on Sept. 18, 2012, along with a copy of the film script. http://www.vice.com/read/here-is-what-we-believe-to-be-the-final-2011-screenplay-for-innocence-of-muslims#tips

Jimmy Israel believed. "I believe his goal was to expose those who have killed Copts and to warn the world of the danger of the extremist interpretation of the Koran."

The central character of the screenplay he read in 2011 and turned over to VICE was named "Mo" and "Mohammad." His first wife was called "Khadija," her uncle, a priest who helped write a book for him based on the Torah and parts of the New Testament, is called "Warraqa." Mohammad takes a young girl for a wife in the screenplay, where she is named "Aisha." His companions are called "Omar," "Abu Bakr," "Ali," and "Abu Mutaleb."

All of these are the authentic names of the founder of Islam and his immediate family and friends, as reported in Muslim scriptures. The notion that Mohammad's wife's uncle or a Christian monk had written the Koran for him as a means of attracting Jewish and Byzantine followers in seventh century Mecca has long been acknowledged in Islamic tradition, although it is not widely known to ordinary Muslims.[3]

Jimmy Israel says that after reading the script, he "could not justify working on the film as it was written. I told [Nakoula] that if I was going to be involved, I wanted to make the screenplay better, specifically by cutting the enormous amount of brutality and gratuitous sex scenes. He said that he would 'consider' my suggestions after the casting was completed."

And so, the work began. Jimmy Israel placed the ads for the casting call along with a synopsis he wrote after a quick read of the screenplay. Nakoula texted him a list of roles to place in the ad. The characters were now called George (for

---

[3]   I incorporated stories of the Christian monk Bahira, whose contributions to the writing of the Koran appear in Ibn Ishaq's definitive Life of Mohammad (the Sura), in my fictional account of the origins of Islam, *St. Peter's Bones*. A research note detailing these sources is available here: http://kentimmerman.com/Research_note.pdf

Mohammad), Condalisa (for Khadija), Solymon (for Warraqa), and Hillary (for Aisha).

Through his real estate contacts, Jimmy Israel found a location on La Cienega they could use for the auditions. Nakoula was in a hurry to choose the actors and film the movie. "He wanted to shoot. Basseley wanted to shoot the film right away and cast it right away and da ra ra," and so together they went to the La Cienega location and signed a rental agreement for the auditions on the spot.[4]

But that evening, Nakoula spoke to Brownell again by phone. He convinced Brownell to come back to direct the film, and so Jimmy was out. "And that was fine with me because I hated the screenplay," Israel said in his deposition.

Jimmy Israel tells two different versions of his story. To Vice, just days after the September 11, 2012 attacks in Benghazi, he said that the film script Nakoula showed him had the names of Mohammad and other Islamic characters. Two years later, when he was deposed in Cindy's lawsuit by Cris Armenta, he couldn't recall and thought that the main character was called Master George. But he admitted that in one of the versions of the script he had seen the character was called Mo. "That's all that I know. That's all I recall," he told Armenta.[5]

Nakoula told me that he changed the names to make it easier for American actors unfamiliar with Middle Eastern names to pronounce them as they acted their scenes. ("Imagine an American trying to say, 'Abu Mut'aleb!'" he said to me with a laugh.) The actors, of course, accuse him of duplicity and dupery.

But Jimmy Israel thought he understood Nakoula's motivation right from the start. In his deposition with Cris

---

[4]   Deposition of Jimmy Israel, *Garcia v. Nakoula*, p22.
[5]   Ibid, p29.

Armenta, he said that Nakoula had spoken to him about his purpose in making the film. "He was a Coptic Christian, and he was – you know, he said that they were – the Muslims were beating up and killing Coptic Christians. He wanted to get the word out."[6] And all versions of the film, including the 14-minute trailer that became infamous after the Benghazi attacks, start with a scene in modern-day Egypt, where a Coptic Christian pharmacist who has helped his Muslim neighbors is brutally beaten by an angry Muslim mob who sack his pharmacy and threaten to rape and kill his wife and daughter, while the "Islamic police" look on.

In the end, Israel says the filmmaker still owes him money – "$300 for the day that I worked."

But he denied having any legal interest in the film as a copyright owner or in any other capacity. "I have absolutely no interest in this film at all," he said. "I think it's a piece of shit, and I don't even want to think about it anymore."[7]

That's a sentiment he shares with most of the people who eventually got involved with *Desert Warrior*, aka *Innocence of Muslims*.

---

[6]   Ibid, p42.
[7]   Ibid, p60

CHAPTER 9
ON THE SET OF
DESERT WARRIOR

Like most of the 80 or so actors who participated in making the film, Gaylord Flynn was not a professional actor. In fact, he had been a physicist for most of his professional life and had worked for the Naval Research Lab during the 1980s on missile defense projects, right next to Bolling Air Force Base in Washington, DC. "We all teamed with Europeans so our research could be used by the NATO allies," Flynn told me. "My partner was a Brit. He liked to joke that in his previous job he made fuses for nuclear bombs."

Flynn began acting as an extra in commercials out in Palm Springs, where he and his fiancé lived. When he saw the casting call on Craigslist, he decided to audition for the part of the bearded, older priest. "So I played Solymon, the guy who wrote the Koran," he said.

I asked Flynn if he had figured out what the movie was all about when they were on the set. "I saw this small, elderly guy. He had his granddaughter serve us lunch on the set. I figured it was this guy's bucket list. Maybe we would all get to the end of it and they would say, 'Surprise, you're on *Candid Camera*,' and we'd all laugh.[1]

Flynn remembers being summoned to an industrial warehouse next to a Walmart in Duarte, California. "The whole thing was like a family affair. The producer clapped me on the back when he saw me perform, telling me I was a good man."

The premises used for the shoot belonged to Media for Christ, a non-profit production company run by Joseph Nasralla Abdelmasih, an Egyptian Coptic Christian who has partnered with pastors and activists seeking to turn Muslims away from Islam and toward Jesus.

Nasralla offered Nakoula the use of his studio and green screen facilities for free, but insists he was not involved in the production of the movie or aware of its content. Activist Steve Klein, who hosted a TV show on Nasralla's satellite television network called The Way TV, would later agree to become a spokesman for Nakoula once the national media started hounding him in the wake of the Benghazi attacks. (An early Daily Beast "investigation" that identified Nasralla mentioned "several other strange videos of [Nasralla]... that depict him singing hymns." Actually, the YouTube video the Daily Beast links to is not a hymn, but a common-place Arabic-language music video, similar to what you might hear in an upscale Cairo restaurant or nightclub.) [2]

So much disinformation and confusion by people with little if any experience in the Middle East.

Gaylord Flynn recalls no mention of Media for Christ on

---

[1]   Actually, it was Nakoula's daughter, Thoriya, who served lunch.

[2]   Marlow Stern, "Media for Christ, Company Allegedly Behind 'Innocence of Muslims,'" Daily Beast, Sept. 14, 2012. The link Stern provided is here: https://www.youtube.com/watch?v=KtG2i1UCEO4&feature=related

the set or anywhere. "There was nothing religious anywhere," he recalled. "We never heard anything about any religious involvement of any kind," with the film or with the facility. He parked his antique Mercedes 500k special roadster in the parking lot and posed for pictures with other actors. It was a very special car – only 342 of them made – which he had acquired by a stroke of extraordinary good fortune at a storage locker auction. "It was absolutely trashed," he likes to tell people. "An animal had been living in the back of it. I bought it for $1,000!" One of these 1930s era collector's models fetched $1.45 million in 2007.

Flynn thought the Assistant Director hired to manage the actors, Jeff Robinson, seemed professional, as did his production assistant, Steve Goldenberg. "They all seemed to know what they were doing. The set was real. The camera crew were real. The producer was real. It was pretty clear to me it wasn't their first rodeo."

Several things stand out in Flynn's memory about the filming.

He remembers watching the scene where Khadija, the 40-year-old merchant who is about to marry her 25-year-old servant, Mohammad, hides him between her legs as he flees what he thinks is a devil seeking to torment him. On the set, they were called Condalisa and Master George.

This is one of the scenes that made it into the 14-minute trailer. It might seem comic, even sexy, to Americans with no knowledge of Muslim hagiography. Khadija is wearing a loose dress that exposes her legs up to the hips, and drapes her bare legs around Mohammed's head for what appears to be a sexual embrace. (Alan Roberts had a reputation for making soft porn movies, and revealed those talents here). But the scene accurately reproduces a famous moment in *The Life of Muhammad*, where Khadija has the future Prophet hide his face between her legs, unveils her face, and makes the "demon" disappear. That is proof that the being tormenting Mohammad was not a devil, but an angel, she says, and that Mohammad is a Prophet. Why? Because a devil would have continued to look upon her unveiled face.

The next day, Flynn was supposed to marry Khadija and Mohammad on the set, since he was the bride's uncle and a priest. "And so the guy who is playing Mohammad asks the actress, 'Is it okay if I kiss you?' and the woman cracks up. 'After what we played yesterday, are you kidding?'"

"No one had the sense of doing anything nasty," Flynn said. "Everybody was easy going, even normal. Everything seemed on the up and up, with the producer and the directors coaching us how they wanted us to deliver our lines."

Later, the actor who played the young Mohammad turned to Flynn on the set. "When this is over, everybody here is going to be a Smith."

Although Flynn didn't see what he was getting at, it was at that point he realized something very serious and very wrong was going on.

Only later would he realize that his colleague probably meant it as a subtle warning. "You know, like John Smith, Jane Smith. Anonymous," he told me.

+++

When they arrived on the set in Duarte, California, half-way out to the San Bernardino Valley, none of the actors had the slightest idea what the movie was actually about. No one had shown them the entire script, nor was there any kind of general meeting to build camaraderie. "We weren't even introduced to one another," Cindy recalls. As a result, the actors fended for themselves, finding their partners and running through their lines. The actors were "like ants crawling on a hill," Dan Sutter, who played the part of a desert chieftain, told *Vanity Fair*. "No one knew anything."

Even the shooting schedule was a mystery, with actors getting schedules by email or phone the day before they were supposed to appear. "Out of nowhere, while on lunch at work, I get a call," one actor said. It would be Jeff Robinson or Steve Goldenberg, the assistant directors, reminding him that his call time was at 7 AM the next morning. "Uh, excuse me? Reminder? I didn't even know I was cast!"[3]

The ADs emailed most of the actors "sides," or pages, for the scene they were going to shoot the following day, along with the schedule to let them know the time their scene was going to be shot. As Robinson told me, "the casting was done on the fly, with the next day's actors being cast the day before."

Some of the actors wondered about the use of Anglo-Saxon names for ancient Arab characters. "I asked, 'Who, 2,000 years ago in the Middle East, was named George?'" one female actress recalled. "And I was told, 'Oh, don't worry about it.'"[4]

Several actors told *Vanity Fair* that they "simply checked out, making a game of mocking the production on set" because they were getting virtually no real direction from Alan Roberts or from Nakoula. "We were talking kind of like, 'Aaaarrr!'" one of them said, mocking a pirate's growl. "We would openly ridicule it because the dialogue was so atrocious, and we weren't getting direction from anyone."

Some of the actors playing Mohammad's companions began to joke that they were making a pirate musical, "because of the amount of times that we were going 'Aaarrr!' when we came back from a battle. We would cheer and yell and raise

---

3   "Disaster Movie," op cit.
4   Ibid.

our swords up high at the beginning of every take." And then, one day they arrived on scene and were told they were all gay. "And then it was a gay pirate musical. And we did it. 'Okay, we're all gay!' What the fuck," another actor said.[5]

Tim Dax recalled just one mention of religion during the entire filming, and that was from Nakoula himself. "Do you know what Muslims, where I come from, would do to a person like you?" Nakoula asked him, indicating his tattoos. When Dax said he didn't have a clue, Nakoula said they would murder him. "I'm against that."

Dax rolled his eyes, revealing the tattoos on his upper eyelids. "I said, 'Uh, yeah... I am, too,' and went to lunch."[6]

+++

Cindy recalls not receiving her sides until she actually arrived on the set at Media for Christ. She had been cast in the role of a mother. *That's pretty safe, right? A mother?* she thought. When she reached Duarte, a four-hour drive from her home in Bakersfield, she located the other actor in her scene. He was playing her husband, and so they began to run their lines. That was all the rehearsal they got.

An hour before shooting, at 11:30 AM, she was called upstairs for costume, hair, and make up. "I remember we were all in robes with belts or sashes as well as scarves for head coverings for the women," she said.

The filming was done against a green screen, with the exception of two ancient looking tents and a single swing set up outside. Cindy recalls looking around inside the tent before her scene and finding bits of the drapery that weren't hanging

---

5   Ibid.
6   Ibid.

right. "I wanted to run over there and fix it. I mean, I was going to be in this film and I wanted it to look perfect." But she realized that would be out of place, so she brought it to the attention of the crew. They just shrugged.

Everything felt rushed to her. That only contributed to her confusion later on.

Cindy managed to watch some of the other scenes filmed on the two days she was on set, but she never put two and two together, as some of the other actors did. Just before she went on for her first scene they filmed a sword-fight. The warriors were fighting one another and kicking each other, but everything seemed so fake. *They are not making the fight look real*, she thought. She wanted to jump and show them how to fight. Instead, she kept her peace.

Then she was called inside the tent to film her scene. She was Om-Roman, the mother of Hillary, a young girl. Her "husband" comes into the tent in great joy.

"What is wrong with you, husband?" she says. "We do not have that much to be happy about."

Her husband, Mohammad's companion Abu Bakr, replies that they have great cause for rejoicing. "The Messenger of Allah has asked for our daughter's hand in marriage."

In the script that Cindy read, her husband is called "Kero" and the words "of Allah" have been deleted. But he is still called "The Messenger." Anyone with a cursory knowledge of Islam should have understood the story. But Cindy is adamant that she did not.

"And this makes you happy?" *Cindy's character says.*

"Yes, of course it makes me happy! My daughter shall have the stars!"

"Are you crazy? Is George crazy?" *Cindy read.* "Your daughter has not yet reached her thirteenth year. He must be over 50 by now!"

When Cindy read those words the first time, Nakoula intervened. "Your daughter has not yet reached her *seventh* year," he said. "*Seventh*," he repeated, reading from his version of the script. But Alan Brownell shouted him down. "She's 13. 13!" he said. "Or, say, "she is but a child."[7]

This was one of many differences Cindy observed between Nakoula and Alan Brownell, the director. "I remember referring to George as a child molester," she said, "and it was in reference to George that I said that. I mean, for God's sake, the man was 55 and my husband was arguing with me saying, no, George was just 53, like there was some big difference. I begged and pleaded with my husband to put a stop to this, but he would not. My husband wanted the prestige that George had offered him by doing this."

Cindy really got into her part. In the next scene, Master George (Mohammad) entered their tent with an evil smirk on his face, announcing a blessing on their family. Their daughter, Hillary (Aisha in the original) was outside playing, and Cindy was supposed to fetch her and hand her over in marriage to Master George. So many emotions were going through her mind as the scene developed. She realized she didn't want to go outside to get the girl, that it was wrong. She was embarrassed that her husband was so submissive. Finally, her husband yelled at her again, "Go get her, now!" and Cindy left, summoning all the hatred and contempt she felt in her heart into a searing glare she offered the two men.

And then, she found her daughter, and she was thinking, *This is my baby girl, how much I love her.* She pushed her on the

---

[7]   Jimmy Israel gave a copy of the screenplay Nakoula was using to Vice, who published it online just two days after the Benghazi attacks (*supra*). This passage occurs on page 63. It can be accessed directly, here: https://issuu.com/vicemag/docs/warriorrewrite3_30_11-vice/53?e=5285225/4100336

swing, wanting the moment to prolong itself forever, anything to keep her from giving up the girl to the sexual pervert waiting inside. Finally, she stopped pushing her and gathered the girl into her arms. She held her face in her hands and looked deep into her eyes, wanting her to feel her love. Then she kissed her on the forehead and took her hand and walked her into the tent.

In the next scene they were back inside the tent, and Master George was asking for his bride. Cindy tried to shelter the girl behind her. Her maternal instincts kicked in, and the whole scene became so real to her, she felt she was living a part of her childhood all over again, only this time she was the mother trying to protect her daughter, and failing. In the script, she is just supposed to come inside and take her daughter's hand and place it in the hands of Master George, saying that he is to be her husband. But something wouldn't let her do that and she kept trying to protect the girl. Finally, Kero, her husband, got annoyed and the director broke off filming.

"Look, you're supposed to take your daughter's hand and place it in his."

"Sorry, yes, I know," Cindy said. But it no longer felt like she was acting. It was all too real. She could feel the pain in her heart that she had felt as a child when the older man molested her. She could feel the fear in her daughter, and the lasciviousness of this Master George and the weakness of her husband, who was looking forward to the benefits this Master George was going to bestow on him in exchange for his child.

As she placed the girl's hand in Mohammad's her daughter cried out, "Mama, I am hungry," and her heart was aching. She could feel physical pain in the pit of her stomach as she watched this big man swoop up her beautiful little girl in his arms to rape her. She started to follow them out the tent, but the director cut the scene again. "Cindy, step back. Just let them go," he said. So they redid the last part and it took all of her strength to step back out of the way. "Is your George a child molester?" she wailed.

"That's a take," the director said.

At that moment, an older man she hadn't noticed before clapped appreciatively. He jumped over the props and introduced himself.

"That was great!" he said enthusiastically.

Cindy couldn't believe it when he said his name. He was the son of a famous actor from the 1950s.

"It looked like you really connected with your character. Like you really felt it," he said. "I could feel every emotion that you were feeling."

Cindy was proud, but also emotionally drained. "I've lived life," was all she could think to say. The man said he made films, too, and he would like to call her. So she gave him her contact information, and she began dreaming of future roles where she could pour out her heart, breathing life and passion into fictional characters that without her would be just words on paper.

She never heard from him again.

+++

Her second day on the set was pretty much a replay of the first, except that the actress who played her daughter, Hillary, was caught in traffic and arrived late for their shoot. So this time Brownell had her stand outside the tent, and pretend she was listening to Master George speaking with her husband inside. Those scenes never made it into the final movie.

They also shot close-ups inside the tent. It was mid-August and hot, and the air was stifling with the bright lights they used on the set. She had to dab at her face to keep her make-up from dripping. Every chance she got she went outside, and stood in front of a giant fan they had set up to cool off the actors.

At one point, during a break by the fan, she met up with the handsome, younger actor who played Master George, and started telling him about her faith in Christ.

"Has anyone ever told you that you look like paintings of Christ?" she said.

He just glanced at her, and shook his head no.

"Cindy, if you only knew what is really going on here."

"What do you mean?"

He gave her an incredulous look, like *you've got to be kidding*. But he said nothing.

Later that second day, she asked Nakoula about her IMBD credits. After all, that was the main reason she had taken the part. They were paying her gas money, $75 a day. They hadn't even asked her to sign a release because she wasn't getting paid for her acting.

"Miss Cindy, I'm going to show the film in my home country, Egypt," Nakoula said. "I am so happy to do this. People there will understand how important it is."

But he never said a word about why he wanted to do that, or what the movie meant. And never did he say a word about Islam, as far as Cindy can recall.

+++

Anna Gurji, who played Aisha in the movie in the scenes with Cindy, also has no recollection of any religious overtones or content during the filming. In the days after the Benghazi attacks, when *Innocence of Muslims* was being blamed by Secretary of State Hillary Clinton and President Obama for the deaths of Americans in Libya, she was scared. Like Cindy, she told a good friend, she felt shattered. "I don't know, I feel very dead inside," she said.

She remembered auditioning for a role in an indie low budget feature movie "about a comet falling into a desert and ancient tribes fighting over it for they thought that the comet had some magical powers."

A year later, she said, "the movie was dubbed without the actors' permission, the lines were changed drastically and the movie was morphed into an anti-Islam film. Even the names of the characters were changed. And the character I had scenes with, GEORGE, became MUHAMMAD."

Her character was called "Hillary" on the set at Media for Christ. When the movie was released onto the Internet, she became "Aisha," the child-bride of the Prophet Mohammad.

Like most of the actors, Anna was never shown the entire script, just the pages with the scenes involving her character. "I did not consider this to be an unusual thing, seeing as I have had an experience with something like this before," she said. "I did a movie once where the script was written in a foreign language and only my parts were translated into English and accordingly, I was provided with my scenes only."

She thought the same thing was going on with *Desert Warrior*. From his thick accent, she thought that Sam Bassil, the producer, was a foreigner. "I thought that the original script was written in his native tongue and that not all scenes were translated into English."

And then, she had an additional, personal reason. She had a scheduling conflict with filming for another acting job, and so the *Desert Warrior* scenes where she appeared had to be rescheduled at the last minute to fit her schedule. "Because of this rushed rearrangement, I thought that the [producers] first forgot and then did not consider it necessary to send me the script, and again, I did not find this unusual."

However, she did seem to have an overview of the plot, and knew that the character George "was a leader of one of those tribes fighting for the comet" that had fallen to earth and was believed to have supernatural powers.[8]

Like so many of the others, including Cindy, Anna clearly had no understanding of Islam and was not familiar with the Muslim prophet. She had never heard the story of the enormous black comet that had fallen to earth in the Arabian desert and became an object of veneration for 1.6 billion Muslims worldwide who to this day make an annual pilgrimage to Mecca to express their homage to Allah for showing them such a sign of his greatness.

The comet and its enclosure, know as the Kaaba, is the holiest site in all of Islam and sits at the center of the Masjid al-Haram in Mecca. Mohammad himself is said to have restored the comet onto its foundations after a flood damaged it around 600 AD. Before Mohammad fled Mecca, persecuted by the local inhabitants who rejected his new religion, he and his followers knelt in the direction of Jerusalem when they prayed. But once he "migrated" to Medina, he and his followers prayed in the direction of Mecca, as do 1.6 billion Muslims today.

Anna knew none of this, apparently. "There was no mention EVER by anyone of MUHAMMAD and no mention of religion during the entire time I was on the set," she said. "I am a hundred percent certain nobody in the cast and nobody in the U.S. artistic side of the crew knew what was really planned for this *Desert Warrior*."

Jeff Robinson, the assistant director, was working off the same script with the phony names. He called it, "the hidden version." But if you read through it, "you know what it's really about," he said.

---

[8] Anna Gurji's letter is here: http://journal.neilgaiman.com/2012/09/a-letter-from-scared-actress.html

Hollywood is a funny place. Aspiring actors will take parts in just about any production that puts them in front of a camera, in hopes of getting an IMBD film credit they can use on their resume, as Cindy told me again and again she had done. They shut off any intellectual curiosity as to the content of the production, whether it be a soft porn version of *Lady Chatterley's Lover* (one of director Alan Roberts' credits), or a *Desert Warrior* version of *The Life of Mohammad*. Anna Gurji, like Cindy and countless others, seemed to understand little about the film she was part of, and showed little if any curiosity while she was on the set to find out. Later, of course, she was outraged that she had been part of a film about the founder of Islam.

As Anna wrote:

"It's painful to see how our faces were used to create something so atrocious without us knowing anything about it at all. It's painful to see people being offended with the movie that used our faces to deliver lines (it's obvious the movie was dubbed) that we were never informed of, it is painful to see people getting killed for this same movie, it is painful to hear people blame us when we did nothing but perform our art ... I feel awful that a human being is capable of such evil. I feel awful about the lies, about the injustice, about the cruelty, about the violence, about the death of innocent people, about the pain of offended people, about the false accusations."

In the aftermath of the Benghazi attacks, it became painful for Anna, Cindy, and many of the other actors to be confronted with the consequences of their own ignorance, their innocence. But it became truly frightening to see the naked face of an

Islam that motivated its followers to slaughter innocents over a YouTube video they found offensive. How could that be? How could such innocent actions as making an ageing man's "bucket list" film lead to such death and destruction?

For Cindy, it was her introduction to a world beyond Hollywood, beyond America, that she never dreamed could exist. It was a world of hatred and violence that seemed almost an institutionalized version of her own younger years.

It was her introduction to the Muslim world.

CHAPTER 10
"SAM" DISAPPEARS

After shooting *Desert Warrior*, Cindy periodically called Nakoula, whom she still called "Sam," to ask him how things were going. He kept telling her he would let her know when it was finished and looked forward to inviting her to the premiere. At one point she dropped her cell phone in the pool and lost his number. By the time she finally called one of the other actors to get his number, months had gone by.

"Cindy," he said, "I am so happy you called me. I have been trying to contact you. We had some problems with the sound during the filming. I need you to come re-record your voice."

Nakoula explained that while her voice was normally strong and clear, for some reason it had been too soft during the filming so they needed to redub it. "Can you come back to Duarte?"

She said yes. They arranged to meet on March 2, 2012, for lunch then drove together to Media for Christ.

Cindy was surprised when they arrived at the studio. It looked so different than it had during the filming. There was no set, no green screen that she could see. Only a sound booth with foam on the walls and a microphone and a control room.

Nakoula introduced her to his 20-year-old son, Abanob.

He was working the mixing board along with other people Cindy didn't recognize.

"Where's Alan?" she asked.

"They all left me," she remembers Nakoula telling her. "We have to finish the film by ourselves. Do you know anyone who can edit in HD?"

Cindy said she did, and would look into it once she got home.

Nakoula had her go into the sound booth while he joined the others in the control room. Instead of giving her a script, Nakoula and another man said words into her headset, and had her repeat them into the microphone. They coached her how to pronounce them, and for the proper inflection they wanted.

Cindy thinks the sound session lasted less than ten minutes. The new takes seemed odd and out of context since they were mostly single words or short phrases she did not remember speaking on set. When it was finished she said good-bye to Nakoula. He promised to send her a check for her travel expenses, so she gave him her mailing address. Then she drove back to Bakersfield.

She didn't give serious thought to the dubbing session until January 2016, when I helped her to locate the audio CD of the session in a bunch of boxes in her car and we listened to it together in a parking lot in Venice Beach, California.

+++

For several months after that, Nakoula dropped out of her life. Cindy got pulled into other projects, including a family drama called *Broken Roads* written and directed by Justin Chambers. She auditioned for dozens more parts, landed a couple, and saw her acting career take off.

In July 2012, Nakoula phoned her again and said that he had posted the movie to YouTube, where she could find it under the name "Sam Bacile." Cindy looked him up on YouTube, but all she found was a 13'03" trailer for something called "The Real Life of Muhammad." That had to be it, she thought, although she didn't recognize the title. When she watched it, she didn't understand.

"Honey, this is crazy," she told her husband, Mark. "None of this looks familiar."

And then she saw her own face in the scene in the tent.

"You look good," Mark said. "Just go out there and keep auditioning for new roles."

And that's what she did. She was thankful because he believed in her. She didn't remember the unfamiliar title of the trailer or anything else until the morning of September 12, 2012, when her face filled the TV screen on every news channel on air.

+++

Steve Klein recalls meeting Nakoula briefly in the summer of 2011, just as the Egyptian-American was about to embark on making his movie. It all began with a cold call, no more than three minutes long. Nakoula had gotten his number from a mutual friend, Joseph Nasralla, and said he had an urgent matter he needed to discuss. He suggested that they meet at the offices of Media for Christ in Duarte, California, where Klein taped his TV show on Islamic terrorism, *Wake Up America*.

A former U.S. Marine Corps officer who had served in Vietnam, Klein was an outspoken critic of Islam, who titled his Facebook page "Abolish Islam." Nakoula told him about his project to make a video about the life of Muhammad, and said he was worried that he might get arrested for it, since that is what would happen in the Muslim world. When they met, he asked Klein what would happen under American law if he made such a movie here. "I said I'm not an attorney. I can't tell you. You need to talk to an attorney," Klein told Cindy's lawyers later. When Nakoula pressed him for more, Klein said that he had never had that kind of problem, because the First Amendment protected free speech.[1]

Over the next year or so, they spoke several times by the phone about the film project, but Klein did not get involved in the filming itself. "I didn't make the movie. I had zero to do with it," he told Cindy's attorneys in a sworn deposition. Anything he had said in public to the contrary "was just talk in an interview, and that's all," he added.[2]

In June 2012, Nakoula called him again, this time asking him to come to a screening of the entire two-hour movie at the Vine Theater on Hollywood Boulevard on June 23. Nakoula told me that he paid the owner of the theater to screen the movie.

Nakoula made a flyer for the film, which he was then calling *Innocence of Bin Laden,* and had it distributed it at prominent mosques in Southern California. The flyer featured a photograph of Osama Bin Laden, and in Arabic said it would reveal "the real terrorist... who caused the killing of our children in Palestine and our brothers in Iraq and Afghanistan." The idea was to attract young Muslims to see the movie, in the hope it might jolt them enough to change their attitude toward the Koran and toward Islam, Nakoula explained to me. Klein told a reporter that their intent was to enrage and flush out "suspected terrorists" in the United States.

"We passed out flyers at mosques around California where we knew there was a small percentage of terrorists," Klein told

---

[1]   *Garcia v Nakoula,* Deposition of Steven Klein, July 11, 2014, 18.
[2]   Ibid, p31.

the *Los Angeles Times* just days after the Benghazi attacks. "And the idea was to locate, which we did, those folks who believed Osama Bin Laden was a great guy, and to try to get them to come to the movie."[3]

In a videotaped interview that appeared on YouTube at around the same time, Klein went further: People who think of Osama Bin Laden as a hero "will come to watch the film thinking that it's going to be a ra-ra-ra Osama Bin Laden film" and would thus be unmasked. Klein didn't say who he expected would benefit from the unmasking.[4]

Nakoula's friends also placed the flyer as an ad in the Anaheim-based *Arab World* newspaper. When an *LA Times* reporter called the newspaper, he was told that "a man named Joseph" had paid $300 to run the ads three times. The *Times* then noted that the "president of Media for Christ is named Joseph Nasralla Abdelmasih."[5]

The advertisement attracted the attention of Oren Segal, director of Islamic Affairs for the local chapter of the Anti-Defamation League. "When we saw the advertisement in the paper, we were interested in knowing if it was some kind of pro-jihadist movie," Segal said.

Klein came to the Vine Theater for the screening, but sat outside in his car across the street wearing a disguise. "I was afraid if somebody showed up and recognized – 'cause I do that TV show, and I know I'm being monitored by some people that are not too friendly with my points of view, that I might get beat," he told Cindy's attorneys.[6] Afterwards, he called

3   Phil Willon, "Anti-Muslim film poster in Hollywood surprised locals," *LA Times* blogs, Sept. 14, 2012.

4   https://www.youtube.com/watch?v=fHxUBaOxyBM

5   Mona Shadia and Harriet Ryan, "California Muslims hold vigil for slain ambassador," *LA Times*, Sept. 15, 2012.

6   Ibid, p33

Nakoula. 'Hey, Sam. Nobody came. Not one person came,'" he said.

A local blogger heard about the flyer and the screening and raised it with the Los Angeles City Council on June 29, 2012, the night before the film was scheduled to be shown a second time. Considered a gadfly because of his frequent interventions on a broad range of subjects at the public hearings, the blogger stood up to warn of "an alarming event occurring in Hollywood on Saturday." He said that some group had rented the Vine Theater "to show a video entitled 'Innocence of Bin Laden.' We have no idea what this group is."

As a result of his intervention, the owner of the Vine Theater cancelled the second screening.

No more than a dozen people ever showed up at the Vine Theater to watch the movie. Nakoula himself was in the building, but not inside the theater itself. Given the scant turnout, Nakoula concluded that he needed to change the title of the movie so people wouldn't think it was somehow sympathetic to Osama Bin Laden.

He refused to condemn Joseph Nasralla and Steve Klein for distancing themselves from the movie. "When something like this is successful, everybody wants to be the father. But when it happens like this, nobody wants to be reminded of their involvement," he told me.

+++

Sometime after the Vine Theater fiasco, Nakoula called Klein again, this time asking him to endorse the movie. He also asked Klein to call Pastor Terry Jones, whom Klein identified as "the guy that burns the Korans," for an endorsement. "It was hard to understand him, especially on the phone, and I hadn't even seen the video," Klein testified. Nakoula didn't know Jones, which is why he asked Klein for the introduction.

In the meantime, Nakoula's son, Abanob, had uploaded a thirteen-minute trailer of the video to YouTube. Klein found it "so pathetic that I only watched it for five minutes, and I shut it down, and I didn't call [Nakoula] back because I was too embarrassed, and I didn't want my name affiliated with the video."[7]

Klein became a witness in Cindy's lawsuit because he was widely quoted in the media in the aftermath of the Benghazi attacks as the official spokesman for the movie. He told me that when Nakoula first approached him, he was enthusiastic about the project. "Nakoula told me he wanted to make a movie that would expose the real side of Islam to Americans. I thought, wow, that would be like exposing who Hitler really was in 1937. So I signed on."

The first call he received from the media was at 9 PM Pacific Time on the night of the attacks, just two hours after Hillary Clinton blamed the video for the death of the U.S. Ambassador. An Associated Press reporter "wanted to know if I was a spokesperson for the video. I said I had agreed to help out," he said.

The AP quoted him as saying that he had warned Nakoula that he would become "the next Theo van Gogh." The AP explained that this was a reference "to the Dutch filmmaker killed by a Muslim extremist in 2004 after making a film that was perceived as insulting to Islam."

"We went into this knowing this was probably going to happen," the AP quoted Klein as saying.[8]

The next morning, September 12, 2012, a reporter from the UK woke him up at 5 AM. Klein asked the reporter to call

---

[7]   Ibid, p25.
[8]   This is from the original AP story on the evening of Sept. 11, 2012 by Shaya Mohajer, op cit.

back in an hour after he checked the Internet for news. After that call, he got "swarmed" by reporters. Asked by Cris Armenta, the attorney, how many, Klein replied: "About 47 billion... They started storming the beach" at his office and home.

At about 10 AM his time, a CNN reporter called and "accused me of having blood on my hands and that I was directly responsible for killing the ambassador."

That got Klein's back up. "I explained at length that, had Hillary Clinton done her job, the ambassador would have never been injured." And then he tried to turn the tables. "It was Hillary Clinton and President Obama's fault 100 percent for the exposure of the video," he said. "They were the publicists, and they were the ones that caused all of the lies to happen and further mayhem."[9]

Klein was right, as we will see.

+++

The media found Nakoula in less than 24 hours and camped out in front of the house in Cerritos, California where he lived with his family. The LA Sheriff's Department took him into what they told him was "protective custody" shortly after midnight on September 15.

"They brought me to a hotel," Nakoula told me.

Almost immediately, federal agents took over and began interrogating him, trying to make a case for a formal arrest. For the next two weeks, they moved him from hotel to hotel, out of reach of the media. They held him in secret, without charge, without an attorney or possibility of bail, an extrajudicial prisoner in the United States of America. "They told me they wanted me to stay far away from the media," Nakoula said. "I

---

9   Ibid, p46.

wanted to go home."

It was unheard of and unconstitutional. But Nakoula was afraid it would get worse if he refused to comply.

Hillary Clinton had kept the vow she made to Charles Woods, the father of former U.S. Navy Seal Ty Woods, when she met him at the ramp ceremony at Andrews Air Force Base, to "find the people responsible for this and throw them in jail."

She was referring to the filmmaker behind *Innocence of Muslims,* not the terrorists.

CHAPTER 11

CAIRO AND ISTANBUL: SETTING THE TABLE

Majid Nawaz, a former Islamist and co-founder of the Quilliam Institute in London, told CNN's "Connect the World" on September 13, 2012, that he had watched the trailer a few days before the Benghazi attacks "and it only had a few hundred views, and now it's gone over a million." It was only after Benghazi that interest sparked in the "amateurish" and "poorly-made" video, he said. Politicians and others talking about the movie were "making the maker of this film far more famous than he otherwise would have been."[1]

He was right. The movie only went viral *after* the Benghazi attacks and *only because* the U.S. government promoted it. Exactly how they propelled Nakoula's crudely made film from total obscurity to world-wide fame in a matter of days is the subject of the next two chapters.

+++

On July 1, 2012, Nakoula's son, Abanob, created a YouTube

---

[1]   https://www.youtube.com/watch?v=dOcQF9QxULo

channel for Sam Bacile and uploaded a 13'03" trailer titled "The Real Life of Muhammad." The following day, he uploaded a second, slightly longer one, called "Muhammad Movie trailer" to the same channel. Cindy Garcia and Steve Klein saw one of these trailers over the summer.

After two months, the movie was still languishing in obscurity, having received just a few hundred views. So on September 4, Nakoula had his son upload a version of the longer trailer, dubbed into Arabic by Egyptian actors speaking the distinctive Cairo dialect, onto the "Sam Bacile" YouTube channel. The title clearly identified it as a "dubbed" version of the Muhammad movie. Nakoula brought the Arabic actors to the sound booth at Media for Christ for the dubbing. On the Sam Bacile YouTube channel, the "director" left a brief challenge in the description box: "The story of the life of Muhammad, the Messenger of Islam, according to the approved Islamic books. We are fully ready to receive all criticisms and to respond with all the factual evidence, based on references to Islamic texts." He even left a toll-free U.S. telephone number for inquiries!

That same day, one of Nakoula's close friends, Morris Sadek, made a phone call to a journalist in Egypt, telling him about the movie. The Egyptian Muslim Brotherhood government had stripped Sadek of his Egyptian citizenship earlier that year because of his anti-Islam rants.

On September 5, Sadek began promoting the film on his Narcopticas blog site. He posted invitation-only links to the Arabic and English trailers and emailed the links to several hundred contacts in Egypt and the United States, including Gamal Girgis, the journalist he had phoned the day before. The front page of his blog included one of the famous Mohammad cartoons that had enflamed Muslims worldwide, and an advertisement for "International Judge Muhammad Day," an event Sadek planned to attend at the church of Pastor Terry Jones in Gainesville,

Florida, on the September 11 anniversary. The Arabic-language title of the dubbed trailer on Sadek's blog was "World-Renowned Film on the Life of Muhammad, Prophet of Islam."[2]

Still nothing. No one was watching the movie in either Arabic or English.

When Girgis still didn't publish anything on the movie, Sadek called him again the following day, this time with success. Later that day, September 6, Girgis published a three-paragraph story about the trailer in al-Youm al-Sabaa, a newspaper devoted to the activities of Egyptian expatriates. Here is a translation of the article by a DailyKos blogger who uses the screen name "angry marmot."

Copts Produce a Film Offensive to Islam and to the Life of the Prophet Muhammad

Thursday, 6 September 2012, 20:49

By Gamal Girgis

In a shocking move that confirms their plans for harm against Egypt, calls for sectarian discord and [sic] fuels the feelings of hatred between Muslims and Copts, just as they have worked against the attainment of stability for Egypt since President Muhammad Morsi took up the reins of state, a number of expatriate Copts led by 'Ismat Zaqlamah (who has called for the division of Egypt and names himself the president of a so-called "Coptic State") and by Morris Sadek (who has never ceased to attack Egypt in every international forum and provoke foreign sentiment against it) allied

---

[2]   http://nacopticas1.blogspot.com/2012/09/blog-post_5.html

with the bigoted Reverend Terry Jones (who has burned the Qur'an numerous times) have produced a film about the life of Muhammad, Peace Be Upon Him, which contains profound abuses and extensive deceptions against the Holy Prophet, confirming the deep hatred that the producers of this film hold for Islam and the sublime Prophet.

At this time a number of Egyptian Coptic leaders have already denounced the film, emphasizing that the producers of the film are advancing their own agenda, and these leaders have rejected any abuse of the Holy Prophet and have denounced the production of the film as an offense against God, just as it is an offense against Islam.

Dubbed in fluent Arabic by the producers, the film represents Muslims as terrorists and as bearing collective responsibility for the attacks of September 2009. In this way, the film opens with the killing of a Coptic doctor and his daughter in Egypt by the hands of Muslims with encouragement from Egyptian police officers, a scenario that does not exist in reality because Egyptians, both Muslims and Copts, are woven together in a single nation and are not separated by sectarian strife. Whatever happens is nothing more than a passing crisis and imperils neither the unity nor commitment among Muslims and Copts.[3]

The Girgis story gives a very different picture of the movie from what we have been accustomed to hearing. In fact, it made the *Mohammad Movie* appear like it was specifically tailored "to

---

[3]   http://www.dailykos.com/story/2012/09/24/1135744/-From-Film-to-Protests-the-Publicization-of-Innocence-of-Muslims-in-Egypt#?friend_id=228932&is_stream=1

stir up sectarian conflict within Egypt," not that it was a broadly anti-Islam movie. (The "angry marmot" whose Arabic was good enough to translate the Girgis story showed up at a Bernie Sanders rally in Duluth, Minnesota, in February 2016, and offered to caucus for the socialist presidential contender.)[4]

Girgis later told a McClatchy News Service reporter that Sadek claimed *he* had produced the movie and wanted to screen it on September 11 "to reveal what was behind the terrorists' actions that day, Islam." This detail is important for what follows.[5]

On September 8, al Youm and other newspapers in Egypt started referring to a 1'32" Arabic-language clip, which had been culled from the 14-minute Arabic-language version of the trailer. But as the McClatchy account pointed out, "the story remained off the front pages, still considered a local piece about an Egyptian in America fueling a sectarian crisis here, not about how the West treats Islam."

That evening, Sheikh Khalid Abdullah, a cleric who co-hosted a show of Islamic commentary on al-Nas television, held up a newspaper headline that claimed a new film made by expatriate Copts attacked Islam. Along with his co-host, Mohammad Hamdi, he warned viewers that he was going to show them something disturbing, then they aired the 1'32" clip in Arabic from the "Mohammad Movie" trailer. The Coptic

4 http://www.dailykos.com/story/2016/01/27/1475756/-Espying-a-Ghost-at-Sanders-Duluth-Event

5 See Nancy A. Youssef and Amina Ismail, "Anti-U.S. outrage over video began with a Christian activist's phone call to a reporter," McClatchy, Sept. 15, 2012. Speaking through a family member because of his poor English, Morris Sadek said he had "nothing to do with making this movie," but acknowledged posting it to YouTube and to contacting Egyptian reporters. He confirmed that he was not the one who changed the name to *Innocence of Muslims,* but just grabbed the version already up on Sam Bacile's channel.

Church in Egypt had already condemned the movie, Morris Sadek, and Florida pastor Terry Jones, he said.

The Salafist TV network blurred the face of the woman in the clip, apparently to suit the Salafist notion that women should not be allowed to appear uncovered in public. But it made no attempt to obscure the image of the actor who played Mohammad, even though the Salafists believe Muslims are forbidden to show any image of their prophet.

The scenes showed Mohammad discovering the "first Muslim animal," a donkey; Mohammad claiming that "the inspiration was gone" now that Warraqa, the priest, was dead; and a brief battle. Cindy's segment, calling Mohammad a child molester, was not in the clip.

"What is this stupidity?" Abdallah asked after airing the brief clip. He asked his co-host if anyone had apologized for making the film. Hamdi replied, "An apology is not enough. I want them convicted."[6]

Hillary Clinton and the Obama Justice Department agreed.

On Sunday, September 9, the Mufti of Al Azhar University, considered the "Vatican" of the Sunni Muslim world, condemned the video for "insulting the prophet." However, instead of linking the film to the United States, he said merely that it had been produced by "Copts living abroad."

Despite that qualifier, the first calls for protests in front of the U.S. Embassy in Cairo for September 11 appeared on Facebook and on another Islamist TV channel, al-Hikma, later that day. Wisam Abdel Waris, another Salafist television preacher, demanded an official American denunciation of the film and an apology. He was also pushing for world-wide adoption of laws banning blasphemy that would make it illegal to criticize Islam.

---

[6]   https://www.youtube.com/watch?v=InM_NuW0r9M

But the protest appeal called only for the immediate release of the Blind Sheikh, the Egyptian Muslim cleric jailed in the United States since 1994 for his role in organizing the bombing of the Lincoln and Holland tunnels. That was a long-standing demand of the Muslim Brotherhood in Egypt, whose supporters had started organizing a September 11 protest in front of the U.S. Embassy in Cairo many weeks earlier. *It was crystal clear that the 1'32" Arabic-language trailer, which virtually nobody had actually seen, was only tacked on at the last minute to attract additional bodies to a demonstration in front of the U.S. Embassy in Cairo that had long been in the works. It did not drive the crowds, or the organizers. It was simply an afterthought.*

The social media buzz caught the U.S. Embassy in Cairo unawares. "People were writing to us asking what the role of the U.S. government has in this video. What are you going to do? Who produced this?" an unnamed official at the Embassy contacted by the McClatchy reporter said. "Our initial response was: What video?"

In a Twitter message using the official @USEmbassyCairo handle, an Embassy spokesperson responded later that day, September 9, to someone asking about the video, "We've never heard of this movie, what is it?" That and subsequent tweets by the embassy apologizing for the movie and for those who "hurt the religious feelings of Muslims" were deleted on orders from Washington after Republican presidential nominee Mitt Romney accused the State Department of apologizing to terrorists rather than protecting U.S. diplomatic facilities abroad.[7]

It is extremely significant that the chronology above emerged so quickly after the Benghazi attacks. Stories capturing most of the details I have related above appeared within 12 to

---

[7]   https://factreal.wordpress.com/2012/09/13/images-deleted-tweets-by-us-embassy-in-cairo-egypt-september-11-2012/

36 hours of the attacks in McClatchy, the left-wing blog site Daily Kos, *U.S. News*, the *Washington Post*, and the *New York Times*. (Indeed, the first one actually appeared *before the first shots* had been fired in Benghazi, as I detailed in Chapter 2, above).[8] It had all the appearances of a narrative that had been pre-cooked, spoon-fed to journalists by anonymous sources at the State Department and the U.S. Embassy in Cairo. *Focus on the Youtube,* they were saying. *Don't pay attention to the fact that the brother of al Qaeda leader Ayman al-Zawahri, who had recently been released from an Egyptian prison by President Morsi, was calling on jihadi sympathizers to "burn down" the U.S. Embassy and "kill everyone inside," to pressure the U.S. government to release the Blind Sheikh and al Qaeda detainees in Guantanamo Bay.*[9]

CNN reporter Nic Robertson was one of the few reporters who took notice of the protesters who had been camped out in front of the U.S. Embassy in Cairo for several days. In his astonishing interview segment on September 10, neither Zawahri nor the son of the Blind Sheikh mentioned a YouTube video as motivating their protest. Robertson walked with Zawahri toward the small crowd in front of the embassy in the set-up shot, where they joined up with the Blind Sheikh's son. "This is the protest calling for the release of Sheikh Omar Abdel Rahman," Robertson explained.[10] Once the media had adopted

---

[8]   In addition to those cited in previous notes, see also: Elisabeth Flock, "How 'Innocence of Muslims' Spread Around the Globe and Killed a U.S. Diplomat," U.S. News, Sept. 12, 2012; and Pamela Constable, "Egyptian Christian activist in Virginia promoted video that sparked furor," *Washington Post*, Sept. 13, 2012.

[9]   See *Dark Forces*, p281-282. Zawahri and other well-known al Qaeda figures in Egypt used al Qaeda-affiliated media outlets to incite their followers to ransack the U.S. Embassy. See also Thomas Jocelyn, "Al Qaeda-linked jihadists helped incite 9/11 Cairo protest," Long War Journal, Oct. 26, 2012. http://www.longwarjournal.org/archives/2012/10/al_qaeda-linked_jiha.php#

[10]   https://www.youtube.com/watch?v=tPszLCEyu-I

the *YouTube-video-is-responsible-for-Muslim-violence* narrative, CNN stopped linking to Robertson's interview and it has all but disappeared from the CNN website, except for the brief clip above.

+++

Many have speculated that the original goal for planting the narrative that a "hateful" YouTube video was responsible for violent Muslim protests was to promote Mrs. Clinton's well-known hatred for Pastor Terry Jones and his efforts to wake up U.S. public opinion to the violent nature of Islamic doctrine. Indeed, she had publicly crossed swords with Jones in the past over his Koran-burning ceremonies, and regularly used him as an example of the type of behavior that should be banned under the type of Sharia-compliant blasphemy laws proposed by the Organization of Islamic Cooperation. References to Pastor Jones appear periodically in Mrs. Clinton's now-released emails, so we know that he was on her mind and on the radar screen of her top aides, who had standing orders to send her any newspaper articles mentioning Jones.[11]

Mrs. Clinton actively embraced news laws banning blasphemy as Secretary of State and instructed the United States Ambassador to the United Nations to vote in favor of them, reversing years of U.S. opposition. Adopted by the United Nations Human Rights Council on April 12, 2011, United Nations Resolution 16/18 is cloaked in outwardly benign language. Read superficially, it appears to support religious tolerance. For example, it bans religious profiling and promotes

---

[11]   See, for example, the Sept 12, 2012 email from Cheryl Mills, "Anti-Muslim film director in hiding, following Libya, Egypt violence," in which she sent Mrs. Clinton a *Washington Post* article claiming that Jones was "among those promoting" the film.

outreach to religious minorities. But Muslim states have never exercised religious tolerance: indeed, it is illegal to hold a Christian worship service in Saudi Arabia, while most Muslim states such as Iran and Pakistan actively persecute Christians and other religious minorities.

Resolution 16/18 includes serious restrictions on free speech in the only countries that actually respect it: the United States and its Western allies. For example, it calls for measures "to criminalize incitement to imminent violence based on religion or belief," precisely the charge levied against *Innocence of Muslims* and its makers. It also calls for the training of government officials in "effective outreach strategies" to Muslim communities, and for widespread indoctrination of Muslim religious beliefs in schools and government-controlled institutions in the West.

When Egypt's Muslim Brotherhood president, Mohammad Morsi, had the Public Prosecutor issue arrest warrants against Nakoula, Terry Jones, Morris Sadek and others involved in making the movie on September 19, he served them through Interpol, undoubtedly expecting that Mrs. Clinton would agree to enforce the arrest warrants in compliance with Resolution 16/18[12]. Resolution 16/18 also calls on Western governments to curtail surveillance of potential terrorists if the surveillance

---

[12]   "Egypt's Interpol office seeks warrant against anti-Islam filmmakers," Egypt Independent, Sept. 20, 2012 (translated from al-Masry al-Youm). Morsi was advised on how to deal with Mrs. Clinton by Clinton Foundation Cairo City Director, Gehad el-Haddad, who was also a top Muslim Brotherhood operative. El-Haddad stayed on the Clinton Foundation payroll from 2007 through August 2012, even though he officially joined Morsi as an advisor in May 2011. El-Haddad was arrested after Morsi was deposed, and in August 2015 he was sentenced to life in prison. See: http://www.globalmbwatch.com/2015/04/14/egyptian-muslim-brotherhood-advisor-and-former-clinton-employee-gets-life-in-prison/

was tied in any way to their religious beliefs. This is precisely why the feds didn't identify the San Bernardino shooters ahead of their murderous rampage at a Christmas party in 2015, despite all the warning signs: the feds shut down an early warning program that had identified the mosque where the shooters had met as a fertile recruiting ground for potential jihadis.[13]

The OIC had been trying to criminalize any criticism of Islam since at least 1999, by seeking to outlaw "defamation of religions." Mrs. Clinton actively participated in these efforts, throwing U.S. support behind the OIC's "Istanbul Process." She blasted Pastor Jones during the 2010 midterm elections, when he organized his first Koran burning. "It's regrettable that a pastor in Gainesville, Florida, with a church of no more than fifty people can make this outrageous and distressful, disgraceful plan and get, you know, the world's attention," she told the Council on Foreign Relations.[14]

In a July 2011 speech in Istanbul devoted to enforcing the restrictions on free speech included in Resolution 16/18, Mrs. Clinton praised the resolution for its moderation, since it "only" criminalized speech when there was "an incitement to imminent violence." It was necessary for the United Nations to take "concrete steps to fight intolerance wherever it occurs [since] we have seen how the incendiary actions of just a very few people, a handful in a country of nearly 300 million, can create wide ripples of intolerance," she said.[15] She was directly referring to Pastor Jones and his Koran-burning ceremonies.

---

[13] See "Whistleblower: DHS Pulled Plug on Surveillance That Could've ID'd CA Terrorists," Fox News, Dec. 10, 2015.

[14] Lucy Madison, "Hillary Clinton, Joe Lieberman Denounce Florida Pastor's Planned Quran Burning Event," CBS News, Sept. 8, 2010.

[15] Video of the speech has been archived, here: http://web.archive.org/web/20110718110721/http://www.state.gov/secretary/rm/2011/07/168636.htm

A word search of the emails from her private server she was forced to turn over to the State Department for public release shows 26 separate entries containing the string "Terry Jones," and another 35 with the string "Koran burning."

The notion that the United States was responsible for the violence of Muslims around the world was deeply ingrained in the mindset of Mrs. Clinton and her entourage. Former aide Sid Blumenthal sent Mrs. Clinton a three-page letter from former U.S. Ambassador Joe Wilson, the husband of former CIA officer Valerie Plame, after a "reality check" visit he made to Baghdad in September 2010. Wilson described going to a U.S. military PX to look for t-shirts for his kids, "but it was hard put to find any that were not horribly bellicose or racist in nature." Most bore slogans referring to Arabs as "camel jockeys," or depicted a nuclear mushroom cloud enveloping Baghdad. "Were I the commander those shirts would not be on the shelves as they convey adolescent macho Pastor Terry Jones attitudes," Wilson wrote Mrs. Clinton. "The service people don't see themselves there to bring peace, light, joy or even democracy to Iraq. They are there to kill the 'camel jockeys.'" [16]

Pastor Jones for his part played right into Mrs. Clinton's scenario, goading her in public and organizing outlandish events. His latest, in preparation for "International Judge Mohammad Day," included a video presentation of the "charges" against Muhammad, whom he was planning to put "on trial" on the 2012 anniversary of the 9/11 attacks. Behind him as he

---

[16]   The emails can be searched at the State Department's FOIA reading room, here: https://foia.state.gov/Search/Results. aspx?collection=Clinton_Email

The Joe Wilson letter was relayed to Mrs. Clinton on Sept. 13, 2010. She liked it so much she asked aides to print three copies but to "remove the heading from Sid so it is just the memo from Joe to me." Sidney Blumenthal email to Hillary Clinton, "H-Joe Wilson's memo to you on his trip to Baghdad: Sid," Sept. 13, 2010.

spoke was an effigy of the prophet of Islam wearing a Devil's mask. Jones finished the video by declaring that he planned to "execute" Mohammad because "Islam, Mohammad, and his teachings are of the Devil."[17] Cheryl Mills, Mrs. Clinton's chief of staff, believes to this day that the "hateful video" that had "caused" the Cairo protests and Benghazi attacks was this brief promotional film made by Pastor Terry Jones, not Nakoula's trailer. That's how obsessed Mrs. Clinton and her inner circle had become with Pastor Jones.[18]

On his website, Jones carried extensive criticism of Mrs. Clinton and her devotion to the "Istanbul Process," calling her and other Obama administration officials who supported it the "puppets" of the OIC. In one blog posting that August, he carried a video of a remarkable exchange in which Rep. Trent Franks (R, AZ) repeatedly asked a senior Department of Justice official, Tom Perez, a simple question: "Will you tell us here today that this administration's Department of Justice will never entertain or advance a proposal that criminalizes speech against any religion?"

That should have been a no brainer, right? *Yes, Congressman, of course I can give you that assurance. We would never think of such a thing.*

Instead, Perez, an assistant attorney general, refused to answer. Not once, not twice or even three times: but four times. He started talking about "hate speech," and "racist

---

[17]   https://www.youtube.com/watch?v=ImHqkfLMohY. The Internet archive of that video showed that it had received just 8,151 views as of September 12, 2012. https://web. archive.org/web/20120912204432/http://www.youtube.com/ watch?v=ImHqkfLMohY

[18]   Interview of Cheryl Mills, Select Committee on Benghazi, Sept. 3, 2015; pp81-84. The transcript of Ms. Mills closed-door testimony was leaked by committee Democrats shortly before Hillary Clinton's public testimony on October 22, 2015.

speech," but Representative Franks cut him off and asked the question again. The blog post noted that Perez in the past had shown support for "a legal declaration that U.S. citizens' criticism of Islam constitutes racial discrimination." Such a declaration would allow anyone deemed to have made anti-Islam statements to be prosecuted under existing hate crime laws, a chilling assault on our First Amendment freedoms.[19]

Just days before the September 11, 2012 attacks in Cairo and Benghazi, yet another OIC-sponsored meeting on criminalizing any criticism of Islam was held in Istanbul. Cloaked in mumbo-jumbo "interfaith" rhetoric, even the Vatican's final statement recognized that a key subject was "discourses and languages used in the media, popular culture, and religious centers" about religion. "Religious leaders and decision-makers should lead a process of reforming these areas." In clear language, that meant new laws to govern speech. It was an open door to imposing Sharia-compliant blasphemy rules on the West.[20]

Indeed, several emails to Mrs. Clinton immediately after the attacks show that her staff was tracking any comments by Muslim leaders who favored new blasphemy laws. For example, a September 13, 2012 memo that circulated among Clinton staffers mentioned an Al Jazeera interview with President Obama's emissary to the OIC, Rashad Hussein, and a subsequent commentary by historian and political analyst Dr. Mohamed al-Jawadi. "When asked how to prevent future violent incidents at U.S. Embassies, [al-Jawadi] emphasized the

---

[19] The video is here: https://www.youtube.com/watch?v=0wwv9l6W8yc&feature=youtu.be. The blog post has been archived here: https://web.archive.org/web/20130408225456/http://www.standupamericanow.org/articles/2012/07/will-obama-criminalize-criticism-of-islam-terry-jones-holds-international-judge-muh

[20] The full Vatican communiqué is here: http://www.news.va/en/news/full-text-final-communique-from-istanbul-interfait.

importance of strong judicial institutions to address charges of breaking laws and denigrating religions, so the cases may be settled within legal systems," an aide wrote.[21]

There's just one problem with this analysis: while it shows clear motivation and intent, up until September 11, 2012, almost no one had seen the movie. A "hateful video" seen by a handful of Muslim clerics in Cairo, and shown on an obscure, Saudi-funded television station, wasn't enough. Indeed, so few people had watched the al-Nas TV show that the State Department and the U.S. media accredit with having made Nakoula's video go viral, that the YouTube archives of the Arabic language versions of the clip don't even begin until September 12, 2012.[22]

For the "hateful" video to become an issue, for it to create a backlash against "anti-Muslim bigotry," it needed to go viral. It needed to go global. It needed millions of views.

And first of all, it needed a new name.

---

21   Email from Thompson, Rebecca B to Clinton staff, Sept. 13, 2012, titled, "Rashad Hussein on Al Jazeera, Sept. 13."

22   See for example, John Hudson, "The Egyptian Outrage Peddler Who Sent an Anti-Islam YouTube Clip Viral," TheWire.com, Sept. 13, 2012. The archive for the Al Nas (1'32") version is here: https://web.archive.org/web/20120912033920/http://www.youtube.com/watch?v=lnM_NuW0r9M&feature=youtu.be&t=1m45s, while the archive for the longer (13'53") version posted to the Sam Bacile channel was here: https://web.archive.org/https://www.youtube.com/watch?v=GsGPOTpU-dU&feature=youtu.be\

CHAPTER 12

HOW THE MOVIE WENT VIRAL

Max Fisher, the reporter from the Atlantic who published the first piece in English about the YouTube video, was the first to use the title, *Innocence of Muslims*.

> "The movie is called *Innocence of Muslims*, although some Egyptian media have reported its title as Mohammed Nabi al-Muslimin, or Mohammed, Prophet of the Muslims. If you've never heard of it, that's because most of the few clips circulating online are dubbed in Arabic."

Remember, he wrote this article as the protests were underway in front of the U.S. Embassy in Cairo on the afternoon of September 11, 2012, hours *before* the Benghazi attacks.

Who told him the movie was called *Innocence of Muslims*? That remains unclear. He claimed in his article that the movie was "associated" with Pastor Terry Jones in Florida, but Jones didn't use that title in reference to the movie until later. Nakoula told me that it was his title, and that he had "probably" discussed it with Terry Jones and Morris Sadek by phone. Were those phone calls intercepted by the U.S. government, scrubbed, and passed on to Max Fisher through cut-outs? Fisher, who was reporting from Washington, DC, told me in an email exchange that he simply doesn't recall where he first heard of the movie title but that it was probably from other reporters.[1]

The YouTube channel that Max Fisher linked to in that initial piece was a very obscure one, called MarsadIslami. And although Fisher claimed that most postings of the movie were in Arabic, which he didn't understand, MarsadIslami posted the 14-minute trailer in English under the title, "The Coptic Abroad insulting the prophet in doing Movie Trailer." In the description box, the owner of MarsadIslami wrote, "We do not encorage [sic] this movie as they are insulting our Prophet (PBUH) and have uploaded it to show what the Coptics are saying about our blessed Prophet (PBUH)."[2]

Why hadn't Fisher seen that, or mentioned it? *Because it didn't fit the agenda.* MarsadIslami made no mention of Nakoula or Sam Bacile, no mention of Terry Jones, no mention of the United States, no call for protests. And garnered just 405 views as of September 11, 2012.

YouTube took down the Marsad account a few months later for an unrelated violation of its community guidelines, but not before lawyer Cris Armenta and her Internet sleuths, David Hardy and Eric Bulock, managed to track it down.

It was associated with an Islamist news site called the Islamic Media Observatory, aka the Islamic Information Centre,

---

[1]   Fisher cited Adrien Chen at Gawker.com as the probable source. But Chen's stories were all posted well after Fisher's. Fisher was following *NY Times* reporter Liam Stack as well, as mentioned in Chapter 2. But Stack was being tipped off or getting his information second-hand.
[2]   Archived here: https://web.archive.org/web/20120911205509/http://www.youtube.com/watch?v=4sQPRtS2h7k

and a website called MarsadPress.net. They were cited in the al-Wakeel newspaper article that was held up by the hosts of al-NAS TV in Egypt on September 8, calling on the Egyptian authorities to prosecute the film-maker, Morris Sadek, and Pastor Terry Jones, so it makes sense for them to have posted the video on YouTube. They accused the filmmaker and his Coptic allies for "wanting to extinguish the light of Allah with their mouths."[3]

A WhoIS search run by Armenta and her team showed that MarsadPress.Net had been registered in February 2012 by Yasser al-Sirri, a well-known al Qaeda sympathizer, using a London address. Al-Sirri was an Egyptian with a long pedigree of Islamist activities. He had traveled repeatedly to Peshawar, Pakistan, during the Soviet war in Afghanistan in the 1980s, where he worked for Islamic relief agencies tied to Osama Bin Laden. The Egyptian government sentenced him to death a first time in 1994 for his alleged role in the attempted assassination of Prime Minister Atef Sedki, causing him to flee to England where he was granted political asylum. They again sought his arrest for his alleged involvement in the 1997 terrorist attacks in Luxor, carried out by Gamaa Islamiya (Islamic Group) with help from Iran.

That's not a typo. I learned first-hand about Iran's involvement in the Luxor attacks, and with al-Qaeda more generally, from Egyptian government officials during a reporting trip to Cairo in early 1998 for Reader's Digest. When the Digest published my profile on Osama Bin Laden in the July 1998 issue, they couldn't even acquire a public source photo of Bin Laden and used an artist's sketch. Three weeks later, he became world famous for the simultaneous bombings that

---

[3]   The original al Wakeel article and a rough translation were provided
by Cris Armenta to the author.

destroyed two U.S. embassies in Africa, attacks we now know were joint operations between al Qaeda and Iran.[4]

Assistant United States Attorney James Comey indicted al-Sirri in New York in 2002 for allegedly conspiring to help the jailed Blind Sheikh communicate with terrorist supporters outside the United States. That same year he was named as a co-conspirator with Osama Bin Laden in the sprawling lawsuit by victims of the 9/11 attacks known as *Burnett et al v. Osama bin Laden et al.* During the revolution that ultimately ousted strongman Hosni Mubarak in Egypt, al-Sirri joined the ranks of Muslim Brotherhood supporters from his exile in London, calling on Egyptians to shut down the Suez Canal. The Iranian regime was wildly supportive of the Muslim Brotherhood takeover of Egypt and the government of President Mohammad al-Morsi.

Many analysts in the West point to the sectarian differences between al Qaeda and Iran as proof they have no operational relationship. But that has been proven wrong again and again.

The U.S. Treasury Department first accused Iran of aiding al Qaeda financial networks in 2005. On January 16, 2009, it revealed that Bin Laden's eldest son Saad was being sheltered in Iran, and on July 28, 2011, Treasury sanctioned a major al Qaeda financial network in Iran, noting that they were moving "money and recruits from across the Middle East into Iran, then on to Pakistan for the benefit of al-Qaida senior leaders." On February 16, 2012, Treasury designated the Iranian Ministry of Information and Security (MOIS) for its support of terrorist groups, "including al-Qaida." Bin Laden himself, in a letter seized by Seal Team 6 at his headquarters in Abbottabad,

---

[4]   The information on Iran's involvement in the embassy bombings is detailed in the Opinion and Order by Judge John Bates in *Owens v. Republic of Sudan*, 826 F. Supp. 2d 128 - Dist. Court, Dist. of Columbia 2011. The 1998 Reader's Digest story, "This Man Wants You Dead," is available here: http://kentimmerman.com/news/rd_OBL.htm

Pakistan, scolded a follower for making idle threats against Iran. "We expect you would consult with us for these important matters, for as you are aware, Iran is our main artery for funds, personnel, and communication, as well as the matter of hostages," Bin Laden wrote.[5]

Like Hillary Clinton, the Iranians needed to cover their tracks. Blaming the video was an easy call.

As I first revealed in *Dark Forces: the Truth About What Happened in Benghazi*, a significant body of evidence confirms the presence of an Iranian special operations team in Libya that played a direct role in the Benghazi attacks. That evidence includes accounts from U.S. intelligence officers, U.S. special operations officers and private military contractors who were on the ground in Benghazi, as well as banking records provided by defectors from Iranian intelligence. We now know that multiple U.S. intelligence agencies were tracking the presence of an Iranian Revolutionary Guards Corps-Quds Force team in Benghazi and were reporting up the food chain to their superiors in Washington, DC.

As I will reveal in the Afterword, Iran's role in the Benghazi attacks was confirmed in a recently-declassified memorandum to Defense Intelligence Agency Director, General Michael T. Flynn, dated September 29, 2012, which was obtained under the Freedom of Information Act by the public interest group, Judicial Watch.

Could al-Sirri have been operating on behalf of the Iranian regime when his YouTube channel posted Nakoula's video? The official Iranian media was certainly quick to blame the Benghazi attacks on the video. Early reports, in Iran Press TV and elsewhere, also mentioned the "Jewish donors" lie.

---

[5]   The Bin Laden letter regarding the support Iran was providing him is available in English translation here: http://www.dni.gov/files/documents/ubl2016/english/Letter%20to%20Karim.pdf

Yasser al-Sirri certainly knew Western reporters, and he may have called them to alert them to the video. But whatever his motives in posting the trailer, he was not aware of the title, *Innocence of Muslims*. And he lacked the reach and the audience to make the video go viral, as the traffic of his MarsadIslami YouTube channel shows.

+++

For nearly a full day after the Benghazi attacks, U.S. reporters were still having a hard time finding the movie, complaining this was "because most of the clips are in Arabic."[6]

Cris Armenta's Internet sleuths found that the first English-language YouTube upload using the name *Innocence of Muslims* appeared on a little-known but apparently very well-funded YouTube channel called NewsPoliticsNow.

NewsPoliticsNow had three separate YouTube channels, known as NPN1, NPN2, and NPN3. It used NPN3 to launch the 1'32" English-language version of the trailer, which it uploaded at some point during the early afternoon of September 11, 2012, Eastern Time. When users hovered over the title, *Innocence of Muslims,* a subtitle appeared: "Egypt Protest film." So it appears that it was uploaded sometime after the protests in Cairo began, but before the Benghazi attacks.[7]

The NPN3 version of the trailer was dramatically different from the one posted by al-Nas TV. It began with the scene where Mohammad plunges his head between the legs of his wife,

---

6   Billy Hallowell, "This is the Anti-Muhammed Movie That Sparked Deadly Islamist Protests in Egypt and Libya Yesterday," The Blaze, Sept. 12, 2012 8:19 am ET.

7   An archived screenshot of the NPN3 video on Sept. 12, 2012 can be viewed here: https://web.archive.org/web/20120912231853/http://www.youtube.com/user/NewsPoliticsNow3

Khadija. "It is definitely more vulgar and shocking," said Eric Bulock.

The owners of NewsPoliticsNow joined YouTube on June 18, 2012. Until *Innocence of Muslims*, NPN3 had showcased a few anti-Mitt Romney clips, some Obama clips, sensationalist footage of storms, and a shooting of a Sikh temple. None of them got significant traffic.[8]

Innocence of Muslims went from zero to over 4.5 million views in just three days. That is a phenomenal performance, and it shows that whoever was behind the channel was a pro.

"Something that goes viral has a signature. It's almost impossible to fabricate. It's an organic thing, social behavior. I don't think it went viral until it was blamed," Bulock told me.

"The primary trigger was the Egyptian TV host who put it on TV. But when people searched YouTube, it wasn't Sam Bacile's channel that got the hits, but NPN3, which was owned by a government-related social media company," he added.

The owners of NPN3 were Internet-savvy, and boosted viewership of their channel by using the key words "Egypt protest movie" and "Muhammad movie" that people were initially searching. They may also have embedded links to the movie in advertising for mass market products in Arabic-language markets, knowing that viewers would then flock to

---

8   An archived capture of the Channel on Sept 12, 2012 can be viewed here: https://web.archive.org/web/20120912231853/http://www.youtube.com/user/NewsPoliticsNow3

watch the YouTube, Bulock said.

By September 18, *Innocence* had received 8.9 million views on NPN3. So many people were looking for the movie that online guides with website addresses started popping up everything. The original Sam Bacile YouTube channel also took off once NPN3 got things going, and received several million views. By September 20, hundreds of YouTube channels now featured the movie, and it was widely available on fast download torrent sites.[9]

It was all over the world. It had gone viral with an active

---

[9]   Eric Bulock provided me with the following table tracking the hits on the video on the NPN3 channel during this period:

Date	Views	Likes	Dislikes
9/12/2012	102229	1847	4355
9/12/2012	326046	2212	5536
9/13/2012	545741	2547	6574
9/13/2012	1630636	4543	15017
9/13/2012	1977709	5169	17306
9/14/2012	1977709	5529	18588
9/14/2012	2559392	5858	20129
9/14/2012	3628725	6841	24846
9/14/2012	3931091	7673	27421
9/15/2012	4242815	7809	27810
9/15/2012	4968083	8655	30323
9/15/2012	5289779	9102	32083
9/15/2012	5785379	9885	34527
9/16/2012	5978062	10000	34915
9/16/2012	6854105	11100	39681
9/17/2012	6974556	11227	40217
9/17/2012	7154271	11273	40360
9/17/2012	7289693	11415	41243
9/18/2012	7457325	12129	43749
9/18/2012	8512621	12291	44302
9/18/2012	8935286	12487	44978
9/19/2012	9397493	12790	46101
9/19/2012	9489209	12882	46383
9/19/2012	9598387	13169	47132

assist from Hillary Clinton and Barack Obama, who continued to blame the YouTube video for the widespread violence sweeping throughout the Muslim world in multiple public statements.

"The biggest boost to the NPN3 YouTube channel would have been the result of advertising spent by the White House," Bulock told me. During the week of the attacks, the United States government "bought $70,000 worth of air time on seven Pakistani television channels to air an ad showing Barack Obama and Secretary of State Hillary Clinton denouncing the anti-Islamic video and denying any U.S. involvement in its production," he pointed out.

As they say in the marketing business, there is no such thing as bad publicity. All of those public statements and the advertising buy only served to further inflame Muslims and to spark more violent protests: 83 in all, by the time it died down a month later.

The owners of NPN3 had accomplished their goal. The video had spread like wildfire. And so on September 20, NPN3 removed the video, and disappeared.

The channel didn't just go off the air, but erased all trace of its existence – at least, to ordinary users.

+++

So who was behind NewsPoliticsNow?

"We have never been able to find out for sure who owned NPN3," Bulock says. "But we believe it could be traced back to a company called Stanley, Inc."

The United States government spends several billion dollars every year on "Information Operations." Most of that money is doled out to private contractors by the Department of State, the Department of Defense, and the Central Intelligence Agency. Stanley Inc. "provides services to the U.S.

federal, civilian, defense and intelligence agencies," according to its website.[10] Indeed, corporate parent CGI credits Stanley Inc. for bringing to the merger enormous no-compete federal contracts, including multiple highly-classified programs.[11]

CGI won the initial $678 million contract to build the Obamacare website, by all accounts a massive failure. The Daily Caller and other center-right news organizations claimed that CGI won the Obamacare rollout as a no-compete contract, because of its personal and political ties to the Obama White House.[12] Senior CGI Vice-President Toni Townes-Whitley had long-standing ties to First Lady Michelle Obama through Princeton University, the Organization of Black Unity, and the Third World Center, ties acknowledged even by the left-wing Snopes.com.[13] Top Stanley and CGI executives are big Democrat party donors, according to the center-left Sunlight Foundation.[14]

When U.S. government officials pointed journalists to the movie, they pointed to this particular trailer on this particular channel, NPN3. "How did they know to point there? *Because they put it there,*" a YouTube analyst using the handle "Montagraph" said.[15]

---

[10]   This is also the language used when mega-contractor CGI announced its merger with Stanley in 2010. See: http://www.cgi.com/en/stanley. CGI Federal, a Canadian subsidiary of CGI Group, botched the $678 million Obamacare rollout.

[11]   CGI lists the contract "vehicles" for shareholders and subcontractors here: http://www.cgi.com/en/us-federal/contracts

[12]   See: http://dailycaller.com/2013/10/25/michelle-obamas-princeton-classmate-is-executive-at-company-that-built-obamacare-website/

[13]   See: http://www.snopes.com/politics/obama/whitley.asp

[14]   See: http://sunlightfoundation.com/blog/2013/10/09/aca-contractors/

[15]   Montagraph created his own YouTube video to show how he traced the NPN3 avatar to Stanley Associates, here: http://www.tatumba.com/blog/archives/8656

NewsPoliticsNow had a TM marker, indicating it was a trademarked channel set up by a commercial entity that sought to protect its intellectual property. But a trademark search with the U.S. Patent and Trademark Office turns up empty. If it ever was actually registered with the U.S. patent office or any other authority, that registration also has vanished. It is possible that the owners of NPN3 included the TM marker as a pre-emptive warning, not an actual registration, so they could reserve the right to sue in the event someone infringed on their "brand." As it turned out, of course, the owners of NPN3 decided it was more prudent to simply vanish.

But before they did, Montagraph did a search through the Google Image data based on their trademarked avatar, the stylized graphic they used to identify the YouTube channel. Only one name turned up in the vast Google image data base: Stanley, Inc., the government intelligence and services contractor, with close ties to the Obama White House.

image size:
106 × 104

No other sizes of this image found.

Best guess for this image: *stanley inc*

Stanley Associates
www.stanleyassociates.com/
We are pleased to announce that **Stanley Inc**. is now part of CGI. For more information, please visit www.cgi.com/Stanley and CGI solutions for the U.S. federal ... 2 images
+ Show stock quote for SXE

Stanley, Inc. - Wikipedia, the free encyclopedia
en.wikipedia.org/wiki/Stanley,_Inc.
Stanley, Inc. (NYSE:SXE), acquired by CGI Group in 2010, is an information technology company based in Arlington, Virginia. Founded in 1966, it operated as a ...

According to the Washington Examiner, CGI Federal president, Donna A. Ryan, "enjoyed high-level access to top Obama administration officials," access documented by White House visitors logs. Before her company was selected to design the Obamacare website, Ms. Ryan visited the White house six times, the logs show.[16]

Ms. Ryan had been Vice President of Stanley Inc. before the two companies merged in 2011. She brought with her years of expertise in the defense and intelligence sectors, including black Information Operations (I/O).

"The Obama administration needed to be involved in making the video go viral while creating the perception that it "had absolutely nothing to do with it," former Muslim terrorist turned Christian evangelist Walid Shoebat wrote. The video was supposed to invoke "peer pressure and shaming" without the hint of government involvement," the very terms used by Hillary Clinton in her 2011 Istanbul speech referenced above.[17]

A spokesperson for CGIA/Stanley, Linda F. Odorisio, said in an email exchange that she was "not aware of any relationship" between Stanley and NewsPoliticsNow.

+++

I contacted the Associated Press reporter in Los Angeles whose early story on the Cairo protests and the filmmaker was picked up by the national media. I wanted to know how she could be sure that the person she interviewed, who claimed he was Sam Bacile, was actually the filmmaker. She's the one who first claimed that he told her he was an Israeli-American writer

---

[16]   See: http://www.washingtonexaminer.com/obamacare-website-firms-execs-had-white-house-access/article/2537235

[17]   See: http://shoebat.com/2014/06/17/company-botched-obamacare-website-tied-benghazi-video/

and director who made the movie with $5 million in donations from 100 Jewish donors, a fairy-tale that went wild all over the world.

Remember, Nakoula told me several times that he was too afraid to speak to the media. That's why he had asked Steve Klein to serve as his spokesperson. Having been brought up in Egypt where blasphemy laws were very real, he was afraid he would go to jail for making the movie. Or worse.

The AP correspondent, Shaha Tayefe Mohajer, left the AP a few months after that story and now works for a left-wing digital magazine called "TakePart," which links its news coverage to "related actions that can be taken to participate in positive social change." The online magazine is a project of Participant Media, founded by eBay billionaire Jeffrey Skoll. George Soros is a major donor. Both have a long history of funding left-wing causes.

Could she have invented the bit about Nakoula being an Israeli-American as part of an activist agenda, perhaps to provoke Palestinians to launch violent demonstrations against Israel? Or more generally, to provoke Muslims?[18]

"I decline to be interviewed, as I did while I was at the AP, per their policy on outside interviews of their reporters," she told me in an email. "You are welcome to contact corporate communications at AP for further details."

I sent her a follow-up email, to make sure that she understood that the filmmaker had denied talking to her, but received no reply.

A few hours after her initial dispatch appeared, the

---

[18]   Participant media itself also funded a Netflix documentary about the pro-democracy movement in Egypt that toppled Hosni Mubarak. "The Square," named after Tahrir Square in Cairo, claims the Muslim Brotherhood was in cahoots with the army to put down a less-radical Islamist movement that sought to bring freedom to Egypt.

Associated Press put out an "updated" version that included an important correction: "New information has come to light regarding *Innocence of Muslims* and its creators. "Sam Bacile" is a pseudonym used by Nakoula Basseley Nakoula, identified by authorities as the man behind the project." Then they included a "breaking news update" that walked back Ms. Mohajer's claim that "Bacile" was an Israeli-born Jewish writer.[19]

Less than 48 hours after her initial story appeared, the AP issued a full correction as a stand-alone story – a highly unusual thing for the AP to do. The correction read as follows:

Correction: Egypt filmmaker story

Sept. 14, 2012

LOS ANGELES (AP) — In a Sept. 12 story about a film that sparked deadly protests in Libya and Egypt, The Associated Press quoted a man who identified himself in several phone conversations as Sam Bacile, and who said he wrote and directed the film. The AP story quoted him saying he was an Israeli Jew.

In later reporting, the AP was unable to find any public records confirming the existence of a person with that name.

The AP subsequently reported that Nakoula Basseley Nakoula was the key figure behind the film. Federal authorities confirmed that finding. A federal law enforcement official told The Associated Press on Thursday that authorities had connected Nakoula to the man using the pseudonym of Sam Bacile. Federal

---

19   The most widely viewed version is here: http://www.huffingtonpost. com/2012/09/12/sam-bacile-in-hiding_n_1876044.html

court papers filed against Nakoula in a 2010 criminal prosecution noted that Nakoula had used numerous aliases, including Nicola Bacily and Robert Bacily. Nakoula told the AP on Wednesday that he is a Coptic Christian.

The person claiming to be Bacile said in his conversation with the AP that the film was financed with the help of more than 100 Jewish donors. According to Film L.A. Inc., which grants filming permits in Los Angeles County, the production company for the film was a Duarte, Calif.-based Christian group, Media for Christ. The president of that organization is a Christian from Egypt.

Usually if a breaking news reporter gets a fact wrong, the AP will update the wires with the correction incorporated into a new header, along with the original story as it appeared. They did that initially, but ultimately removed Ms. Mohajer's original story from the wire.

In her initial email to me, Ms. Mohajer claimed that she was "not the first" to whom "Sam Bacile" made his claim about being an Israeli-American. "Reporters from the *Wall Street Journal* spoke to him before I did and published an interview before I did, as did a reporter in AP's Cairo bureau," she wrote.

I found that odd, since the dateline on the Cairo-based report on the video is 4:35 PM on September 12, 2012 – a full fifteen hours *after* Ms. Mohajer's story.

The author of the Cairo report, Maggie Michael, told me in an email exchange that since Nakoula was not in Cairo "for sure I didn't interview him." Any interview with Nakoula would have been done by "our colleagues in the States,"

One thing is clear: the AP was embarrassed by Ms. Mohajer's reporting and subsequently walked it back, ultimately providing multiple, conflicting explanations for how they had mistakenly reported Nakoula's identity.[20]

They finally appeared to admit that it was Klein who had spoken with the AP for their initial story, not Bacile. "Klein had told the AP on Tuesday that the filmmaker was an Israeli Jew who was concerned for family members who live in Egypt."

But that's not what Ms. Mohajer wrote. In her initial story, she said that *Bacile* told her he was "a real estate developer and an Israeli Jew." The first "corrected" version toned down his racial identity, calling him "an Israeli-born Jewish writer and director." She never quoted Klein as saying that Bacile was Jewish or Israeli. She claimed that Bacile had told her that.

Nakoula's phone records, obtained by Cindy's attorney, show no calls from anyone from the Associated Press either the night of September 11, when Ms. Mohajer says she spoke with him, or the following day. All the numbers that called the number he was using belonged to known associates.

The only reporter who tried to phone him was an ABC News correspondent in Los Angeles named Joshua L. Paris, but Nakoula didn't pick up the phone because he didn't recognize the number.

As for the *Wall Street Journal*, they also printed a correction to their earlier story but did claim that a reporter had reached Nakoula by phone that Tuesday evening. The reporter who

---

[20] The corrected AP story started by saying that a federal law enforcement official told them that "Nakoula was connected to the persona of Sam Bacile, a man who initially told the AP he was the film's writer and director." Next, when Bacile turned out to be a false identity, they "traced a cell phone number Bacile used" to a house in Cerritos, CA, where they found Nakoula. When AP showed up at his house on Sept 12, he told them that "he managed logistics for the company that produced the film [but] denied he was Bacile." Lower down in the story, they reveal that they had gotten Bacile's phone number from Morris Sadek, the Coptic activist in Virginia. See: http://bigstory.ap.org/article/california-man-confirms-role-anti-islam-film-0

wrote that story, Dion Nissenbaum, told me that his editors would not allow him to comment on his reporting. When given a second cell phone number that Nakoula was using at the time, he would not say if that was how he had contacted Nakoula.

Steve Klein told me what actually happened, because he was the one who told reporters initially that the filmmaker was an Israeli Jew.

"When the woman from the AP called me the evening of September 11, this was before the shit had hit the fan," he said. She called at 9:30 or 10:00 that night and started badgering him, saying that he wasn't the spokesman for the movie. "So I said, fine, you can call Sam yourself, and hung up. Five minutes later, she called back and said that Nakoula had told her to speak to me. That's when I told her he was an Israeli Jew."

Why did Klein invent that story on the night of September 11, 2012? He had been working with Coptic Christians in Egypt for several years. When he saw the intensity of the violence at the U.S. Embassy in Cairo that afternoon, he realized that thousands of lives were at stake and that he had to do something to protect them.

"I'm a U.S. Marine Corps officer. There's an old Latin phrase Marines are familiar with: *necessitas non habet legem*: Necessity knows no law. There come times you have to mislead some people to save others. I felt I had to deceive her, deceive the media, in order to save lives, just like Churchill and Patton did in World War II."

Klein insists, however, that he never told Ms. Mohajer or anyone else that the film was financed by 100 Jewish donors. "This is the first I've ever heard of that," he told me as I was researching this book. Nakoula also insisted he never said that or even knew about it, as did Morris Sadek, who said he never spoke with Ms. Mohajer. "I think she made it up," Sadek told me.

I can understand Ms. Mohajer, the AP, and the WSJ for making an honest mistake: who doesn't. But shame on her, when presented with the evidence, to refuse to acknowledge it and to attempt to shift the blame to someone else.[21]

+++

One final note on Stanley Inc.

On March 20, 2008, the *Washington Times* revealed that three contract employees had been disciplined by the U.S. Department of State for having improperly accessed the passport application files of presidential candidates, Barack Obama, John McCain, and Hillary Clinton. The State Department subsequently revealed that two of them worked for Stanley, Inc., and were fired. A third worked for a Stanley subcontractor called The Analysis Corp (TAC), run former CIA officer, John O. Brennan.[22]

Stanley, Inc. acknowledged the firings in a press release. The company had been handling security of the State Department passport files for some 15 years, and had just been awarded a

---

[21] A journalism professor at the City College of New York, Devin Harner, also smelled a rat and corresponded with the AP Director of Media relations at the time, Paul Colford, who claimed that the AP had already spoken to 'Sam Bacile' and "his name was on the AP wire before Shaya picked up the story in L.A. and continued with it. She did not 'break' the story." There is zero evidence that this is true. Klein categorically told me that Ms. Mohajer is the only reporter who called him on the night of September 11, 2012. But that's her story, and she is sticking to it. See Devin Harner's excellent blog post, which I discovered after I had written this section. http://mediashift. org/2012/09/how-sam-bacile-bamboozled-the-ap-wall-street-journal-over-anti-muslim-film258/

[22] "Obama passport files violated; 2 workers at State fired; 1 rebuked," *Washington Times,* March 20, 2008. *The State Department revealed*: see http://www.nytimes.com/2008/03/22/us/politics/22passport.html?_r=0

five-year, $570 million follow-on contract.[23]

As I wrote shortly after Obama took office in 2009:

> Sources who tracked the investigation tell Newsmax that the main target of the breach was the Obama passport file, and that the contractor accessed the file in order to "cauterize" the records of potentially embarrassing information.
>
> "They looked at the McCain and Clinton files as well to create confusion," one knowledgeable source told Newsmax. "But this was basically an attempt to cauterize the Obama file."
>
> "This individual's actions were taken without the knowledge or direction of anyone at The Analysis Corp and are wholly inconsistent with our professional and ethical standards," Brennan's company said in a statement sent to reporters after the passport breach was made public.
>
> The State Department chalked up the passport file snooping discovered in March 2008 to "imprudent curiosity" by contract employees hired to help process passport applications.[24]

The State Department's Office of Investigator General conducted a probe into the passport breach that reportedly zeroed in on Brennan's employee. What type of information had been targeted? "The breaches involved electronic files that contained personal information about the three candidates... [including] biographical information and passport applications.

---

23   Kate Bolduan, "Chief of firm involved in breach is Obama adviser," CNN, March 22, 2008.

24   Ken Timmerman, "Obama's Intelligence Adviser Involved in Security Breach," Newsmax, Jan. 12, 2009.

The files also contained Social Security numbers, addresses, dates of birth and other personal information," the *NY Times* reported.[25]

But the story doesn't stop there. Just five days after the breach was revealed, Officer William A. Smith Jr. of the D.C. Metropolitan Police Department's Narcotics Special Investigation Division made a fortuitous traffic stop of a suspicious car with dark-tinted windows. When the driver put down his window, a wave of marijuana smoke billowed out. Officer Smith asked if he could conduct a search, and discovered that the driver, 24-year-old Leiutenant [sic] Quarles Harris Jr., had stuffed a large zip-lock bag into his jacket pocket that contained 13 smaller zip-lock bags, each filled with marijuana.

Officer Smith also found 19 credit cards with names different from Harris and his female companion, and eight State Department passport applications.

That's when he called in the feds.

Officer Smith took Harris down to the D.C. Metropolitan Police Sixth District headquarters for booking, where investigators from the Secret Service, the Department of State, and the U.S. Postal Service soon arrived to question him about the passport breach. In the original charging document, Harris "admitted he obtained the Passport information from a co-conspirator who works for the U.S. Department of State," and that he used stolen passport information to make fraudulent credit card application. He also agreed to cooperate with the federal investigation, and over the objection of prosecutors was released on personal recognizance at his arraignment the next day.[26]

---

25   Helene Cooper, "Passport Files of 3 Candidates Were Pried Into, " *NY Times*, March 22, 2008.

26   The charging document was obtained by a news organization which has since removed it from its website. An archived copy is here: https://web.archive.org/web/20101212024630/http://acc-tv.com/sites/wjla/news/stories/videos/harrischargingdoc.pdf

Less than one month later, Harris was murdered. D.C. Police found his body on April 18, 2008, inside his locked car, dead from multiple gunshot wounds fired through the windshield, the *Washington Times* reported.[27]

The DC police said they did not know whether his death was a direct result of his cooperation with federal investigators. "We don't have any information right now that connects his murder to that case," Cmdr. Michael Anzallo told the *Washington Times*.

Of course, it's only a coincidence, comrade.

The State Department Inspector General released its 104-page report on the passport breach in July 2008[28]. Page after page were heavily redacted or totally blacked out, including an entire 30-page section. A former Passport Office employee, 26-year-old Rodney P. Quarles Jr., of Charlotte Hall, Maryland, was formally charged for stealing passport information that October.

The identity of the John Brennan employee involved in the breach has never been revealed.[29] At the time of the Benghazi attacks, Brennan was Obama's top counter-terrorism and intelligence advisor at the White House. Since 2013, he has been Director of the Central Intelligence Agency.

---

[27] "Key witness in passport fraud case fatally shot," *Washington Times*, April 19, 2008.

[28] United States Department of State and the Broadcasting Board of Governors Office of Inspector General, Office of Audits: "Review of Controls and Notification for Access to Passport Records in the Department of State's Passport Information Electronic Records System (PIERS), AUD/IP-08-29, July 2008; Sensitive but Unclassified.

[29] For a more detailed account, see: Jerome R. Corsi, "Did CIA Pick Sanitize Obama's Passport Records?" WorldNetDaily, Jan. 8, 2013. http://www.wnd.com/2013/01/did-cia-pick-sanitize-obamas-passport-records/

CHAPTER 13
REAL WORLD IMPACT

As the video swept across the Muslim world, thanks to the promotional efforts of the United States government, so did riots, anti-American protests, and murder.

In Egypt, president Mohammad Morsi stoked the fires by calling for the prosecution of the "madmen" behind the video. The political arm of his Muslim Brotherhood, known as the Freedom and Justice Party, issued a statement that strongly condemned the film "promoted by U.S. Coptic Christian individuals," and considered the film "a racist crime and a failed attempt to provoke sectarian strife between the two elements of the nation: Muslims and Christians."

It should come as no surprise that the Muslim Brotherhood used almost identical language as Mrs. Clinton to define anti-Islam "hate crimes." Nor should it come as a surprise that they called for the U.S. to restrict First Amendment freedoms if those freedoms were used to "insult" Islam.[1] The State Department drew the line, however, when it came to Egypt's demand to extradite Nakoula, Morris Sadek, and the others so they could

---

[1]   Erica Ritz, "Remorseful? Read the Muslim Brotherhood's Statement on the Embassy Attacks," The Blaze, Sept. 12, 2012. 11:05 AM ET

face prosecution in Egypt. "Because we were U.S. citizens, the State Department refused the deportation request that they received from Egypt via Interpol," Nakoula confidant Nabil Bissada told me. Bissada, who is an active voice within the Coptic community in the United States, had been forced to leave Egypt in 1990 after spending 16 months in jail for helping Muslims convert to Christianity. "I still can't go back to Egypt, even today," he told me.

74 protests took place over the two weeks following September 11, 2012, and another nine in the two weeks following President Obama's United Nations speech.

Here is a brief rundown, which was compiled with help from independent researcher Paul Webb.

Wednesday, September 12:

The protests began on September 12, with angry crowds gathering in Cairo, Tunis, and Khartoum. The Egyptian police were ready for the protesters this time around, and reinforced the security perimeter around the U.S. Embassy compound. Instead of allowing the jihadis to storm the walls and raise the black flag of Islam, as they had the previous day, the police succeeded in preventing any large-scale demonstration.

In Tunis, police fired tear gas and rubber bullets to disperse some 200 protesters who had gathered outside the U.S. Embassy in Tunis. The crowd threw rocks at police, burned U.S. flags, and chanted Islamist slogans. There were no reports of casualties.[2]

In Khartoum, around 300 protesters gathered in front of the U.S. Embassy in Sudan, demanding that U.S. officials deliver

---

[2]   http://www.irishtimes.com/news/protest-at-us-embassy-in-tunisia-1.736095

"an immediate apology" and the "removal of the YouTube video," an embassy official said. The protesters remained peaceful and did not seek to breach the walls of the embassy compound.[3]

In Washington, President Obama told a hastily-called press conference in the Rose Garden that the United States "reject[s] all efforts to denigrate the religious beliefs of others."

Afghan President Hamid Karzai set up a firewall to prevent Afghanis from viewing YouTube videos, while YouTube announced that it had "temporarily restricted access" to the video from inside Libya and Egypt. If true, those actions had little impact on the mounting rage throughout the Muslim world and provide further evidence that the video became infamous because of the U.S. government efforts to blame it for the violence.[4]

Thursday, September 13:

Protests escalated the next day, with large crowds gathered in cities across Iraq to protest the video. Many of them were supporters of anti-U.S. Shiite cleric Moqtada al-Sadr and called on the Iraqi government to close the U.S. Embassy.[5]

In Washington, Hillary Clinton called the video "disgusting and reprehensible," words that were replayed around the world.

---

3   http://www.modernghana.com/news/417110/1/protest-at-us-embassy-in-sudan-over-anti-islam-fil.html

4   Jonathan Allen and Michelle Quin, "Arab Spring: Tech as tinder," Politico, Sept. 14, 2012. Hillary Clinton thanked President Karzai for his statement in response to the video, "[e]specially the point that the people that make these kind of videos are a fringe group," according to a debrief memo of their conversation released under the Freedom of Information Act to Judicial Watch in March 2016. http://kentimmerman.com/IOMdocs/HillaryClinton-transcripts-post-Benghazi-calls.pdf

5   http://in.reuters.com/article/2012/09/13/iraq-usa-threat-idINL5E8KD83Y20120913

In Yemen, several thousand protesters stormed the gates of the U.S. Embassy in the capital, Sana'a, and managed to set fire to vehicles inside the compound. Police opened fire, killing five people and wounding 11 others. 24 guards were also wounded. The U.S. responded by dispatching a USMC Fleet Antiterrorism Security Team (FAST) to Yemen that arrived the next day, in stark contrast to their reaction to the Benghazi attacks.[6]

Renewed tensions erupted around the U.S. Embassy in Cairo, with reports that 224 people were injured in clashes with the police.[7]

In Iran, crowds gathered outside the Swiss Embassy in Tehran, which has represented U.S. interests since 1980, chanting "death to America" and "death to Israel." The protest was organized by a radical Islamic student group, and led the Swiss to evacuate embassy employees. Some 200 police and fire personnel prevented an estimated 500 protesters from breaching the embassy gates.[8]

Friday, September 14:

Fridays in the Muslim world are traditionally a day of protest, kicked off by fiery sermons by radical imams. On the Friday immediately following the Benghazi attacks, 21 separate protests were reported from Tunis to Nairobi, from Khartoum to Kuala Lumpur. It was a worldwide Muslim day of rage against the United States. At least seven people were killed in Khartoum, Tunis, Cairo and Tripoli, Lebanon.[9]

---

6   http://blogs.aljazeera.com/topic/anti-islam-film-protests/us-marines-arrive-yemen
7   http://www.bbc.com/news/world-africa-19584734
8   http://www.dailystar.com.lb/News/Middle-East/2012/Sep-13/187749-iranians-protest-film-outside-swiss-embassy-report.ashx#axzz26MmeScjI
9   "Seven dead as anti-Islam film protests widen," BBC, Sept. 14, 2012.

In Egypt, Muslim Brotherhood Secretary General Mahmud Hussein called for gatherings "outside all the main mosques in all of Egypt's provinces... to denounce offenses to religion and to the Prophet."[10] One person was killed during the fourth day of ongoing protests in front of the U.S. Embassy in Cairo. Another was killed in Lebanon when protesters attacked a KFC restaurant.

In Indian Kashmir, 15,000 Muslims burned U.S. flags and called President Obama a "terrorist" in more than two dozen protests throughout the province.[11] Demonstrators pelted the U.S. consulate at Chennai with stones, breaking windows and forcing it to suspend visa operations for two days.[12] 25 protesters were injured when the police counter-charged. Protesters also gathered in front of the French consulate in Puducherry to denounce the film.[13]

In Khartoum, several thousand people stormed the U.S. Embassy in Sudan, after initially gathering outside the German Embassy and setting it on fire. The protesters also attacked the nearby British Embassy. Three people were killed.[14]

In the Egyptian Sinai, protesters stormed a compound of the Multinational Observer Force in the town of Sheikh Zuwayed, wounding two international peacekeepers. The protesters replaced the UN flag with the black flag of Islam and chanted, "There is no God but Allah, and Mohammad is the Prophet of Allah."[15]

---

10   http://english.alarabiya.net/articles/2012/09/12/237617.html

11   "http://article.wn.com/view/
WNAT0DAD3557FCBCA9E09738B4EF05BD2184/

12   http://timesofindia.indiatimes.com/India/US-consulate-in-Chennai-shuts-down-visa-section-for-2-days-following-protests-over-anti-Islam-film/articleshow/16432296.cms?referral=PM

13   http://articles.timesofindia.indiatimes.com/2012-09-14/chennai/33843064_1_consulate-anti-islam-film-ban-film

14   "Seven dead..." op cit.

15   http://blogs.aljazeera.com/topic/anti-islam-video-protests/ultraconservative-protesters-storm-un-sinai-camp

In Tunisia, two people were killed and another 29 were wounded as police tried unsuccessfully to prevent crowds of protesters from entering the U.S. Embassy compound, where they hurled petrol bombs, set fire to vehicles, smashed windows, and looted offices of computers and telephones. Two armed Americans reportedly watched the riot from the roof, but no U.S. diplomats were inside.[16]

Threats from radical Muslim groups caused the Nigerian police to lockdown the capital, Abuja, during Friday prayers. Some 3,000 protesters gathered in the town of Sokoto to protest the film, and government troops fired in the air to disperse angry crows in Jos, a city where the Islamist group Boko Haram has repeatedly massacred Christians.[17]

In Mogadishu, home of "Black Hawk Down," 3,000 Somalis gathered to protest the film. No injuries were reported.[18]

In Gaza, thousands of angry Palestinians emerged from local mosques after Friday prayers and burned American and Israeli flags outside the Parliament building, in protests reportedly called by the Hamas government. Palestinians also clashed with Israeli security forces in Jerusalem, the West Bank, and in the northern Israeli seaport city of Acre, where thousands of Arab protesters denounced the film and called for an Islamic State.[19]

In the Qatari capital of Doha, prominent pro-jihadi

---

[16]   http://www.reuters.com/article/us-film-protests-idUSBRE88D0O320120914

[17]   "Nigerian troops fire to disperse Muslim protesters in Jos," Chicago Tribune (Reuters), Sept. 14, 2012.

[18]   http://www.presstv.com/detail/2012/09/14/261526/antiislam-film-sparks-protest-in-somalia/

[19]   http://www.timesofisrael.com/palestinians-protest-against-anti-islam-film-in-east-jerusalem-and-gaza/?utm_source=The+Times+of+Israel+Daily+Edition&utm_campaign=38bf368868-2012_09_14&utm_medium=email

cleric Sheikh Yusuf al-Qaradawi, who had his own TV show on al Jazeera, called for protesters to gather in front of the U.S. Embassy. (Qaradawi was reportedly working at the time as a secret Obama envoy to the Taliban to negotiate a U.S. withdrawal from Afghanistan and the release of Gitmo prisoners.)[20] Police estimated some 2,000 people answered the call of the Egyptian cleric sometimes called the "Dear Abby" of the Egyptian Muslim Brotherhood.[21] Some chanted, "Obama, Obama, we are all Osama," a reference to Osama bin Laden.[22] Qatar hosts a major U.S. Air Force base in the Persian Gulf region used to launch air strikes in Iraq and elsewhere.

In Islamabad, security forces clashed with protesters outside the U.S. Embassy in the Pakistani capital. Protesters called for the execution of the filmmaker and the expulsion of all U.S. diplomats from Pakistan. Demonstrators at a separate protest in Lahore burned American flags in front of the U.S. consulate. [23]

Smaller protests were organized by Muslim clerics in front of U.S. diplomatic facilities in Kuala Lumpur, Nairobi and Muscat. In the Maldives, several hundred protesters gathered in front of the UN building to protest the film.[24] Muslims in Europe also held protests in front of U.S. diplomatic facilities in Amsterdam and London.

A diplomat at the U.S. Embassy in Tripoli, Libya, sent a very different message back to the State Department on this day, calling on his colleagues to "not conflate" the video with the

---

20   See: http://www.thehindu.com/news/article2755817.ece
21   http://www.spiegel.de/international/world/islam-s-spiritual-dear-abby-the-voice-of-egypt-s-muslim-brotherhood-a-745526.html
22   http://dohanews.co/qatar-residents-join-protests-against-anti-islam/
23   https://web.archive.org/web/20150924204043/http://presstv.com/detail/2012/09/14/261518/pakistan-police-attack-antius-protesters/
24   http://www.straitstimes.com/breaking-news/asia/story/anti-islam-film-sparks-protest-maldives-20120915

attacks across the region. "The overwhelming majority of the [Facebook] comments and tweets we've received from Libyans since the Ambassador's death have expressed deep sympathy, sorrow, and regret... Relatively few have even mentioned the inflammatory video. So if we post messaging about the video specifically, we may draw unwanted attention to it. And it is becoming increasingly clear that the series of events in Benghazi was much more terrorist attack than a protest which escalated into violence."

That message was suppressed by the State Department until the Benghazi Select Committee uncovered it and released it in April 2016.[25]

Saturday, September 15:

The protests continued to spread to Muslim communities far beyond the Middle East. In Sydney, Australia, violent protests broke out in front of the U.S. Consulate General at the urging of local imams. Protesters held signs with messages such as, "Behead all those who insult the Prophet," and "Our Dead are in Paradise. Your Dead are in Hell." Six policemen were among the dozen people injured as police deployed police dogs and battled protesters with pepper spray.[26] 250 protesters were arrested outside the U.S. Embassy in Paris,[27] while Canadian Muslims held a peaceful protest in Calgary, Alberta.

In the teeming Pakistani port city, Karachi, one person died and nine were injured after protesters broke through security

---

25 I've posted it online here: http://kentimmerman.com/
    IOMdocs/2012_09_14-Tripoli-email.pdf
26 http://www.dailytelegraph.com.au/police-use-pepper-spray-on-
    anti-islamic-film-protesters-in-sydney-at-the-us-consulate/story-
    e6freuy9-1226474744811
27 http://www.nydailynews.com/news/world/100-protest-anti-islam-film-
    u-s-embassy-paris-article-1.1160497

cordons outside the U.S. consulate. Police fired live bullets in the air and used tear gas and water canons to disperse an estimated 1,000 protesters.[28]

At renewed protests outside the American Embassy in Tunis, four people were killed and 46 injured. The U.S. government ordered the evacuation of all but emergency U.S. government personnel from the embassies in Tunisia and Sudan and "warned Americans not to travel to those countries."[29]

Sunday, September 16:

This was the day that U.S. Ambassador to the United Nations Susan Rice went on the Sunday talk shows, blaming the Benghazi attacks on the YouTube video. Rice claims she just repeated talking points prepared for her during an intense back-and-forth between senior officials at the CIA, the State Department, and the White House. The subsequent release of 100 pages of emails showed that White House and State Department officials were anxious to remove any suggestion that the Benghazi attacks were carried out by terrorists.[30]

Tempers in Pakistan had reached a boiling point, with protests turning violent all over the country. Massive protests erupted on Sunday at The Mall in Lahore, at a rally in front of a local mosque. Speakers including Muslim clerics and opposition political leaders. One of the speakers, identified as Hafiz Saeed, claimed the film had been produced with the

---

[28] http://www.humanevents.com/2012/09/16/anti-us-protests-in-karachi-turn-violent-1-dead-9-wounded-video/

[29] https://www.washingtonpost.com/world/most-us-government-workers-families-evacuated-from-tunisia-sudan/2012/09/16/4284b4ba-fff5-11e1-b257-e1c2b3548a4a_story.html

[30] I covered this subject extensively in Chapter 15 ("The Cover Up") of *Dark Forces: The Truth About What Happened in Benghazi*.

backing of the U.S. "establishment" and that the producer and all those involved must be hanged publicly. "The U.S. must make a law against blasphemy, or we will not let the U.S. consulates in Pakistan function," he said.[31]

In Greece, an estimated 600 Muslims clashed with riot police in front of the U.S. Embassy in Athens. 40 people were arrested.[32]

Monday, September 17:

Protest over the film kept spreading far and wide. Muslim protesters "totally trashed" the largest Catholic church in Niger's second city, Zinder. Local Christian leaders were taken into custody by police "to ensure their safety." [33]

In the southern Philippine city of Marawi, hundreds of angry Muslims burned American flags,[34] while in Azerbaijan, police detained 30 Muslim activists leading a crowd toward the U.S. Embassy in the capital, Baku, as they chanted "Allah-u Akbar." The embassy had issued a warning earlier to U.S. citizens about a protest assumed to be "connected to other anti-American demonstrations ongoing worldwide."[35]

In Belgium, the leader of an Islamist group known as Sharia4Belgium was among some 230 people detained by

[31] http://tribune.com.pk/story/437772/ultimatum-to-us-criminalise-blasphemy-or-lose-consulate/

[32] http://www.keeptalkinggreece.com/2012/09/23/athens-muslims-clashed-with-riot-police-in-anti-mohammed-film-protest-videos/?utm_source=feedburner&utm_medium=feed&utm_campaign=Feed%3A+KeepTalkingGreece+(Keep+Talking+Greece)

[33] http://www.lemag.ma/english/m/The-largest-Catholic-church-in-Zinder-Niger-s-second-city-destroyed_a2267.html

[34] http://www.mindanaoexaminer.com/news.php?news_id=20120917042710

[35] http://www.naharnet.com/stories/53890-azerbaijan-arrests-30-at-protest-over-anti-islam-film/print

police in Antwerp during violent protests where they set fire to U.S. flags.

Tuesday, September 18:

400 protesters gathered outside the U.S. Embassy in Bangkok, responding to a call from a group called the International Al Quds Federation of Thailand. They carried signs that read, "We love Prophet Mohammad, " and "Stop insulting our religion," and chanted "Down with America." Protest leader Said Sulaiman Husseini said the world could become a "sea of fire" if the American government did not stop distribution of the film.[36]

Friday, September 21:

Deadly clashes erupted across Pakistan after Friday prayers, killing 23 people, even though the government had decreed a public holiday they called "Love the Prophet Day" in an effort to quell the violence. In Karachi, a crowd of 15,000 angry Muslims torched "six cinemas, two banks, a KFC, and five police vehicles," while killing two police officers.[37] Muslim leaders called for nation-wide marches that led to violence in several cities. In Mardan, a mob of 1,500 Muslims threw fire bombs into St. Paul's church.[38] The violence only escalated when television channels in Pakistan began broadcasting an advertisement featuring President Obama and Hillary Clinton. "The United States government had absolutely nothing to do

---

[36]   http://newsinfo.inquirer.net/273082/muslims-stage-peaceful-film-protest-in-bangkok

[37]   http://www.aljazeera.com/news/asia/2012/09/20129219618263113.html

[38]   http://au.christiantoday.com/article/pakistan-christian-leaders-appeal-for-calm-after-church-attack-in-retaliation-for-mohammed-film/14140.htm

with this video," Mrs. Clinton said in the ad. "We absolutely reject its content and message."[39]

At this point, after more than a dozen violent attacks on U.S. diplomatic outposts around the world and 41 deaths, mostly Muslims, the movie had been launched worldwide.

For ordinary Americans, it was a disaster. The State Department had issued a worldwide travel alert warning Americans to stay away from U.S. embassies and consulates and other known facilities tied to the United States unless they absolutely had to go there. However, it was a great success if your goal was to impress upon public opinion in the U.S. and around the world the need to limit anti-Muslim "hate" speech.

The record was clear: when followers of the Religion of Peace felt their Prophet had been insulted they would go on a murderous rampage, killing innocents, torching American restaurants, storming embassies, sacking churches.

It was also a great success for another reason.

Of the 85 violent Muslim actions against the United States, only two were *not* actually set off by the movie: the original Cairo protest, called by al Qaeda supporters and radical jihadis; and the Benghazi attacks, which were coordinated and planned by Iran.

So why were Obama and Hillary Clinton even talking about the movie, especially when the record is now abundantly clear that they knew full well the video had nothing to do Benghazi?

Elementary, comrade. To cover up the truth, to distract the public. That's why I have called the story to blame *Innocence of Muslims* for the Benghazi attacks, the "original spin."

Mission accomplished, it was time to takedown the NPN3 YouTube channel.

---

[39]   http://www.telegraph.co.uk/news/worldnews/asia/pakistan/9557390/Pakistan-protests-US-air-Barack-Obama-advert-condemning-anti-Islam-film.html

CHAPTER 14
DAVID VERSUS GOLIATH

On September 26, 2012, after Cindy appeared on *The View*, her lawyer, Cris Armenta, had a lightning round of phone calls before they boarded separate planes to fly back to the West Coast. She wanted to find out from her new-found Internet sleuths, David Hardy and Eric Bulock, if YouTube had responded favorably to their takedown requests.

"No. They sent us a letter with vague language questioning Cindy's copyright interest in the film, but that's it," Hardy said.

"That's pretty unusual," Eric added. "They normally respond to these requests almost immediately by taking down the content."

"So that's it. We file the injunction," Cris said.

"That should get their attention," Eric said.

"You think they aren't paying attention after what President Obama said yesterday at the UN?" Cris said.

Indeed, Obama had gone on and on about the video in his address to the annual United Nations General Assembly gathering in New York the day before. He called it "crude and disgusting," and summoning all the pompous self-righteousness of which he was capable, declared: "The future must not belong to those who slander the prophet of Islam."[1]

Cindy's temper boiled over when they watched that. Obama was so smug, so condescending, so sure in the way he dismissed her and everyone involved in the movie as racist bigots, she wanted to reach out to the TV screen and whack him. *And he never once called the people who murdered our four brave men in Benghazi "terrorists" or condemned their actions as a "terrorist attack." If it weren't for the video – if it weren't for me –* he seemed to be saying, they would still be alive.

Armenta's last call, after entrusting Cindy to the LaGuardia airport police officers who escorted her to her flight, was to her law partner, Credence Sol. They had decided to put Nakoula's real name, as well as the alias "Sam Bacile" on the complaint. But the big deal was the corporate defendants. After her discussions with David Hardy and Eric Bulock, she had no more doubts.

"We're going after YouTube and Google," Armenta said.

"Are you sure? They are going to come down on us like a ton of bricks."

"We're not going to let them," Cris said. "We're going to hit them in the eye first. Like David."

"Oh yeah. And Goliath," Credence said. She liked it when the two of them were in sync.

"Let's e-file this while I'm on the plane. Suit up!"

Take that, Google!

+++

Armenta thought she had gotten the tone of the complaint just right. She was not a Hillary-hater. And she actually admired

---

[1]   "Obama tells United Nations it is 'time to heed the words of Gandhi...'" op cit.

President Obama. They both repeatedly condemned the video. So she was asking the court to do the right thing, what the president and his secretary of state would want. *Right?*

The film was "hate speech," she wrote. "In the film, Mohammed, the founder of the Islamic religion, is painted in a light that is considered to be blasphemous by many Muslims. Specifically, the Film portrays [him] as a child molester, sexual deviant, and barbarian. Immediately after the Film received worldwide recognition... violence erupted in the Middle East."

Taking her lead from the U.S. government, Armenta blamed the film for causing the attacks on Benghazi. (Only later would she realize that was incorrect). She also noted that the film had provoked violence in Algeria, Australia, Azerbaijan, Bahrain, Bangladesh, Belgium, Canada, Denmark, Egypt, France, Greece, Hong Kong, India, Indonesia, Iran, Iraq, Israel, Japan, Jordan, Lebanon, Kuwait, Macedonia, Malaysia, the Maldives, Mauritania, Morocco, the Netherlands, Niger, Nigeria, Oman, Pakistan, the Palestinian territories, the Philippines, Qatar, Saudi Arabia, Serbia, Somalia, Sri Lanka, Sudan, Switzerland, Syria, Thailand, Tunisia, Turkey, and the United Kingdom.

Cindy appeared in the film to accuse "your Mohammad" of being a "child molester," words that she "never spoke."

"In fact, the Plaintiff was led to believe that she was appearing in a film titled *Desert Warrior*," Armenta wrote, "an adventure film set in ancient times." Cindy found the words attributed to her "repugnant, vile, and hostile," things she "would never say in any context, even during the course of a performance." What's more, Cindy was "an ordained minister and would never debase another person's religious beliefs. It is not in her character, and the thought that she would blaspheme any religion or god is profoundly distressing to her."

In short, she was "duped."

Armenta laid it on with a trowel, painting Cindy in as

sympathetic light as possible for the district court judge. Then she eased into her novel legal theory.

"Because she did not assign her rights in her dramatic performance, or her copyright interests, nor was the Film a 'work for hire,' her copyright interests in her own dramatic performance remain intact," Armenta argued.

In fact, Cindy had already filed an application with the U.S. copyright office to register the rights to her dramatic performance in *Desert Warrior*.

Beyond that, YouTube's Terms of Service specifically required that users uploading content must warrant that they "own or have the necessary licenses, rights, consents, and permissions to publish Content." They also remind users that YouTube "does not 'permit hate speech.'"

She concluded: "Plaintiff previously requested that YouTube take down the Film because it constitutes hate speech and because the unauthorized dubbed depiction of her violates California state laws pertaining to her right to privacy and right to control the use of her likeness, among other protected rights that the continued exhibition of the Film violates. YouTube refused Plaintiff's request."[2]

There it was, Armenta thought. How could the court possibly oppose their request, especially since YouTube appeared to be in violation of its own Terms of Service by allowing the film to remain online?

---

[2]   Armenta included the multiple "takedown notices" sent by Hardy and Bulock's DMCA Solutions to YouTube, listing scores of YouTube channels where they had found copies of the movie trailer. Complaint, *Cindy Lee Garcia v. Nakoula Basseley Nakoula, Google, Inc., YouTube LLC et al*, California Central District Court, 2:12-cv-08315 (MWF-VBK), hereafter *Garcia v Google et al*, September 26, 2012. Many of the court documents in the docket can be accessed for free here: http://www.plainsite.org/dockets/nj7ni6a8/california-central-district-court/garcia-et-al-v-google-inc-et-al/

She was asking them to do the right thing, not just for her client, but for their country. After all, isn't this exactly what the president and the secretary of state would want? For the video to disappear so no one could blame the United States any longer or attack our diplomatic facilities because of the movie?

None of them – not Armenta, or her law partners, or Cindy – could have conceived that the U.S. government might have an interest in keeping the video up on YouTube, precisely *because* it was provoking Muslims to violence.

But as time went on, and especially once they saw how Google responded, that was the only conclusion left.

+++

The same day that Armenta filed the complaint in federal district court, Nakoula got a call on his cell phone from someone in the Romney campaign. "They told me they wanted to meet with me, to hear my story," he told me.

Nakoula thought that perhaps the Romney people could provide him some kind of protection. But before that could happen, the feds arrested him officially the following day, September 27, 2012, after more than two weeks of off-the-books detention and surveillance by federal agents.

The arrest warrant, signed by U.S. Magistrate Judge Suzanne H. Segal, jailed him on "allegations of violations of conditions of probation or supervised release" from a previous fraud conviction. Judge Segal determined that Nakoula posed a flight risk (despite the fact he was already being illegally detained!) because he had "not shown clear and convincing evidence that he will abide by conditions of release." Her hand-written order continued: "He appears to have engaged in a pattern of deception. He lacks stable employment or residence. He does not have an adequate surety or bail resources. He has some ties to foreign countries. He has used aliases. Thus, dependant poses a risk of flight."

Ponder those words for an instant. He hadn't been convicted of anything. Even the judge acknowledged that accusations against him were just "allegations." He was considered a flight risk because he didn't have a job? Really? The claim that he had no stable residence was flat-out not true. The only reason he didn't appear to have one was because federal agents had removed him from the home that he shared with his family in Cerritos, California two weeks earlier!

Judge Siegel also found that he posed a "risk to the safety of other persons or the community" because federal agents "alleged he failed to use his true name" and "may have committed new crimes while on release."

Nakoula had received a reduced sentence on a credit card conviction in 2010 on condition that he cooperate with federal agents by testifying against co-conspirators still at large, and that he use only his legal name, which he had changed years earlier to Mark Basseley Youssef. "When they took me in for questioning, they asked me if I was using a different name. I told them, no. All of my documents had the name Mark Youssef," Nakoula told me. "I told them, that is my name. My legal name is Mark Youssef."

But the feds told him he was lying. "They said, 'you never told us your name was Mark Youssef.' How could they not know that Mark Youssef was my name, since they had seized my U.S. passport in the name of Mark Youssef and had it in their possession since 2009!" he said.

It was a *Catch-22* situation. Or perhaps, more ominously, it was directly out of a Kafka novel. The feds wanted him off the streets, far from the media, and damn the pretext – and the law. Whatever they could get a judge to sign off on was good enough.

National Review editor Rich Lowry later wrote that Nakoula deserved a place in American history as "the first person in this country jailed for violating Islamic anti-blasphemy laws."[3]

Robert Spencer, who has authored numerous scholarly and popular works on Islamic ideology, agreed. "The increasingly common claim that 'hate speech is not free speech' is paving the way for blasphemy laws. Hillary, as you know, tried to apply UN Resolution 16/18 by jailing the filmmaker of the Mohammad video she scapegoated for Benghazi," he wrote in an email to the author.

Nakoula's arrest on a trumped-up charge of a parole violation was the fulfillment of Hillary Clinton's promise to the Organization of Islamic Cooperation, and her vow to the father of slain U.S. Navy Seal, Tyrone Woods to put those responsible for his son's death behind bars.

It was disgraceful, un-American, illegal, and a clear violation of Nakoula's constitutional rights.

Nakoula's journey to Hell was just beginning.

+++

Google stayed quiet for over a week. After their initial response questioning Cindy's copyright interest in the film, Armenta's Internet sleuths sent them multiple takedown notices identifying another 171 YouTube channels where they had found the film, but heard nothing back.

David Hardy thought they had succeeded in boxing Google into a corner. "With Nakoula in jail and barred from using a computer, he can't assert his copyright interest in the film or issue a counter-notice," Hardy argued to the team.

"And so once they take down the film, he has no means of

---

3   Rich Lowry, "The Benghazi Patsy," Politico, May 9, 2003.

putting it back up," Eric Bulock added. "Checkmate!"

But that didn't explain why Google had remained silent, or why Hardy and Bulock were finding new YouTube channels streaming the film every day.

A new channel set up by an Internet gamer stood out for the enormous number of views it was generating (at its peak, the gamer boasted he had received 17 million views). His YouTube handle was DARTHF3TT. At a related Twitter account, he described himself this way: "I like to make fun of fat people and Islam." And he was aggressively promoting the video.[4]

When "Darth" saw that the video had upset actress and comedian Bette Midler, he taunted her, generating even more views. Here is their brief exchange.

> **Bette Midler** @BetteMidler 13 Sep 2012 Who are the idiots who made the video and put it on YouTube? When do we meet them? They should be charged with murder.
>
> 120 retweets 25 likes   Reply Retweet 120

> **Darth F3TT** @DarthF3TT@BetteMidler I uploaded the *Innocence of Muslims* to YouTube. When would you like to meet?

"Darth" used provocation to expand his reach, taunting angry (and foul-mouthed) Arabs who tweeted to him. "The point is," he wrote on September 18, 2012, "Islamic society WILL LEARN... if you kill Americans to achieve an objective, THE OPPOSITE WILL HAPPEN!" Or again, when asked when he would take down the video: "The video will be removed when the 4 innocent Americans are brought back to life."

---

[4]   https://twitter.com/DarthF3TT/status/248097142630125571

Until he uploaded *Innocence of Muslims,* Darth F3TT had posted clips of his gamer play in Sniper Elite. Eric Bulock traced him to a small Internet company in Virginia, and discovered that he was a graduate of The Citadel. "In one of his posts, he mentions a gamer video that he was in back in second grade in 1983. He tried reposting a popular rap video to get traffic in October 2012. But *Innocence of Muslims* was his only real success," Bulock told me.

"Like NPN3, he didn't really exist before posting the video," he added. Since then, "Darth" has started his own Internet consulting business, specifically aimed at promoting YouTube videos through "ad-words" and segmented demographic targeting. For him, Nakoula's movie was career-enhancing.[5]

When Google finally responded to David Hardy on October 2, it was with a blanket refusal to take down the film. Armenta was angry when Hardy called her with the news. Why had they taken so long to respond? By now, the damage to Cindy and the other actors was done.

"Let me call Tim Alger," she said. That was Google's lead attorney. "It's time to lean into him a bit harder."

The more she thought about it, the less she was surprised by Alger's response. After all, this was a guy who had the gall to blame Cindy in open court during their first appearance for bringing the death threats down upon herself by going public. *Like she should have done what, crawl into a hole and hide?* On the contrary, Armenta was convinced it was far more likely that Cindy's public appearances condemning the film had kept her out of harm's way.

Still, she wasn't prepared for what Alger told her that day.

"I was told... that the decision to keep the video on the

---

[5]   Bulock was able to unmask the true identity of DARTHF3TT and shared that with the author.

site was made 'at the highest levels,'" she told the court after speaking with Google's attorney. *What exactly does that mean?* she wondered. Alger also told her that YouTube "was not obligated" to even respond to the takedown notices, a position Armenta said she found "highly unusual."[6]

Hardy soon found out what Alger had meant. Google Executive Chairman Eric Schmidt was staking out a position as the film's defender. At a conference in Seoul, South Korea, the week before, he swept aside charges that the film had sparked violent protests around the world.

"Google has a very clear view on this, which is that we believe the answer to bad speech is more speech," he told reporters.[7]

Schmidt acknowledged that YouTube had blocked access to the video in some countries, where it violated local laws. Others, including Pakistan and Sudan, had blocked it themselves.

As Armenta and her team mulled over Schmidt's position, they couldn't help but wonder whether the Google exec was acting on his own accord.

"Look, this guy is very close to the president," Armenta said. "He's not just a big donor; he actually goes to the White House and talks to Obama."

Eric Bulock pointed to the fact that former State Department official Jared Cohen had gone to work as a strategic policy advisor to Schmidt at Google. Cohen became famous during the June 2009 protests in Iran for having called up Twitter management and asking them not to take the system down for

---

[6] Declaration of M. Cris Armenta in support of ex parte application, Oct. 16, 2012; *Garcia v. Google et al.*

[7] "Google's Schmidt defends hosting of anti-Islam film," The Express Tribune (AFP), Sept. 27, 2012. http://tribune.com.pk/story/443336/googles-schmidt-defends-hosting-of-anti-islam-film/

planned maintenance so the Iranian protesters could use it.

Armenta and her legal team were beginning to wonder if the White House claim that they had called Google begging them to take down the movie wasn't just another lie, an attempt to mislead the public away from their true purpose.[8] Why would an Obama supporter like Eric Schmidt get crosswise with his biggest political ally, especially when he had every legal reason to respond to the takedown requests? To Armenta it appeared she had wandered into a high stakes political game where the other side was carefully coordinating their actions, and she and Cindy were just patsies.

As it turned out, Armenta's suspicions were well-founded. The State Department has now released an email exchange between Mrs. Clinton's office manager, Nora Toiv, and White House chief of staff Dennis McDonough, detailing her calls to senior Google executives, who ensured her the movie would remain "unblocked" for at least another week. One of these emails included the personal phone number of Eric Schmidt's new policy advisor, Jared Cohen. These calls between the secretary of state's office and Google occurred on the same day Schmidt made his announcement about keeping the movie online.[9]

Just another coincidence, comrade.

+++

Hardy made one more try to get YouTube to relent. In

---

[8] Byron Tau, "White House asked YouTube to 'review' anti-Muslim film," Politico, Sept. 14, 2012.

[9] Email from Nora Toiv to Denis R. McDonough, Cheryl D. Mills, Patrick F. Kennedy, Jacob J Sullivan et al, Sept. 27, 2012. Subject: Google and YouTube. Released under the FOIA by the Department of State on Feb. 26, 2016. See https://wikileaks.org/clinton-emails/emailid/8609

a letter sent on October 3, he suggested that YouTube was stalling "in order to generate more views on a film that has 'gone viral' worldwide" in order to "enhance YouTube's view counts and revenues, at the expense of... the lives of each actor that now has a 'fatwa' issued against them."

He reminded them that Google "has already stepped decidedly outside the safe harbor provisions" of the Digital Millennium Copyright Act by refusing to take down the video. Cindy had not signed a release, and so she retained a copyright interest in her dramatic performance. They were violating her copyright by keeping the video online. "Just as a musician can object to the use of his or her music in a film trailer to which he or she did not consent, Ms. Garcia has the right to object to the reproduction or publication of her copyrighted dramatic performance," he wrote.

Just in case they didn't get the point, he gave them another analogy. "It would be no different if, for instance, Angelina Jolie acted in one film, and that footage was taken, without her permission, assignment or waiver, to be inserted in a completely different film." Finally, he pointed out that YouTube "ordinarily takes down allegedly infringing content within minutes using its automated system or within 24 hours in other cases. The fact that YouTube has not followed its own internal protocols in this particular situation speaks to YouTube and Google's bad faith."[10]

In their conversations in preparation of that final letter, Armenta thought they should hammer home the profit allegation, since Google had been caught in that trap before. She and her legal team had turned up an earlier case, *Viacom v. Google*, where emails from YouTube executives showed them

---

[10]   David Hardy to YouTube Copyright Takedown Agent, Oct. 3, 2012; letter supplied by Hardy to the author.

acknowledging that if they removed all copyrighted content from their site, their views would drop by 80 percent.

YouTube finally responded after that letter, saying it had no intention of taking down the video, in effect acting as judge and jury of Cindy's copyright claim. When Hardy got the letter, he phoned Armenta immediately. "Google has decided to abandon the safe-harbor of the DMCA and is heading for open waters," he said.

In fact, they were all heading for open waters and into a storm the likes of which none of them could have imagined.

+++

Given Google's hard line, Armenta filed an amended complaint on October 4, 2012, alleging copyright violation, fraud, unfair business practices, libel, and intentional infliction of emotional distress.[11] She followed that up on the 17th with a new application for a temporary restraining order, an emergency action aimed at getting immediate relief for Cindy from the constant death threats and obscene slurs angry Muslims were hurling at her over the phone and the Internet. Cindy told the court about the extraordinary security measures she had been required to take in New York, and how the New York Port Authority Police wouldn't even allow her to enter the public terminal at LaGuardia because she would become "an instant target" if she showed her face in public.

"I have been advised by security personnel and law enforcement to move my personal residence, which I have done," Cindy said. "I also moved my church's location where I preach." She included a 25-page sampling of the death threats

---

[11]   Only the copyright claim was asserted against Google; the other claims were asserted against Nakoula.

she had received over Facebook.[12]

Armenta included statements from two other actors, Dan Sutter and Gaylord Flynn, who corroborated Cindy's account of how she had been duped by the filmmaker, and a lengthy presentation by Khaled Abou El Fadl, a Professor of Islamic Law at the UCLA School of Law and the chair of the Islamic Studies program at UCLA. He was a real find, with a resume up the yin-yang that included serving on the Board of Directors of Human Rights Watch and a presidential appointment under George W. Bush to the Commission for International Religious Freedom. Professor El Fadl revealed for the first time the text of the fatwa against Cindy's life by an Egyptian cleric, and translated it into English (see chapter 6).

"More than *fatwas* or threats that are reported by or to the media, what concerns me to a much greater degree are unannounced or secretive calls by extremist and fanatic groups to inflict harm upon Ms. Cindy Lee Garcia," he wrote. "As a result of her involuntary appearance in this hate film, she cannot easily travel internationally, especially in Europe or in any Muslim country. She is a marked woman. Her public statements condemning the film have been received in the Muslim world with controversy. There are many who believe that she is, in fact, part of the conspiracy to hurt, harm, and denigrate Muslims."

Professor El Fadl then explained that the lawsuit was "critically important" for her safety because it was the only way of proving to doubters that her apologies were sincere. "If she is successful in pulling the content down from the Internet, it will likely help her in terms of believability of her message condemning the film and its message," he said. He then

---

[12]   Declaration of Cindy Lee Garcia, Oct. 16, 2012; *Garcia v. Google et al,* Docket 14.

professed to be "shocked" at YouTube's refusal to take down the film. "The film is absolutely, without any question in my mind, bigoted hate speech," he wrote. "Therefore, YouTube's position to protect the rampant posting and reposting of the film throughout the world is not only contrary to their established guidelines, but remarkably appalling." The film was nothing less than "insidious and malicious incitement against the sacred symbols and beliefs of Muslims."

He argued that no one would have participated in the film if they had understood its true content or intent, unless of course they shared the bigoted views of the filmmaker, which Cindy did not. But her appearance, albeit against her will, had placed her "in a global political, and even what many perceive to be a cosmic, controversy that will and has changed her life forever. In many countries, for example, in the United Kingdom, there exist anti-blasphemy laws. It would not be surprising, therefore, that if she traveled to Britain, she could be arrested, detained, and charged, for being in this film."

El Fadl was essentially arguing that the United States should adopt similar laws banning blasphemy, if for no other reason than to prevent Muslims from killing other Muslims in foreign countries. The film's impact on the Muslim world "is reasonably foreseeable," he noted.[13]

The very next day, the U.S. district court denied Armenta's request for an emergency ("ex parte") restraining order, noting that the film had been up on YouTube since July 2, 2012. But they set a tight schedule for the two parties to file their briefs on the merits of the case.

+++

[13]   Declaration of Khaled Abou El Fadl, Oct. 15, 2012; *Garcia via Google et al*, Docket 14.

What happened next might surprise some readers.

"Google decided to make this a First Amendment case," Armenta told me. "They argued that this was all about free speech, whereas we had been arguing a more narrow issue of copyright violation."

Tim Alger, Google's lawyer, dismissed Cindy's claims as "really nothing more than a pretext to seek removal from YouTube of material that she considers offensive." He then launched into a full-throated defense of Nakoula and his right to make an offensive movie, invoking "broader social policy" in favor of free speech. Cindy and her attorneys were using copyright law "as a means of stifling speech about a matter of public concern simply because she objects to that speech. Irrespective of the Film's artistic or social merits, Plaintiff's own allegations demonstrate that the Film is now part of important public debate, even becoming an issue in this year's presidential campaign," he wrote. "Indeed, Plaintiff's involvement in the Film (which she herself has aggressively publicized on television) is newsworthy in itself."[14]

Beyond the dripping sarcasm, Armenta found his arguments bizarre. Did Google really want to go to the mat for a movie that was such obvious trash as *Innocence of Muslims*? The political implications were starting to make her head explode. First, the president and the secretary of state and just about everybody in the administration were blaming the video for the Benghazi attacks, so you would think they would want it taken down. Then their pals at Google do everything in their power to ensure that the video stays up so it can enflame more Muslims around the world. Did the Obama administration actually want that violence to occur? What was really going on?

---

[14]   Opposition of Google Inc. and YouTube LLC to Plaintiff's Motion for a Preliminary Injunction and Order of Impoundment," Oct. 29, 2012, *Garcia via Google et al*, Docket 22.

Armenta wasn't a political junkie. Nor was she a conspiracy theorist. But here was Google calling black, white, and white, black. There had to be something much bigger at stake. But what?

CHAPTER 15
GOOGLE'S
SKULLDUGGERY

Google is one of the largest corporations in America in terms of market capitalization. In the second half of 2015, it ranked only second after Apple. At the time Google chief Eric Schmidt unleashed his legal team on Cindy, Google was expanding at breakneck speed. On October 1, 2012, Bloomberg reported that Google had surpassed Microsoft as the world's second-largest technology company, making it the ninth biggest publicly-traded corporation in the world.[1]

So money was no object in making Cindy's lawsuit go away. And Google attorney Tim Alger had a plan.

He pulled the trigger on a Sunday afternoon, in a terse email he sent to Armenta, claiming that Cindy had filed a copyright release form with Nakoula, the producer.

---

[1]   Brian Womack, "Google Passes Microsoft's Market Value as PC Loses to Web," Bloomberg Business News, Oct. 1, 2012.

Armenta had already left Los Angeles for the Thanksgiving holiday week, and was en route to Bozeman, Montana with her two children. The document he attached to his email was a scanned copy of what appeared to be a "Cast deal" contract and a copyright release form, signed by "Cindy Garcia." Armenta was floored. Cindy had assured her repeatedly she had never signed such a release, only a single-sheet form that would guarantee she received IMBD picture credits for *Desert Warrior*. She called her client immediately.

"No way did I sign anything like that," Cindy said. "It's a forgery. Sam is a convicted con artist, how can anybody believe anything he says or does?"

"This is getting stranger by the moment," Armenta said. "Google is demanding that we dismiss the case."

"No way!" Cindy said.

Now Google was stepping in as if they were representing the producer. Why were they doing this, Armenta wondered. Would they actually take the risk of forging such a document? Or had they gotten it from the producer? How? He was in jail!

Over the holidays, she conferred back and forth with her

legal team. They agreed that the best approach was to wait and see if Alger came up with the original of the purported copyright release forms, and then to hire a handwriting expert to compare the signature to Cindy's.

When the whole week went by without any word from Alger or the court, Armenta sent him an email reply on Monday, November 26.

"Based on what we have learned from our client and from others who worked on the this film, we have serious doubts as to the authenticity of the document(s) you sent. What do you offer as the provenance, or ability to authenticate, this document?" She also demanded to see the originals.

Armenta's legal team agreed that this was the best response. Let Google show a little leg. After all, they couldn't introduce the documents into evidence unless they authenticated them anyway.

Alger got back to her almost immediately, saying that he had obtained the release forms from the attorney who had defended Nakoula in criminal proceedings two years earlier. "I would think your client would be able to confirm or deny its authenticity," he wrote. "If you are not inclined to dismiss the [case], let me know this morning and I will file it with the court with appropriate authentication. It's been a full week since I provided this document to you."

Armenta stood her ground. Cindy could *not* confirm the authenticity of the document; she fired back. And besides, he had only provided a *copy* of the document, and for just three business days, "one of which was the day before Thanksgiving."

She thought she saw where Alger was going with this, and wanted that statement on the record so he couldn't accuse her of foot-dragging in front of the court.

But Alger wasn't planning to accuse her of foot-dragging. Instead, in a three-line email, he revealed that he and his

KENNETH R. TIMMERMAN

corporate bosses were prepared to file fraud charges against her.

It was a shocking turn of events none of them had seen coming.

"I think you're going to have to decide right now whether you want to challenge the authenticity of the document at the risk of Rule 11 sanctions and a damages claim under 17 USC 512(f), both of which my clients are prepared to pursue," he wrote.[2]

Rule 11 sanctions are extremely serious. They were created primarily to prevent frivolous lawsuits. As the American Bar Association explains, they require an attorney to "stop, think, and investigate" before filing a paper with the court. "[A]s a young lawyer, there is nothing more petrifying than learning that opposing counsel is seeking Rule 11 sanctions against you because you failed to do an adequate pre-filing investigation into your new client's claims."[3]

While Armenta found the threat to be heavy-handed, she figured it was bluster. Most telling was the fact that Alger hadn't offered to provide her with the original document for independent examination, as the law required. That probably meant he didn't have it.

+++

Seeing Armenta's intransigence, Alger didn't stand still. He filed what he now claimed was the original of the purported release document on November 28, just three days before they all were supposed to appear in court for the hearing.

---

[2] Email from Timothy Alger to Cris Armenta, Nov. 26, 2012 10:28 AM. *Garcia via Google et al*, Docket 37, p31.

[3] Melissa L. Stuart, "A Young Lawyer's Guide to Rule 11 Sanctions," June 20, 2012, American Bar Association.

He authenticated it through a sworn declaration from Nakoula – a convicted fraudster, Armenta noted – and his own five-page statement explaining how he had gone to Nakoula's jail cell to acquire it.

He's been a busy boy, Armenta thought as she read.

Alger said that he got the initial photocopy, which he had emailed to Armenta on the Sunday before Thanksgiving, from Nakoula's criminal attorney, Steve Seiden. He then hired a private investigator to check public records to determine if the social security number written on the release was indeed Cindy's. He claimed that he had tried repeatedly to call Armenta to urge her to drop the case, without success, and only heard back from her by email on the 26th.

Given that Armenta had challenged the authenticity of the document, Alger shifted gears and made arrangements to visit Nakoula/Mark Youssef in the Metropolitan Detention Center (MDC) in downtown Los Angeles, which he did on November 27. "Mr. Youssef is in the Special Housing Unit at MDC, segregated from the main population and unable to visit with family or friends," Alger wrote.

Nakoula was terrified when the Google attorney came to visit him. He had been held incommunicado for over two months, insulted as a "murderer" by his jailors and spat upon whenever he crossed paths with other inmates. It was so bad, he told me, that he wasn't even allowed to use the showers and had to wash as best he could using cold water in his cell. "Everybody hated me in that holding cell," he said. "They told me openly that they hated me because I had caused the deaths of Americans."

He had been formally sentenced just ten days earlier and was still reeling from receiving one year hard-jail time. His lawyer thought they had negotiated a deal where he would receive home confinement. Instead, they sent him to MDC where he was treated like a murderer – and where he feared for his life.

So when Alger appeared and asked him to sign a document, he thought that the attorney had been sent by the government and that he had better do whatever he was told. As his criminal attorney warned him years ago, once the government had its claws into you, you had better cooperate if you ever wanted to be a free man again.

Nakoula had used the name "Sam Bessi" and a production company called "Matthew Metta" in the purported release document Alger brought with him to prison – names unfamiliar to Cindy and the other actors. Alger also brought along a sworn declaration he had Nakoula sign, in which Nakoula stated that he "personally provided this document" to Cindy and that she had signed it in his presence on August 9, 2011. Alger noted that Nakoula told him that "he believes in the message contained in the film and he does not want the trailer to be removed from YouTube."

But that wasn't all. Alger then drove back to Nakoula's house in southern Los Angeles County to meet with his son, Abanob. "He brought with him a binder, about four inches thick, containing contracts relating to the film, including releases by other actors identical in form to that which was signed by Ms. Garcia," Alger claimed.[4]

Armenta was floored when she read Alger's declaration carefully. He was calling her client a liar. That's why he had threatened Rule 11 sanctions. The only way she could turn this around was by hiring the best handwriting analyst they could find, and having him testify that the handwriting on the document was not Cindy's.

But they were running out of time. *Damn Alger for dropping*

---

[4]   Declaration of Timothy L. Alger, Nov. 28, 2012, *Garcia via Google et al*, Docket 34.

this so close to the hearing!

Armenta looked at the binder of resumes her assistant Heather Rowland had compiled over the past week of different handwriting experts. One of them stood head and shoulders above all the others.

James A. Blanco was a nationally prominent Forensic Document Examiner who had worked for the ATF and the California State Department of Justice. He had been qualified to testify in federal and state courts in the United States, Mexico, Singapore, and South Africa, and now worked as a private consultant. His personal examiner error rate, according to the American Society of Crime Laboratory Directors, was zero. While in government practice, he regularly worked on joint task forces with the DEA and the FBI. Blanco was the State of California's exclusive document examiner in voter-fraud cases. He also worked with the State of Montana and federal criminal defenders' offices in Alaska, Florida, and Puerto Rico. He had rendered opinions on questioned documents in more than 7,000 cases. He was their guy.

Blanco said he needed a "significant sample" of Cindy's actual handwriting for comparison purposes, so she had Heather work with Cindy to gather notes and documents he could use.

After reviewing Cindy's handwriting sample and the release forms submitted by Google, Blanco called her and said they were not a match. Even better, he wrote in his opinion: "Cindy Garcia is eliminated as the writer" of the release forms. "An 'elimination' is a term of art in Forensic Document Examination opinion rendering and represents the highest degree of confidence expressed by document examiners in handwriting comparisons. That is, the examiner has no reservations whatever... that the writer of the known material did not write the materials in question."[5]

Bolstered by his unequivocal opinion, Armenta prepared a blistering response to Alger's declaration, ripping into it line by line. She noted that Alger was in violation of court rules because he had filed new evidence just three days before an evidentiary hearing, without giving her the ability to cross-examine him or Nakoula, who she called "[Google's] new ally." She informed the court that she had just received Blanco's oral report finding that the documents were "a forgery," and would file his written report as soon as she received it.

She also noted that an Egyptian court had sentenced them all to death that week because of their involvement in the film. [6]

Armenta thought she had nailed it.

But the court didn't agree. Just one hour after she had filed her objection, the court issued a final ruling denying Cindy's request for an injunction.

There would be no evidentiary hearing on December 3, and no further proceedings. It was over. Like that. The court determined that Cindy had "implicitly granted" a nonexclusive license to Nakoula to use her performance, and had "introduced no evidence to the contrary." The only good news was that they also rejected the purported release documents.[7]

Armenta and her legal team were reeling. How could the legal process end up at this conclusion? First, it was bizarre and to their minds, suspicious, that Google had suddenly "found"

---

[5]   Declaration of James A. Blanco, Nov. 30, 2012. *Garcia via Google et al*, Docket 40.

[6]   Plaintiffs Objections to and Request to Strike….," Nov. 30, 2012; *Garcia via Google et al*, Docket 37. See inter alia p16.

[7]   MINUTES (IN CHAMBERS): ORDER by Judge Michael W Fitzgerald: denying Motion for Preliminary Injunction, Nov. 30, 2012. *Garcia via Google et al*, Docket 39. The court rejected the purported release documents in an order issued just minutes before its order throwing Cindy's case out of court. Docket 38.

a release long after all of the legal briefs had been filed with the court. Second, it was unheard of for a major corporation to submit documents to a federal court based on a convicted fraudster's jailhouse signature on a declaration written by company lawyers. Third, when a litigant planned to rely on a document, it was standard practice to allow the other side to examine the original to determine its authenticity. Alger's refusal to allow Cindy's lawyers and handwriting expert to even see the original documents was behavior that Armenta had never seen before. All of these developments occurred against the backdrop of Google's threats to seek financial penalties against Cindy's lawyers personally if they did not suddenly see the case Google's way and dismiss it.

Cindy was an ordinary American suddenly wrapped up in extraordinary events. Now Armenta and her legal team were wrapped up in them with her.

CHAPTER 16
WHO IS SAM BACILE?

Cindy had not spoken to Nakoula, who she still referred to as "Sam," since the day she phoned him in shock at seeing her face on national television as a poster-lady of hate.

As the media began to dig into his criminal past, Cindy became increasingly angry. He was a fraud, a convicted con artist, a liar, and a federal snitch. And he had ruined her life. As far as she was concerned, he could spend the rest of his life in jail. She knew it was an un-Christian thing to think, but there it was.

The federal snitch part is what galled her the most. That's what came out of a previously sealed sentencing transcript, apparently leaked by federal prosecutors to the media just days after the Benghazi attacks.[1] If she had known that, she never would have had anything to do with him.

But Cindy was so wrapped up in her story she didn't understand that the feds had taken Nakoula off the streets so they could turn him into the scapegoat they needed to carry the blame for the deaths of four Americans in Benghazi and the dozens of attacks on Americans and U.S. diplomatic facilities

---

[1] http://www.thesmokinggun.com/documents/investigation/nakoula-cooperation-756920

around the world.

+++

Nakoula emigrated to the United States in 1984 to cheer on the Egyptian soccer team at the summer Olympics in Los Angeles. He married an American named Ingrid Rodriguez soon afterwards and got a green card. The couple had a child, Matthew, and divorced after four years. Nakoula eventually became a U.S. citizen. Their son died during a trip to Egypt when he was 12.

Nakoula's mishaps with the law began shortly after his second marriage in 1990, when he was working as a gas station attendant. In 1991, he was indicted for selling watered down gasoline. As he explained it later, "someone came and took a sample and said the 87 octane was 82 octane. When I took an attorney and went to court, I told the judge, 'I'm not the refinery, I just sell gas.'"[2] He was convicted on two counts.

Six years later, he was arrested for selling bulk quantities of Sudafed over the counter. He claimed he didn't know what it was for, and prosecutors couldn't tie him to any drug trafficking ring. Congress didn't include Sudafed in the scheduler of controlled drugs and stop over the counter sales until 2005.

But in the immediate aftermath of the Benghazi, a vulture media, fed by federal prosecutors and government sources, dished out his criminal record with lurid headlines.

---

[2]   Transcript of Videotaped Deposition of Mark Basseley Youssef, Oct. 6, 2014, in Garcia v. Google et al.

Anti-Muslim Movie Maker a Meth Cooker

The man allegedly behind the film that sparked deadly protests in the Middle East has a sordid criminal past. By Christine Pelisek.

According to a source close to the Los Angeles County District Attorney's office, Nakoula Basseley Nakoula was arrested by the L.A. Country Sheriff's Department on March 27, 1997 and charged with intent to manufacture methamphetamine. He pleaded guilty and was sentenced on Nov. 3, 1997 to one year in county jail and three years probation. The D.A.'s office said he violated probation on April 8, 2002, and was re-sentenced to another year in county jail. [3]

A second article that appeared the next day provided additional detail that could have been right out of a dime story crime thriller. "When the police pulled Nakoula Basseley Nakoula over outside Los Angeles on March 27, 1997, he had $45,000 in hundreds and twenties in a paper lunch bag on the seat beside him." [4]

Helpful government sources provided willing reporters with what they claimed were surveillance records from the investigation. "[T]he Los Angeles County Sheriff's Department had been watching him as he drove a U-Haul rental truck from a storage facility in Downey to a Super 7 liquor store. There, he picked up a liquor store employee named Khaled Abraham. They proceeded to Abraham's house in Lake Elsinore. At the house, Nakoula and the others unloaded 30 boxes of

---

[3]   http://www.thedailybeast.com/articles/2012/09/13/mohammed-movie-s-mystery-director.html

[4]   Christine Pelisek and Michael Daly, "Was 'Innocence of Muslims' Director Also an Informant? Daily Beast, Sept. 14, 2012.

pseudoephedrine, a prime ingredient of methamphetamine. Another 99 cases were found at the storage facility."

Sounds pretty damning, doesn't it? Until the reporter quietly corrected the false information about his arrest record she had included in her initial story. "Nakoula nonetheless only spent just two days in jail," she wrote in the new version, "getting off with three years' probation when he could have gotten hard time."

Why would that be? "Sounds like he's an informant," the Daily Beast quoted a law enforcement official as suggesting.

Hold that thought and fast-forward another twelve years.

In June 2009, Nakoula was arrested on allegations of involvement in a massive credit card and check-kiting scheme. This time the feds built a solid case against him.

It began when in-house investigators from Wells Fargo Bank and Capital One contacted the feds about a "synthetic identity fraud" scheme involving credit card and bank accounts at their companies. Someone, or some group of persons, was matching fictitious names to true Social Security Numbers to apply for credit card and bank accounts, and then withdrawing money. In an affidavit used to obtain an arrest warrant against Nakoula, U.S. Postal Inspector Eric Shen explained that "identity theft suspects open numerous fraudulent accounts so that they can build credit on the credit card accounts by transferring balances and making payments from other fraudulent accounts in order to make the credit card accounts appear to be legitimate and repaid." Often, the perpetrators of synthetic identity fraud will take advantage of "convenience checks" issued by the credit card companies to build up bank balances, then use other credit cards to withdraw cash at ATMs.[5]

---

5   Affidavit of Eric Shen, *U.S.A v. Nakoula Basseley Nakoula*, 2:09-mj-01256, U.S. District Court for the Central District of California, June 16, 2009. Docket 1.

U.S. Postal inspectors started reviewing video surveillance footage at a variety of ATM machines and noticed that the same individual was withdrawing cash from accounts in two different names. When they traced the individual, they discovered it was Nakoula. As Shen continued sleuthing, he discovered that checks from one of the Wells Fargo accounts, in the name of Thomas J. Tanas, were deposited in two different Washington Mutual accounts, one in the name of Nicola Baciley, and another in the name of Erwin Salameh. Video surveillance subsequently showed that Nakoula made those deposits, sometimes accompanied by his former wife, Olivia Ibrahim. That tied him to four fake identities.

As they pursued their investigation, they discovered where Nakoula lived and worked and placed those locations under surveillance, discovering additional synthetic identities involved in the scheme, including "Kritbag Difrat," Matthew Nekola," and "Malid Ahlawi." Because of the ongoing nature of the investigation, federal prosecutors convinced the court to seal the grand jury indictment, which had been issued that February, as well as the criminal complaint, until Nakoula was arrested. He was taken into custody on June 18, 2009. The court determined that he was a flight risk and ordered him to be held indefinitely in pre-trial detention.

But that wasn't all. While in jail, prosecutors interviewed Nakoula repeatedly, offering to reduce his sentence if he would cooperate with their investigation.

Nakoula agreed.

Those debriefing sessions were extensive and detailed. They led to no fewer than 14 separate filings by government attorneys with the court that remain under seal to this day.[6]

---

6   I've placed a copy of the docket at http://kentimmerman.com/ IOMdocs/ USAvNakoula-docket.pdf

Nakoula's testimony allowed prosecutors to expand their case from the handful of identifies mentioned in the original charging documents and a total fraud of just $12,000, to a massive scheme involving more than 640 fraudulent credit and debit cards, 60 different bank accounts in various names, and $794,500.57 in fraudulent profits.

Nakoula also identified the "mastermind" of the scheme, a Palestinian Muslim, who fled to Canada before prosecutors could arrest him.

His name was Eiad Salameh. And because his identity was so sensitive, and the feds wanted him so badly, they kept all mention of him out of the public filings – until September 14, 2012, when they leaked it to an eager left-wing reporter.

Whoever released selected pages from the June 24, 2010 sentencing hearing before Judge Christina A. Snyder, knew exactly what they were doing. They knew it would make Nakoula agree to be taken into protective custody, thus getting him off the street and away from reporters, because he had told them Salameh was a dangerous man and that he had agreed to incriminate him only on condition that the agreement remain secret.

In those pages, Nakoula's lawyer, former Department of Justice official James Henderson, talked turkey about Nakoula's cooperation with the feds and his true role in the credit card scheme. "My argument that the loss significantly overstates the seriousness of the defendant's involvement sort of dovetails with the role and participation. He was the guy as Your Honor knows went in and cashed the checks and then the money would go to Mr. Salamay [sic]," Henderson explained.

He argued for a more significant "downward departure" of the federal sentencing guidelines because "this is the individual who received $60,000 to $70,000 of the proceeds while someone else walked away with 90 percent."

And then Henderson spelled out Nakoula's role as a

federal snitch.

"He's undergone detailed debriefings," Henderson said. "He has implicated Mr. Salamay [sic]. There is no question but that Mr. Salamay at some point is gonna be indicted if he hasn't been already."

Henderson reminded the court that he had been on their side of many plea deals in the past. "We all know what's gonna happen," he said. "Salamay is gonna get arrested some day and based on the debriefing information turned over, he is gonna enter a guilty plea or if he doesn't, then Mr. Nakoula is gonna be called on to testify at trial..."

Nakoula then apologized for his mistakes – to his family, to the court. "I want to cooperate with the government that they can catch with this other criminals who is their involvement," he said in his broken English.[7]

The very same day the plea agreement was illegally released to the media, Nakoula got an angry call from Eiad Salameh, asking him why he had informed on him to the government.

"I told him, no, this didn't happen," Nakoula said. "He said, 'No, there is something that was sealed, and it showed on the Internet. The government mentioned it, and they said that it was sealed and that you said this about me.'"

Nakoula remembers the date exactly: it was September 14, 2012. "After the Benghazi instance [sic], the government showed – the plea agreement with the government. Someone showed it and – and somebody showed it, and it was disclosed."

Cris Armenta asked Nakoula about this incident during his sworn deposition.

ARMENTA: And Eiad Salameh called you about that?

---

7   Sentencing transcript, June 24, 2010. See http://kentimmerman.com/
     IOMdocs/ 2010_06_24-sentencing-transcript.pdf

NAKOULA: Yeah. He called me, and he told me – he said, 'I can kill you.' And he threatened me.[8]

Nakoula went further in his interviews with me. "The judge ordered that document sealed. I was proud that I was working with the U.S. government. My lawyer promised me that only Miss Williams [the prosecutor], the judge, and me would know about the deal. When it was posted to the Internet, I was afraid. Anybody can kill you. Who released the transcript? I am suing the government for $100 million."

Walid Shoebat, the former Palestinian Muslim terrorist turned Christian evangelist, knew Eiad Salameh well. It turns out, they are first cousins on their fathers' side, and they grew up together near Bethlehem, in the West Bank. (Eiad's full name is Eiad Salameh Daoud Shou'aybat). Shoebat revealed Salameh had been arrested in Canada in January 2011, apparently on a warrant from the United States, and was held for seven months awaiting extradition proceedings.

Shoebat claims that he was in contact with the Peel Regional Police, who wrote to him in July 2011 to say that they were still waiting for the U.S. to initiate extradition proceedings. "The feds never responded to the Canadians' last appeal and within a few days, Eiad was sent to Palestine," Shoebat wrote.[9]

If Shoebat is to be believed, this is further proof that the

---

[8]   Deposition of Nakoula Basseley Nakoula, op cit, p28. Armenta went on to ask him if Salameh had invested in the film. (Cindy had become convinced by this point that radical Muslims in the Middle East were behind it, given their wish to impose laws banning blasphemy). But Nakoula didn't see the connection. "He is a Muslim guy. He's a Muslim guy," he answered.

[9]   Shoebat also claims that Nakoula is a Muslim, which is demonstrably false. http://shoebat.com/2012/09/25/innocence-of-muslims-film-was-made-by-terrorists/. Shoebat dug up a 2002 U.S. Trustees report on earlier fraudulent schemes by Salameh, here: http://www.shoebat.com/wp-content/uploads/2012/09/Trustee_Report.pdf.

Obama administration preferred to make a scapegoat out of Nakoula, as part of their agenda to ban "anti-Muslim hate speech" in America, than to prosecute an alleged criminal they had pursued for years.

+++

When the feds finally dragged Nakoula into an open courtroom on September 28, 2012, they handed the case to the chief federal prosecutor in Los Angeles, Robert Dugdale.

If nothing else, it showed the political sensitivity that anything touching the film had assumed. Even today, the U.S. District Court for the Central District of California lists ten "Cases of Interest" on its website. Three of those ten entries involve Nakoula.

It was a high profile, political prosecution.

In ordering Nakoula's detention on a parole violation, Judge Suzanne Segal said that he had "engaged in a likely pattern of deception both to his probation officers and the court."

Nakoula's attorney, Steve Seiden, tried unsuccessfully to convince the court that Nakoula's continued detention put him at danger from fellow inmates. "It is a danger for him to remain in custody at the Metropolitan Detention Center in Los Angeles because there are a large number of Muslims in there," Seiden said. "We are extremely concerned about his safety."[10]

The feds apparently didn't care what happened to Nakoula, who lived in constant fear.

+++

The government kept Nakoula on ice for six weeks, not

---

10   Stan Wilson, "Producer of anti-Islam film arrested, ordered held without bail," Stan Wilson, CNN, Sept. 28, 2012

bringing him back into court until November 7, 2012, the day after the presidential election. With the election in the bag, they counted on an obliging media to turn Nakoula's parole violations into a public lynching.

Assistant U.S. Attorney Robert Dugdale insisted that Nakoula was not being punished for his role in making *Innocence of Muslims*. And then, he couldn't stop talking about it. "[H]is deception actually caused real harm to people," Dugdale said. "[T]he way that he went about making this movie is the problem because he did defraud people." He blasted Nakoula for using false identities, although I seriously doubt any of the actors would have given a second thought if he had presented himself as "Sam Bacile," the name he used during the filming, or "Mr. Nakoula." They were equally unknown.

But Obama-appointed prosecutor Robert Dugdale gave it his best. "So the people who got involved with this – the actors and actresses who answered the casting call that he made – they had no idea that he was a recently released federal felon... And had they known that, had they been given this true name and known his background, they might have had some second thoughts before they joined in on that project. But they didn't have that opportunity because the defendant defrauded them by betraying something as fundamental as his identity to them."

Remember, this case isn't about the movie. *Got that?*

Dugdale then referred to a letter from Nakoula's Probation Officer, which he claimed included an investigation into how Nakoula had actually made the movie. "After they had filmed their scenes, he went back and dubbed in language which made the film the film that people have considered offensive," Dugdale said. "And that's a substantial fraud."

It might be, but it wasn't the fraud that Nakoula supposedly was being charged with.

Dugdale cynically manipulated public opinion and the

feelings of participants like Cindy, who felt they had been wronged by Nakoula. "[A]nd as a result, these people have come forward to the Probation Office and reported that they have experienced death threats, they're afraid for their lives, they feel like their careers have been ruined – all as a result of what this man did to defraud them," he said.

If the U.S. government felt so strongly about the harm the movie had done to the actors and actresses, why had they done nothing to get Google to take it down?

The answer is simple: because they didn't give a hoot about the actors. All they cared about was finding a scapegoat, Nakoula, for the failed policies of the Obama administration and Secretary of State Hillary Clinton that caused the deaths of four Americans in Benghazi.

+++

Nakoula would point to the utter dishonesty of Dugdale's presentation in a "debtor's examination" conducted by the prosecutors four months later while he was in jail.

Dugdale had blasted him for not using the name "Nakoula Basseley Nakoula" with the actors, but then prosecuted him for using it instead of his legal name, Mark Basseley Youssef.

That was the same trap the Probation Officer had sprung on him when he was hauled in for his first interview just after midnight on September 15. She had asked him what name he was using, and he had said "Nakoula Basseley Nakoula," instead of his legal name, Mark Basseley Youssef. She had him, and recommended he be rearrested for violating the conditions of his parole not to use false identiti1es.

As Youssef explained, "I changed my name from 'Nakoula Basseley Nakoula' to 'Mark Basseley Youssef' in 2002, and everything going smooth, everything is going okay, and all of a sudden when they – I get arrested in 2009, the judgment they judged me for 'Nakoula Basseley Nakoula,' that's why I went to Nakoula Basseley Nakoula."[11]

Even the feds couldn't get it straight – or didn't want to get it straight. All they needed was to string him up in public in front of the media, then get him behind bars where he couldn't tell his side of the story. And they succeeded.

Nakoula was confused. He thought his lawyers had worked out a deal, where he would plead no-contest to some of the parole violations, and they would send him to a halfway house or place him under house arrest. He was afraid of the Muslims in the Los Angeles Metropolitan Detention Facility who were threatening him every day. But when his attorney, Steve Seiden, presented the deal he thought they had made, Nakoula watched his Probation Officer shake her head no to the judge.

"She has a problem with my ex-wife," Nakoula told me. "That's because she came one day I wasn't there and started searching the whole house. My ex-wife said, this is his room, you don't have to go around the house. And so my ex-wife kicked her out."

Whatever happened between the Probation officer and Nakoula's ex-wife, who frequently let him stay at the house in Cerritos, I believe the deal was already cooked. The prosecutors, named by the Obama White House, wanted Nakoula in jail. And if something really bad happened to him, then he got what he deserved.

A sympathetic media picked up on that message immediately. "[I]t's probably safe to say that other parts of the world will criticize the United States for not being tougher on Nakoula," a columnist for the left-wing magazine, *The Atlantic*,

---

11   Judgment Debtor Examination of Mark Basseley Youssef," Feb. 18, 2014, in USA v. Nakoula Basseley Nakoula, U.S. District Court for the Central District of California, No. CV 13-08734 CAS-CWx.

wrote. "After all, just a couple of months ago, members of the Muslim community throughout the world were calling for his execution, and one Pakistani cabinet member even put a $100,000 bounty on his head."

The same reporter noted that Nakoula was worried about his safety behind bars, but that prosecutors had denied his requests for special treatment. "Nakoula will have to stay in a cell, hang out in the yard and do all the other things prisoners in Southern California do. It won't matter what Nakoula calls himself there. His reputation precedes him."[12]

Those words were as close to a call to murder as the Pakistani cabinet minister who placed a bounty on Nakoula's head.

+++

After Nakoula was taken out in handcuffs and driven down the street to the MDC, his attorney delivered a defiant one-line statement on the steps of the courthouse. "The one thing he wanted me to tell all of you is President Obama may have gotten Osama bin Laden, but he didn't kill the ideology," Seiden said. Asked what Nakoula had meant by that, Seiden admitted he didn't know and hadn't asked.[13]

Nakoula wanted to explain, but the prosecutors had placed a gag order on him. When a reporter from the *New York Times* tried to interview him in the MDC a few weeks later, he was not allowed to meet with him. Instead, he had to smuggle

---

[12]   Adam Clark Estes, "After Being Sentenced to a Year in Prison, Anti-Muslim Filmmaker Blames it All on Obama," The Atlantic, Nov. 7, 2012; http://news.yahoo.com/being-sentenced-prison-anti-muslim-filmmaker-blames-obama-030400614.html

[13]   "Anti-Muslim filmmaker sentenced to one year for probation violation," CBS News (AP), Nov. 7, 2012.

his written questions and Nakoula's responses past the guards.

Nakoula explained to the *Times* reporter that he had been wanting to make this film for several years. During a first attempt, in 2009, he had hired Alan Roberts the producer and done casting calls with actors, but ultimately had to shut down the project before filming began. He told Roberts and Jimmy Israel, who was already involved at that point, that he had cancer and had to go away for treatment. A family member "shared a similar story with church officials," the *Times* wrote.[14]

Nakoula did have to go away for some months, but it wasn't for cancer treatment. This is when he was jailed for the synthetic credit card scheme.

In one sense, the 21 months he spent in jail was a blessing in disguise, Nakoula told me. He had plenty of time to gather his thoughts and to perfect the script on the origins of Islamic ideology he had been working on for years.

"I have consulted more than 3,000 books by Islamic scholars in the original Arabic," he told me. "You can't understand Islam unless you do this."

The genocide of Armenian and Assyrian Christians, carried out by Turkish and Kurdish Muslims during the final years of WWI, had profoundly affected him. "I read these stories about women who had their babies cut out of their belly. And still the Turkish don't want to admit doing this." Islam and its ideology was the "first terrorism," he said. As a young man, he had seen it every day in Egypt in the way Coptic Christians were reviled and persecuted by Muslims.

While in prison, he found a Chinese comic book artist who dug into the project with him, producing some 1,400 drawings for the storyboard of *Innocence of Muslims*. In that original script,

---

[14]   Serge F. Kovaleski and Brooks Barnes, "From Man Who Insulted Muhammad, No Regret," *NY Times*, Nov. 25, 2012; included in Garcia v. Google et al, Docket 37

the characters were called Mohammad and Khadija, and Aisha, and Abu Bakr, not Condalesa and Master George.

"I wanted to give a warning to Americans through the movie," he explained. "I was not against the terrorists; they are real Muslims! They are just doing what they believe. I am against the people who try to tell us that they are *not* true Muslims, that Bin Laden does not represent the true Islam. He does!"

Nakoula believed that the people who were trying to sell Islam as a religion of peace, who claimed that ISIS and al Qaeda were not real Muslims, were more dangerous than the terrorists themselves. "I call them *tadleem*," Nakoula said. "It means they are hiding. Islam wants pieces, pieces of Christians and Jews, not peace."

+++

Vanity Fair sent a reporter to interview Cindy in Bakersfield that December. He interviewed a number of other actors who seemed somewhat more aware of the movie's message about Islamic ideology than Cindy, and produced a snarky account of how the movie came to be made.

"One actor remembers being struck by lines such as 'There is no God but George's God,' and 'George is the Messenger.'" The actor told *Vanity Fair* he was "able to piece together that there were a lot of similarities to the rise of Islam as far as what we were saying," although he still believed it was not about Islam, but "about two warring tribes in ancient Arabia."

Cindy was a wreck when she agreed to meet the reporter. Her case had been tossed out of the federal district court, she continued to receive death threats, and had moved her church and her home in an attempt to protect her family and her flock. She had even stopped babysitting her great-grandchildren, for fear they would get murdered along with her, "now that a fatwa has been put out against me," she said.

She met him in front of a defunct Peet's Coffee shop, "in a wide-open area with long views in almost every direction," the reporter wrote. "As I arrive, her first words are, 'I'm in a pissy mood.'" That mood only deepened as Cindy felt completely disrespected by a so-called newsman who had come to make a spectacle of her. He mocked her for calling herself a "preacher of the Gospel." In his hands, the fear she felt for her loved ones became paranoia.

She says that a private security firm is now providing 24-hour protection for her, pro bono.

I ask, "Are they watching us now?"

"Ohhh, yes," she answers. In addition to what she calls "My fatwa," Garcia says, she has received "many death threats."

"What kind of death threats?"

"Death threats!"

"By email, phone, letter, or—?"

"Death threats!"[15]

On December 21, 2012, Cris Armenta and her legal team filed their appeal with the Ninth Circuit court, the most liberal appeals court in the land.

But would their liberalism come down on the side of Big Media, as represented by Google? Or would they protect Cindy's rights?

None of them knew.

But it was the only shot they had to protect Cindy and give her some measure of peace.

---

[15] Michael Joseph Gross, "Disaster Movie," *Vanity Fair*, Dec. 27, 2012, op cit.

CHAPTER 17
ATLAS SHRUGGED AND THE JUDGE

While Armenta and her legal team prepared for the appeal, which was set for an oral hearing on June 26, 2013, Cindy tried to reassess her life.

Until now, she had focused all her anger and frustration on Nakoula, who had tricked her by using her brief dramatic performance for a completely different purpose than what she had signed up for.

But the more she read – and she was now reading everything she could find about Islam and the Middle East – the less she understood. What was it about Islam that caused people to commit murder? To go on the killing rampages that had swept through Egypt and Pakistan and everywhere else? To do horrible things, unspeakable things, not just to women, but to children? "When I found out that this Prophet of Islam really did marry a six-year-old little girl and that I was used as a puppet in all of this, it brought back all the pain I had suppressed from what had happened to me as a child," she told me. "I was sickened to think that any religion or person could condone such behavior."

She began to realize that Nakoula had been telling the truth about Islam; he just hadn't told her! She began thinking of what must be happening to innocent children around the world, especially the girls who were sold into slavery and married off to old goats like the "Master George" in the movie. Cindy became consumed by a desire to do something to help them.

At one point, Nakoula sent her lawyer a hand-written letter from prison. "Really I feel sorry for Miss Cindy. But nothing I can do now," he wrote in his broken English. The one bank account he was allowed to keep had only $30.38 in it! "I will never forget the people they worked in the movie as a friends. Especially Miss Cindy. Also I like to let you know the movie defends U.S.A. and all good people."

He told Armenta that he still had big plans. He wanted to show Cindy the entire two-hour movie once he got out. "I'm sure she will feel proud she is in it," he said. He also offered to remove her part from the movie, since it was only 90 seconds out of a 114-minute movie. "I already finish a TV series 200 hours writing for big product[ion]," he ended. If Cindy wanted, he would invite her to play the lead female role![1]

Armenta shared the letter with her, and it touched her heart. As she learned more about all the problems Nakoula had had, his time in prison, the prior convictions, his working as a federal informant, she began to feel compassion for him. "I felt that perhaps he was forced to make this film," she said.

That idea began to grow in her. The more she thought about it, the more she felt that was the only possible explanation. Why would someone make a movie like that, knowing it would cause Muslims to put a death sentence on them and other

---

[1]   Readers will find a copy of the letter here: http://kentimmerman.com/iomdocs/ prison-letter-from-nakoula-to-armenta.pdf

innocent people, unless he were forced? "When I saw that he was arrested and that his life was in danger just as much as mine, I felt the love of Christ in my heart for him," Cindy said. "I have never wanted to hurt Nakoula. I just wanted the truth and my name untied from all of this."

She had such mixed feelings about this man!

"He told a reporter that he was willing to set himself on fire in the public square to show people the evils of Islam. So why did he hide his face when he was arrested?" she asked me. "And why did he lie to the actors?"

Cindy became convinced that someone else was behind the movie and that Nakoula was secretly a Muslim.

As she scoured the Internet, she saw that Walid Shoebat, the former Palestinian terrorist turned evangelist I have quoted above, seemed to know a lot about Nakoula and his background. So she called him. Shoebat convinced her that Nakoula had made the movie as a provocative act, backed by Obama and Hillary, to further their agenda of imposing blasphemy laws in the United States to ban all criticism of Islam.

As Cindy and her attorneys pushed forward with their case, she became convinced that Shoebat was right.

+++

Although Armenta and her long-time colleague, Jason Armstrong, had spent days preparing for their June 23, 2013 appearance before the Ninth Circuit of Appeals, she appeared nervous when she stood up to the bar. The Seattle courtroom was an imposing place, with its elegant wood paneling, double row of benches, and its sheer size. It was packed with spectators and press.

64-year-old Chief Judge Alex Kozinski was a legend. A Romanian Jew born to Holocaust survivors who emigrated to the United States when he was 12, Kozinski was known for his trenchant humor, telling parties from the bench to "chill out." Growing up in a totalitarian society had given him a keen appreciation of our constitutional protections on free speech. He was also notorious – or admired, as the case may be – for his love of the movie industry. He was not just a movie buff; he was a movie *geek,* widely believed to have purposefully worked the titles of more than 200 Hollywood films into a 1990 opinion in *United States v. Syufy Enterprises*![2] As he noted sarcastically in a dissent in one case, "for better or worse, we are the Court of Appeals for the *Hollywood* Circuit." [3]

Appointed by President Ronald Reagan to the bench in 1985, when he was just 35, Kozinski had his own shares of ups and downs. He had taken to posting zoophilic photo montages his friends and family had emailed him on a password-protected website he had set up for his legal writings. When reporters found out, it led to a judicial investigation they dubbed the "cow sex" scandal. (Kozinski was cleared of any wrongdoing, and later said he thought the faked photos were "funny").[4]

While Armenta hadn't read all of his colorful legal opinions, she had read enough of them to realize she would be performing in front of an intellectual giant when it came to copyright law. Kozinski was known for asking seemingly off-the-wall questions that frequently threw attorneys into a tailspin. He also had his own IMBD credits as an actor! The judge with a libertarian bent had made cameo appearances in a number of documentaries. He recently had shown up in *Atlas Shrugged* Part II, playing a

---

[2]   See The Syufy Rosetta Stone, 1992 BYU L. Rev. 457 (1992). Available at: h ttp://digitalcommons.law.byu.edu/lawreview/vol1992/iss2/13

[3]   White v. Samsung Elec. Am., Inc., 989 F.2d 1512, 1521 (Ninth Cir. 1993) (Kozinski, J., dissenting).

[4]   Scott Glover, "9th Circuit's chief judge posted sexually explicit matter on his website," *Los Angeles Times*, June 11, 2008.

judge during the trial of industrialist Hank Reardon![5]

Armenta couched her legal theory in terms she thought would appeal to Kozinski. She and Armstrong had stayed up all night testing potential questions they might get from the judges.

She began by saying that the district court had erred when they concluded Cindy didn't have a copyright interest in her performance "because she was a little person, not the mastermind of the film." Those words were click bait to copyright wonks because of an earlier Ninth Circuit decision in which the "mastermind" was deemed to be the primary copyright claimant.

It didn't take Kozinski more than a minute and a half to bite. Look at the credits that scroll at the end of most movies, he said. "If everybody had a copyright, you would never get a movie done."

Actually, the actors *did* have a copyright, Armenta said. "That's why most reputable studios – all reputable studios – have everyone who participates in a film sign... a release."

"But that's not what happened here. She didn't sign a release," Kozinski said.

Armenta had scored, so she plowed on, more confident now. She cited Kozinski's own Opinions to make her case, arguing that the license Cindy granted the filmmaker was "limited by her intent." Every person who writes, acts, or commits a dramatic performance to film holds a copyright, she said. But those copyrights are usually, at least in the context of a movie, assigned to a studio through a licensing agreement. Since there was no licensing agreement here, the original rights to her performance remained with Cindy.

---

5   David Lat, "A Star is Born: Chief Judge Alex Kozinski, Coming To a Movie Theater Near You," Above the Law, Aug. 29, 2012.

Kozinski cut her off again: "Is she claiming he had no written license?"

"There is no written license," Armenta said.

So it all hinged on whether Google decided to dispute the decision by the lower court to toss out the copyright release forms Armenta's handwriting expert had concluded were forged. Would they actually go there, Armenta wondered? It was a risky approach, since if the handwriting expert was right, Google could get sucked into a legal trap. Shouldn't they have known that the documents were forged? After all, Nakoula was a convicted forger, so how could Google rely on the statement of a guy with a long track record of forging documents and identities, who had been put back in jail for not giving his proper name? *He should be the last person Google should rely on.*

+++

When Google attorney Timothy Alger stepped up to the bar, he could barely get his name on the record before Kozinski interrupted him to ask if he was also representing Nakoula.

"No, I don't believe he's appeared in the case. I don't believe he has even been served," Alger said.

"So why does Google care? Why doesn't Google just pull this thing and save themselves attorney's fees, if nothing else?" Kozinski asked.

Armenta had to keep from doing a fist bump with her colleague, Jason Armstrong. Kozinski was right: why exactly *did* Google care? And whose interests were they actually defending? Was Alger really going to try to make this a First Amendment issue, in front of the King of First Amendment freedoms who just announced it wasn't a First Amendment case?

Alger claimed that Cindy had no copyright interest in the movie, but he pointedly failed to mention the forged release claims. Even if content violated Google's terms of use, Google often refrained from taking it down since "even the terms of use are at Google's discretion," he noted.

Kozinski chewed on that. "You cite discretion. This has obviously caused a great deal of grief to the plaintiff and some danger. Why doesn't Google exercise its discretion to say okay, maybe we don't have to, but we'll take it down anyway?"

Alger circled back to the free speech argument, and claimed that if Google started taking down material because someone who played a minor role objected, "where would we stop?"

Kozinski wasn't having it. The filmmaker had "put words in her mouth and made her say things that she did not utter... There seems to be no dispute that as an actress, she never said these things – never mind her views – but as an actress.... So wouldn't it have been the kinder, gentler, nicer, generous, civilized, civil thing to do to take it down because it's the right thing to do? There's no principle preventing Google from doing the right thing, is there?" Kozinski asked.

Ouch, Armenta thought.

"You're assuming that it's the right thing to do," Alger countered. "This film has garnered the attention of the globe, and the subject of great debate, including the subject of who's going to be the secretary of state.[6] There's clearly debate that goes on around the world about this video and its impact, including on the U.S. government. I think it would be a disservice to people to take it down."

Armenta couldn't believe how well this was going. The chief judge of the court was making her arguments for her. It really

---

[6]   This was a reference to Susan Rice, who had been President Obama's first pick to succeed Hillary Clinton at the State Department, but who was pulled from the running once the White House realized Congressional hearings would expose the Benghazi cover-up.

did all depend on the copyright release form. The fact that Alger missed every opportunity to bring it up meant that her instinct must be right. What if it turned out that Google had actually caused them to be forged, or had somehow participated in the forgery by suggesting to Nakoula that he come up with such a document?

While she thought Alger was too smart to take such a risk, she knew one thing for sure. She had Google over a barrel.

+++

The feds transferred Nakoula form MDC to La Tuna federal prison in Anthony, Texas, sometime after Christmas 2012. Why send him to West Texas? Perhaps they were feeling charitable, and wanted to get him out of the dangerous circumstances he faced at MDC. Others thought it was because the Feds didn't want him talking, "and so the further from a media too indifferent to look hard, the better."[7]

Not long after Armenta's first appearance before the Ninth Circuit, the feds moved him again, this time to a halfway house in the nearby Imperial Valley town of Brawley, California. While it was still hours away from home, his Probation officer allowed him to briefly visit his father in the hospital after he had an aneurism.

In August 2013, Nakoula spoke with CNN's Jake Tapper by phone. Tapper asked his location, but Nakoula told him that the government was "hiding" him so he couldn't speak to journalists. (Tapper reported that he was being held at "an undisclosed halfway house in Southern California."). Nakoula said that President Obama had been irresponsible for blaming his film for the violence in the Middle East. While Nakoula insisted that he liked Obama, "he has a lot of responsibility," he said.

---

[7]   Jack Cashill, "Free Nakoula!" American Thinker, May 10, 2013.

Tapper brought up the subject of Cindy's lawsuit. While it wasn't the reason Nakoula had gone to jail, it had become a big news story. "Nakoula claimed that he had tried to explain to the actors what the movie was about, but they didn't care," Tapper wrote.

When Cindy saw that, she blew her stack – again.

Armenta and her team put together a blistering press release, categorically denying Nakoula's claim, the gist of which CNN later incorporated as an "update" to their original article.[8]

"He never told me squat," Cindy insisted.

+++

Steve Klein, erstwhile "spokesman" for the movie, continued to follow Nakoula's travails. His own life had gotten "interesting" since a gazillion journalists camped out at his home and office the day the story broke.

"They were accusing me of being Nakoula," he said, recalling the pandemonium of that Wednesday. "Then they said it was Morris Sadek. Then they turned to my wife and screamed, 'You are Nakoula!' They were in a frenzy. ABC, NBC, Fox News, the BBC, some guys from Tokyo and who knows where. All just a bunch of piranhas.

"The media definitely had an agenda," Klein said. "That was to make me and Nakoula the fall guys to protect Obama and Hillary."

That night at around 7 PM, he received a text message from the FBI. "It said, like, 'We are FBI. Don't leave your house. We are coming to you.'"

Klein wasn't sure he liked the idea of a bunch of FBI agents showing up at his house. He called the number that had texted

8   Jake Tapper, "Filmmaker of movie initially blamed for Benghazi attacks: Obama administration was irresponsible," CNN, Aug. 13, 2013

him and wound up talking to a former Marine Corps officer, like himself. "'Hey, not to worry, we're not coming out to arrest you, but to protect you,' the guy said."

A couple of days later, the FBI assigned an agent to provide that protection. "It wasn't like the old days, set up a perimeter, guns drawn," Klein told me. "I remember asking the guy, so what are you going to do? And he said, 'Oh, we'll monitor the Internet and see if there are any threats.' Gee, so I am the goat? You're going to tie me to the tree until the lion shows up? He said, 'Yeah, something like that.'"

Klein went to the local sheriff's office out near San Bernardino two weeks later to apply for a concealed carry permit. Obama's speech at the United Nations was playing on the TV behind him as he chatted with the deputy. "He asked me why I needed a concealed carry permit, and so I pointed to the TV. I'm the guy he's talking about, I said. 'You mean, the guy who made the Benghazi movie?' Yeah, that's me."

Klein heard that Nakoula was being transferred back to California from Texas, and phoned Nakoula's daughter on July 4, 2013 to get the details. Then he arranged to meet him in Brawley to take him home the day of his release.

In the meantime, he contacted Pastor Wiley Drake, whose church happened to be in Buena Park, not far from where Nakoula's family lived in Cerritos. "I knew Nakoula needed a place to go when he got out and that Wiley had a big heart. I was pretty sure he would help out."

As they got the ball rolling, the Justice Department called Pastor Drake to make sure he could handle such a high profile guest at his church. They told him that Nakoula's sentence involved four years of supervised release. That meant Nakoula would be remanded to his custody, and he would have responsibility for his actions.

"They didn't want to release him to his family house,

because if anyone attacked him and someone got killed, the family would hold the U.S. government responsible for their deaths," Drake told me. "So they were basically looking for an option. 'Hey, we're not trying to be the good guys, but we don't want his family blown up,' the guy I spoke with said."

The feds had an ongoing relationship with Pastor Drake and his First Southern Baptist Church in Buena Park. They ran a homeless shelter and every day served free meals and provided beds to men in trouble, some of them potentially dangerous. "I said, don't worry, I'll segregate him off from the general population," Drake said.

When I visited Pastor Drake, several employees came through his office who were former felons he had taken under his wing in exactly the same way. White, black, Hispanic, or Arab, Pastor Drake welcomed them all.

Drake is a colorful character in his own right. A vice-presidential candidate on the American Independent Party ticket with Alan Keyes in 2008, and a presidential candidate in 2016, he has fearlessly taken on the federal government for abuse of power. Drake's TV show website, http://thewileydrakeshow.com, includes interviews with many families who claim their children were illegally taken away from them by Child Protective Service workers. He accused CPS of running a "child laundering" racket, abusing the law to collect fees from the federal government for children under its care, much as humanitarian aid agencies such as Catholic Charities collect a fee for resettling Muslim refugees in the United States.[9]

---

[9] A hard-to-watch 14-minute documentary on the abuses of Child Protective Services can be viewed here: https://www.youtube.com/watch?v=sag37aAf1WU. On refugee resettlement, see Ann Corcoran's excellent blog, https://refugeeresettlementwatch.wordpress.com. See also Michael Patrick Leahy, "Unholy Alliance: Christian Charities Profit from $1 billion Fed program to Resettle Refugees, 40 Percent Muslim," Breitbart.com, Nov. 25, 2015

Klein drove out to Brawley on Thursday, September 26, 2013. Nakoula had asked Klein to meet him in front of a store about 300 yards from the halfway house. "He never let me know where he was being housed until I picked him up that day," Klein told me.

Nakoula was a wreck. "We drove through a shopping mall in El Centro, and he was in Stockholm syndrome. He started crying in the mall as he watched children playing in a play area. "I would do it all again if I could save these children from Islam," Klein recalls him saying.

When they reached the modest church in Buena Park, Pastor Drake gave him a warm welcome, and offered him a small bedroom adjoining his office, where he taped his daily Internet TV shows. In exchange for room and board – and security – Nakoula would do chores around the church and the adjoining homeless shelter. For the next four years, that small room would be his home.

CHAPTER 18
VICTORY!

On February 19, 2014, Armenta learned that the Ninth Circuit, led by Chief Judge Alex Kozinski, had ruled in their favor. It was terrific vindication of all their hard work. Her Internet sleuths, David Hardy and Eric Bulock, had been right: the copyright angle was the way to go. *David beat Goliath*, she thought.

But they couldn't start gloating about their victory. In fact, they couldn't even talk about it – not even to Cindy – just yet. The court order instructing Google and YouTube to take down all copies of the video was to remain secret for a full week, so that it wouldn't spark a frenzy of last minute downloads.

The order also instructed Google to "take all reasonable steps" to prevent further uploads of *Innocence of Muslims* to YouTube and any other platforms under its control. "Neither the parties nor counsel shall disclose this order, except as necessary to the takedown process, until the opinion in this case issues."[1]

Armenta and her colleagues were ecstatic. They drafted a

---

[1] ORDER from Ninth CCA filed re: Notice of Appeal to 9th Circuit Court of Appeals [42] filed by Cindy Lee Garcia CCA # 12-57302. Docket 61.

press release they could fire out the minute the court issued its opinion, which occurred exactly one week later.

Here is the text they finally sent over the wires:

"We are delighted that the Ninth Circuit has recognized the significant threat to Cindy Lee Garcia's life and safety caused by Google and YouTube's refusal to remove the propaganda film *Innocence of Muslims* from the YouTube platform after Ms. Garcia made eight separate requests that they do so. Ordering YouTube and Google to take down the film was the right thing to do. The propaganda film differs so radically from anything that Ms. Garcia could have imagined when the director told her that she was being cast in the innocent adventure film *Desert Warrior* that had she known the true nature of the project, she never would have agreed to participate. We look forward to the trial court's entry of an appropriate order making the Ninth Circuit's takedown order permanent."

Not everyone was happy with this outcome. The Electronic Frontier Foundation (EFF), which styles itself as a defender of free speech on the Internet, called it "a prior restraint on speech," since the underlying copyright claim was "doubtful." It also blasted the court for issuing what it called a "gag order" forbidding Google from discussing the ruling for a week. One court watcher called it a "horrific" ruling.[2] Most free speech advocates agreed.

Google didn't take the ruling lying down, but engaged in full-scale legal warfare. Armenta and her team had to work overtime just to keep up. Google filed innumerable briefs with the Ninth Circuit opposing the ruling, calling for the case to

---

[2]   https://www.techdirt.com/articles/20140226/12103626359/horrific-appeals-court-ruling-says-actress-has-copyright-interest-innocence-muslims-orders-youtube-to-delete-every-copy.shtml

be reheard by the entire Ninth Circuit bench. This was called an "en banc" hearing and as a general rule was reserved for extremely controversial cases or cases of public notoriety.[3] For most defendants, even petitioning for an "en banc" rehearing was beyond their means. But if you have Google's deep pockets, it's what you do.

In the meantime, Google didn't seem to be complying with the court order.

One month after the take-down order was supposed to have gone into effect, Armenta and her Internet team found that the video was not only still available in the United States, but was now available in Egypt, "the nation in which the fatwa was issued for Ms. Garcia's execution." In an emergency motion asking the court to find Google in contempt, Armenta spelled out the ease with which "any computer in the world" could still access the film, and then accused Google of dragging its feet.

> "Notwithstanding its vast technical resources and standing as one of the largest and most sophisticated Internet companies in the world, Google and its army of lawyers have taken the position that Google is somehow incapable of complying with the order, that it is "deploying every resource" to comply, and that Ms. Garcia –who has virtually no resources – bears the burden of advising Google of each and every individual URL that remains on Google's platforms in defiance of the takedown order."[4]

---

[3]   Since the Ninth Circuit is so large – around 45 judges in all – it has a special rule to select an "en banc" panel of 11 judges.

[4]   Appellant Cindy Lee Garcia's Emergency Motion for a Finding of Contempt, Garcia v. Google et al, USCA Ninth Circuit, Case 12-57302. Docket 67. Available at http://kentimmerman.com/IOMdocs/ Doc67-garcia_emergency_contempt_motion.pdf

David Hardy sent her an email on March 25, 2014, attaching screen shots of Cindy's scene in the movie that was still up and running on YouTube in Egypt. "This video was posted last September under the name *Innocence of Muslims* – very hard for Google/YouTube to miss it," Hardy noted.

Google responded by saying it had blocked "approximately 1,400 copies of *Innocence of Muslims,* including every one of the 851 channels identified in the takedown notices Garcia's team sent in 2012. They also said that YouTube "does not possess the completely automated system to instantly guard against new uploads," an astonishing statement for the world's largest Internet company.[5]

This time the court sided with Google.

Google not only had deep pockets; it had a deep bench. The Electronic Freedom Foundation (EFF) became a powerful ally to the Internet giant, a clearinghouse for left-wing free speech advocates, news organizations, and law professors who pooled their efforts to keep the movie online. They set up a webpage that kept track of the innumerable legal documents the parties filed in the coming months, as well as the amicus briefs of outside organizations in support of Google.[6]

Scores of organizations filed 25 separate legal briefs. Only the Screen Actors Guild came out in support of Cindy's position that she held a copyrighted interest in the movie. The EFF, the American Civil Liberties Union, Netflix, Adobe, EBay, Facebook, the *New York Times*, the *Washington Post*, the *Los Angeles Times*, Scripps, National Public Radio, the California Newspaper Publishers Association, the First Amendment Coalition, several lawyers associations and others all sided against Cindy and

---

5   Google Inc. and YouTube, LLC's Brief in Response to Cindy Lee Garcia's Emergency Motion for Contempt, March 29, 2014, Case 12-57302. Docket 72-1.

6   https://www.eff.org/cases/garcia-v-google-inc

in favor of keeping *Innocence of Muslims* online, despite the *fatwa* on Cindy's life. A handful of law professors and public interest organizations filed briefs not in support of either party, apparently just wanting to show off their stuff in what was now becoming a case for the law books.

Armenta felt she was riding a rocket. This was history in the making. It was exhilarating, monumental, a case that would be studied for decades.

She felt confident she could ride it out. But she was less sure about Cindy.

+++

In March 2014, fellow actor Gaylord Flynn joined the fray, and asked Armenta to file a companion lawsuit against Google in his name. They began by sending takedown notices with 111 new URLs where the movie could be found online, including "torrent" sites where it could be rapidly accessed and downloaded.

But strange things had started happening as well.

When Armenta started reading through Google's lengthy petition to the appeals court, her eyes popped. She couldn't believe what she was seeing.

Two weeks ago, a divided panel of this Court silenced speech based on a novel theory of copyright law that even the panel conceded was "fairly debatable." That was an understatement. Since the panel ruled, the U.S. Copyright Office has refused registration of the very copyright claimed in this case. It concluded – in a decision Appellant failed to even mention in her brief filed today in this Court – that Garcia's copyright claim was contrary to the Copyright

Act and to the Office's "longstanding practices."[7]

Google's attorneys came right out of the box quoting a letter from the Copyright Office that Armenta herself hadn't yet received!

She went back over her file just to make sure. She had written to the Copyright Office on March 4, 2014, and their response, which they had emailed to her, was dated two days later. But she hadn't yet received the official letter by snail mail, which is why she hadn't put it in her brief.

But Google clearly had obtained it. How?

She had been working on her brief out of her home near San Diego and accessing her Los Angeles office remotely over the Internet. She had her assistant check the logs, and discovered that someone else had accessed the system from a remote location on March 5. She called the server company, and while they saw the intrusion, they were unable to capture the IP address of the hacker.

Two weeks later, on March 26, Cindy received a notice from her ISP that her email had also been hacked. This time, the ISP had captured the IP address, but they refused to release the identity of the hacker without a warrant or a subpoena. Since their case against Google was now on appeal, Armenta was unable to issue one herself. So she contacted the San Diego County Computer and Technology Crime High-Tech ("CATCH") Response Team, asking them to open a criminal investigation into the intrusion and issue a warrant to her ISP to identify the hacker. The CATCH Team had a flashy website, claiming that they were "a multi-agency task force formed in June of 2000 to apprehend and prosecute criminals who use technology to prey on citizens."[8]They invited citizens to report alleged cyber

---

7   Google Inc. and YouTube, LLC's Petition for Rehearing En Banc, March 12, 2014, Case 12-57302. Docket 57.

8   http://www.catchteam.org

crimes, so it seemed the obvious place to go.

One month later, the CATCH team's law enforcement coordinator, Sgt. Mark Varnau, sent Armenta a lengthy email in reply, asking her dozens of very specific questions. He wanted to know everything about the computer intrusion, how they had detected it, why her ISP said they hadn't captured the IP address of the intruder, and whether the letter she suspected had been stolen from her email account could have been acquired by Google by some other means. He also made clear that he had read into the Ninth Circuit case, and gave her a long lecture on why he wasn't going to open a criminal case. ("If law enforcement were to become involved in such allegations, there is a great likelihood the civil case would resolve well before a criminal investigation could be completed AND the likelihood of anyone being prosecuted under such circumstances is slight to none," he wrote.)[9]

Armenta emailed that response to her team, and together they decided to drop it.

So much for your government working for you.

+++

In May 2014, Nakoula through his attorney answered the allegations in the fraud complaint that Armenta served on him shortly after his release from the Brawley halfway house.

He claimed that he had tried to explain the "story of the Film" to Cindy, "but she refused to listen and asked for her check."[10]

Armenta knew hearing that would make Cindy blow her

---

9   Email exchange between Cris Armenta, Mark Varnau, March-April 2014; made available to the author by Armenta.
10   Youssef Answer to First Amended Complaint, May 20, 2014, Case 2:12-cv-08315-MWF-VBK, Docket 75.

stack, so she told her the good news, instead: the fraud case against Nakoula brought them back into the district court, so once again they had subpoena power.

On June 23, 2014, Armenta got the district court to approve subpoenas for the bank records of Nakoula's children, Thoriya and Abanob, as well as his ex-wife's cousin, Mina Sami Imiel, who they believed was involved in financing the movie. She submitted the checks Cindy had received from Nakoula on the set of *Desert Warrior* to identify the accounts.

Cindy came down from Bakersfield to spend a week with Armenta in her house outside San Diego that July as the amicus briefs piled up in the Ninth Circuit case. The more the free speech advocates filed against her, the more dispirited she became.

"I thought we had won," Cindy said.

In the courts, of course, it's never over until it's over. The more Armenta explained the different opposition briefs to Cindy, the more bewildered Cindy became. They all had one thing in common: the news organizations and the First Amendment groups were all accusing Cindy of violating Nakoula's constitutionally-protected right to free speech.

I am a patriot, Cindy told Armenta. *I love the Constitution of this country. I would never do anything to violate anyone's constitutional rights. But he lied. He tricked me. It's not free speech if it's a lie. Is it?*

+++

Armenta decided to bring in an Egyptian interpreter while Cindy was staying with her, so they could also listen to the Arabic-language videos of the Benghazi attacks.

One video in particular had enflamed Cindy's imagination, since it was all over the Internet. It involved two (or possibly more) individuals who spoke in an Egyptian dialect, and frantically told the armed intruders at the diplomatic compound they were friends.

"Don't shoot! Don't shoot! Dr. Morsi sent us!" they said.

Dr. Morsi, of course, was the Muslim Brotherhood president of Egypt. The presence of alleged emissaries of Morsi gave rise to persistent rumors that the attack on the diplomatic compound was aimed at kidnapping the U.S. Ambassador, and exchanging him for "Blind Sheikh" Omar Abdel Rahman, jailed in the United States since 1994 on charges of material support for terrorism.

So Armenta brought in a young Egyptian woman, and they listened to the tape again and again. She stopped it, she amplified it, she asked them to play it in slow motion. And then she concluded: they were speaking in the distinctive Cairo dialect, and that's exactly what they were saying. Don't shoot, Dr. Morsi sent us.

Morsi was Egyptian. Nakoula was Egyptian. The Blind Sheikh was Egyptian. And these people participating in the attacks were Egyptian. Cindy was sure it was not a coincidence and that Nakoula had to be mixed up in the Benghazi attacks.

How could it happen that a guy who just got out of jail after serving 21 months for credit card fraud and identify fraud, suddenly came into a large sum of money that enabled him almost immediately to begin shooting a movie? Cindy asked herself. We know that he was a government snitch. That means he was cooperating with the government. What if the government put him up to it? Had him make the movie so they could blame Benghazi on it, and not their own criminal actions?

+++

Armenta and her team started combing through the bank

records as soon as they came in. Lots of odd things started popping out at them.

First was Mina Imiel, his ex-wife's cousin, who nobody seemed able to find. He was using the same 12608 Park Street address in Cerritos as Nakoula, his ex-wife, and their daughter, Thoriya. Mina turned out to be a landlord, and was depositing rent checks from tenants in Hawaiian Gardens, CA. Many of the checks written from Mina's account were written in a hand that to an untrained eye resembled the cursive scrawl Nakoula himself had displayed in the filming and in his hand-written letter to Armenta from prison.

Shortly after Nakoula got out jail in May 2011, Mina received two deposits for a total of $12,000 from an account controlled by Nakoula's son Abanob for the production company used for the movie, Matthew MTTA. Then in July, the month before shooting began, Mina wrote checks to Abanob for $82,000, and to Thoriya for another $43,000. Were these payments related to the film? Unclear.

The same handwriting appeared on checks written on accounts for Mina, Abanob, Thoriya and the production company, Matthew MTTA. The same cursive scrawl also appeared on cash deposit slips, and on checks written from accounts in the name of Nakoula's ex-wife and her father, and for Basseley Nada, apparently a shortened form of Nakoula's name.[11] All of these accounts showed the same Cerritos address. Some of the payments were a "wash," meaning that two account holders would write each other checks on the same day for the same amount. It was a weird round robin of checks and deposits, checks and deposits, sometimes adding

---

[11] Armenta's investigators discovered that Nakoula's younger brother, Emil Basseley Nada, also lived in the area, and had been granted political asylum by the United States on grounds that he had been persecuted in Egypt for his Christian faith.

up to $25,000 in a single month for children then aged 18 and 21 years old. It resembled in a strange way the check-kiting scheme Nakoula had been jailed for in 2009.

Except for one big difference: they had real money this time, not just convenience checks. The July 2011 statement for Mina's account showed that on July 21, 2011, Mina received an $80,000 wire transfer from the Security Land Escrow Company. When Armenta and her team dug into it, they found that the money, and an additional $24,956 wired to Thoriya's account the same day, came from the sale of a gas station and mini mart franchise Nakoula's ex-wife had owned and put in the name of their 18-year-old daughter. Thoriya sold it to an outfit called Long Beach Willow Inc.[12]

Over the summer that Nakoula filmed *Innocence of Muslims*, he used all six bank accounts to pay the actors, the site location, and the crew. The same person appears to have written most of the checks. While the money may have come from the sale of the "Nobi" gas station and mini market franchise at 11804 East Carson Street in Hawaiian Gardens, California, Nakoula insisted it did not. He said the money for the film "came from Christian people who have been victims of Muslim people, so they want to make a contribution. Some bring food, some bring makeup, some bring uniforms, some bring cash. But the money is not important."

Nakoula's children deposited cash from unknown sources between April and early August 2011. Abanob's account showed close to $10,000 in cash deposits, most of which came in the form of money-grams, a common way of receiving money anonymously. Thoriya deposited just over $28,000 in cash during the same period, and a $1,000 moneygram in September.

---

[12]   The new franchise owners concluded a 10-year lease on the property, which continued to be owned by Mina Imiel, for $5,300/ month. The rent later increased to $8,300/month.

Nakoula has acknowledged that his children's bank accounts were used to pay the actors, the crew, and the set rental fees, with money that came from donors[13]. Many of the expenses were paid in cash. The entire film cost less than $75,000, as far as I have been able to reconstruct it from the bank accounts, with help from Sean Dunagen of Judicial Watch, with whom Cindy also shared the banking records.

No conspiracy. No government involvement. No apparent fraud.

Who would have thought you could make a two-hour movie with nearly 80 actors for so little money?

Welcome to low budget Hollywood.

+++

As Armenta dug further into the banking records, a number of much stranger things popped out. On November 17, 2011, three months after the filming of *Innocence of Muslims,* Mina Imiel received a wire transfer for $6,980 from a Citibank account belonging to someone called Bilal. The same person made a wire transfer for an identical amount the same day into Thoriya's account, and an additional transfer of $1,980 to Mina Imiel on January 6, 2012.[14]

And then, Armenta thought, they hit pay dirt: Eiad Salameh made a series of wire transfers into Thoriya and Mina Imiel's accounts, as did another person named Ali. Both of them had accounts at Standard Chartered Bank. Their transfers, each for $5000, were listed as "settlement of debt."

Cindy began ominously referring to "the money trail" she believed led from Islamic terrorists in the West Bank, Morocco,

---

[13]   Deposition of Mark Basseley Youssef, op cit. p16.
[14]   I have redacted the last names in this section since there is no evidence these individuals participated in any criminal activity.

and London, back to Nakoula and his Coptic Christian family in Cerritos, California. She was sure that Eiad Salameh was the key. "He is a very bad man, we know has ties to terrorists," she said. "Why did the feds want Sam to testify against him and then let him leave Canada?" (Cindy based her claim that Salameh had "ties to terrorists" on vague allegations by Walid Shoebat, who to my knowledge has never provided any evidence to substantiate those claims.)

Thoriya also received $11,000 from Eiad Salameh, similarly identified as "settlement of debt." The only problem was, the transfers from Salameh and "Ali" didn't reach her account until October and December 2013, and Mina Imiel's account until April 24, 2014 – more than two years after the filming of *Innocence of Muslims*. And there was no trace in the bank records that either I or Judicial Watch investigators could find relating to the West Bank or Morocco. "It's in my paperwork," Cindy insisted. I examined five boxes of Cindy's "paperwork" and couldn't find it.

When I asked Nakoula about those transfers, he agreed that they were all Muslim names. "Why would Muslims want to fund my movie?" he said.

Nakoula suggested that the transfers from Salameh to his daughter might be support payments for Salameh's children, who still lived in California and were friends with Thoriya. Whatever their purpose, I could find no evidence showing they were linked to *Innocence of Muslims*.

+++

Shortly after they got the bank records in mid-July, Cindy and her attorney arranged to meet with Nakoula at Wiley Drake's church in Buena Park, south of Los Angeles. They wanted to appeal to him to take down the video, even though he no longer controlled it.

Cindy was totally freaked out about meeting Nakoula face to face again. In addition to Armenta and her colleague, Jason, they brought two bodyguards with them to the run-down church office building. Cindy recalls the meeting vividly.

"I had taken my lawyer's license plate off the back of her car before we pulled into the church where Sam the producer led us to believe he was living," she said. "Sam arrived after we did and was limping, using a cane. He seemed a little confused about which room we were going to meet in. For a moment he walked us into a small, dirty room. I felt uncomfortable there and I had the feeling Sam did, too. So then the people who were there instructed us to use an office area next door."

Nakoula's tiny room, with a single bed, a nightstand, a small chest of drawers and not much else, was right next to Wiley Drake's office, which was dominated by a large desk. Nakoula took a seat behind the desk, walling him off from Cindy and Armenta. He looked very small, very frail, and scruffy.

According to Cindy, Nakoula told her lawyer that he was willing to keep the 14-minute version of the video off the Internet for a price. "He then asked us what we would offer him, what amount of money could he get from us. Cris made him an offer. Sam looked so upset at the offer she made, he grabbed the paper she had handed him off the desk and said that he would think about it."

And then Cindy lost it.

"As I sat there thinking to myself, this man only cares about money, I became infuriated at him. I was holding on tightly to the arm of the chair. I wanted to jump across that desk and grab him by the throat and make him tell the truth about everything. I remember saying to him, 'Sam, how does it make you feel to know that all the Christians are being murdered because of this stinking video?' I said it again, 'how does it make you feel?' I was at the point of yelling, I was so disgusted. My attorney, Cris, said, 'Cindy, STOP!'"

She wanted to strike out at him, to do him physical harm, but instead shut her mouth. Nakoula left the room by a side door not long afterwards, kicking the cane as he walked across the parking lot.

As they drove away, Cindy's blood was just boiling. She who rarely used curse words started to swear at Nakoula. "I called the producer a very bad name and Cris looked at me and said, 'Cindy, you're right, he is a very bad man.'"

Later, Cindy referred to this incident as "dropping my fruit." It was a term Christians used when they become angry and don't act or display the love of Christ.

As Cindy started paying attention to what was happening in the Middle East and heard about the massacres of Christians taking place in Syria and northern Iraq and Egypt and elsewhere, she spent whole evenings lying in her bed, sobbing.

+++

They had another phone conversation with Nakoula and all the attorneys a few months later. The Google attorney Tim Alger was also on the line. Armenta informed Nakoula that she planned to subpoena him and his children to provide sworn video-taped depositions, and that they would be asked about the bank records as well.

Nakoula was clearly upset that his children were being dragged into the lawsuit. "If you want to subpoena them, why aren't you going to subpoena President Obama and Hillary Clinton and Susan Rice?" he asked.

Wow! Cindy thought. He had just dropped the bomb. He had just admitted that the U.S. government was involved in making the movie, just as she had suspected all along. The more she thought about it, the more worried she became that her own government might come after her. And so she began to surround herself with former military people and "Oath Keepers," who she felt could protect her.

But that wasn't what Nakoula had been trying to say at all. He hated this lawsuit. He desperately wanted it to go away, and was hoping that by ridicule maybe the Google lawyer he had met in prison would come down on these crazy women and stop them from dragging his children into it. His son and daughter were barely speaking to him. They accused him of throwing them under the bus. His son had lost a full year in college, hiding in his room so the media couldn't find him. That was the one thing he truly regretted. He had let his own family down.

"This lawyer sent me a document where she was calling Obama and Hillary Clinton and Eric Holder as witnesses in the case, and now she longer had them on her list. I was asking her why she had taken them off the list if she thought they were so important," he told me.

+++

Nakoula drove into Santa Monica on October 4, 2014 for the deposition. Armenta had insisted that Cindy stay home; she didn't want any outbursts or distractions, or for Nakoula to be able to say afterwards that he was under pressure during the deposition. While Nakoula understood and spoke English, he preferred to speak through an interpreter. As you watch him on tape, it's clear he was one unhappy camper.

Armenta was very structured in her questioning. She started by grilling him on his family and on money matters involving his children, and he seemed to become smaller and smaller, as if each question was a hammer-blow driving him beneath the table. Armenta's team had done their research. In addition to the gas station, which they now believed had been sold to fund the movie, they had discovered that Thoriya had just purchased a small apartment complex in Highland, California.

"Can you explain how it is, sir, that earlier this year your 21-year-old daughter purchased a 29-unit apartment building for one and a half million dollars, putting a million dollars down in cash?"

Nakoula said he had "no idea." He claimed not even to know where his daughter lived, although he spoke with her frequently by phone.

Armenta almost felt sorry for him. As she walked him through his criminal record, he was clearly embarrassed and tried to gloss over it as much as possible. But she wouldn't let him. She got the watered down gasoline story, the "over the counter" drug sales, and the synthetic credit card scheme all on the record. She also got him to talk about Eiad Salameh, a subject he clearly found stressful.

Finally, she got him talking about the movie, and it was like a switch went off in his brain. Here was a subject he actually wanted to talk about. It was something that made him proud.

He explained how he had starting working on the script before his arrest on the credit card scheme in 2009, then finished it while he was in jail. The original versions of the script used the actual names of the characters, Mohammad, Khadija, Aisha and Warraqa, not "Master George" or the other names Cindy was familiar with.

Nakoula insisted that he had told Cindy that the movie was about Islam. "I told her that your character – you will play the role of the mother of the young girl that Mohammed is going to marry when he is 53 years old. You will be her mother. Okay. And if you need any references, I have the references in the book.'"[15]

---

[15]   Deposition of Mark Basseley Youssef, op cit, p103-105.

He said what he had liked about Cindy was her honest feelings of disgust when he explained to her that the Prophet of Islam had actually done such a thing. As he remembered, Cindy told him, "Oh, could it be – how come – could this really happen, a guy who is 53 years old married a girl who is 9 years old?" He claims he told her, "There is no Muslim in the whole world whatsoever who can deny or say that this is not true." He came back and told it again. "I told Cindy Garcia that this guy got married to a girl who is... nine years old. And he's 53 years old. She said, 'No way.' I said, 'I have the books. I have the books.' [Cindy said]: 'Are you serious? That's gross.'"

Neither Cindy nor any of the other actors who have come forward have any recollection of such conversations, and Nakoula couldn't remember the specific circumstances or where they had occurred.

Try as she might, Armenta couldn't make head or tails of how Nakoula had financed the movie. He claimed at one point that a few small investors had each given him a few thousand dollars, but never provided any names. Whenever the subject became money, Nakoula managed to turn his testimony into mush.

Still, Armenta was pleased with the results. She had gotten him to establish on the record how he had made the movie, and to name many of the people involved. She got him to make statements about filming the movie that she would be able to corroborate or disprove later on through other witness testimony. And Nakoula proudly assumed responsibility for the movie and the aftermath, absolving the actors of any blame.

"I am the one who made the movie. I am the one who wrote that movie. The idea – it was my idea. I am the one who collected and gathered money so that this movie comes to the light and gets introduced to the whole world. So if there is any responsibility, I'll take the responsibility instead of anyone else."

What Armenta hadn't counted on was Nakoula's cunning. He claimed to have discovered in a box under his bed that he had brought to the church from his father's house after he died a CD with the recording of Cindy's dubbing session.

Armenta had listened to the CD before the deposition began and was troubled. "I don't have any way of knowing whether it is her or not," she said when she introduced it into evidence.

She didn't ask Nakoula a single question about the dubbing session during the entire four-hour deposition. That was what good lawyers did. If you didn't know the answer ahead of time, you didn't ask the question.

CHAPTER 19
WHAT IS TRUTH?

> Pilate saith unto him, What is truth? And when he had said this, he went out again unto the Jews, and saith unto them, I find in him no fault *at all*.
>
> John 18:38 (King James Bible)

On November 12, 2014, the hammer came down. The Ninth Circuit voted to re-hear the case en banc. It was a rare event for the court to question its own decisions. Even worse, their order voided the earlier opinion that Armenta had won, meaning that it could never be cited as a precedent in future cases. That was the brass ring every trial attorney aspired to reach. Now it was beyond Armenta's reach."[1]

The new hearing was scheduled for December 15, 2014 in the federal courthouse in Pasadena, California. Armenta didn't have much time to prepare.

Convinced that she had discovered a terror-linked "money-trail" to the movie, Cindy wanted to send the banking records and other documents she and Armenta had amassed in their

---

[1]   En Banc Order, Ninth Circuit of Appeals, Nov. 12, 2014, Case 12-57302. Docket 128.

investigation to the Benghazi Select Committee in Congress. She sent an initial package through a sheriff's deputy who had befriended her, but lost contact with him and was never sure if it arrived. So she sent another copy by special delivery. When she phoned the committee a few weeks later, they acknowledged that they had received it.

For several nights in a row that November, Cindy noticed heavily armed officers camped outside her home in a cul-de-sac. She felt watched, not protected. She was afraid if she took documents out of the house, they might arrest her or confiscate them. She felt she had gotten the brush off from the Benghazi committee and needed someone who could walk her information into them to get their attention.

Through friends she connected with Scott Winchell, hoping he could help. He edited a blog for Major General Paul Vallely (USA, ret.) called Stand Up America.

Scott drove up from southern California to meet her in the Bakersfield public library, and impressed Cindy right off the bat. She was carrying her .38 special because she didn't trust anyone these days. She showed him her weapon when they sat down and he smiled. "No problem," he said.

They talked for hours as Cindy not only walked him through the case but what she had discovered about "the money trail." After about five hours, her "Zello" went off. This is a cell phone app that mimics a walkie-talkie. Cindy put her caller on speaker: it was a man named Brian she had asked to stand guard for her. He was worried because she was still inside the library, and was checking in on her.

Scott smiled. "I see you have friends."

"Yes, I do," Cindy said.

Scott agreed to walk her document package into the Benghazi committee through friends of General Vallely in Washington who were members of a coalition of former military and intelligence officials, family members of the fallen and conservative reporters called the Citizens Commission on Benghazi.[2]

+++

A few days before the en banc hearing in Pasadena, I contacted Cris Armenta for the first time. She gave me a rundown of the case, and then we discussed Nakoula. "She told my client twice he was a Muslim, then denied it," she said. "Something about him is not quite right."

Armenta had come to the conclusion that Nakoula was a professional liar, in and out of federal custody for decades, a grifter. There was some evidence to suggest he was also an FBI informant, she said. "There are so many dots on the map. We need to connect them."

She had subpoena power. That got my interest, for sure. Just recently they had received bank records showing where Nakoula had gotten the money to make the film. They expected to get email and phone records as well.

But she was spooked.

Their investigation had turned up information showing what they thought was a potential terror link, which they turned over to the FBI. "There are some people involved in this who are really scary. We all have families," she said. "We have all had security breaches on our computers. My client has had people follow her. At first, I thought it was the FBI – but they said, no."

---

[2]   I took part in the early public hearings of the Citizens Commission on Benghazi until I decided to write a book with my own findings on the Benghazi attacks. We jointly agreed to segregate our investigations at that point, primarily for copyright purposes. My book, *Dark Forces: The Truth About What Happened in Benghazi* was published by a HarperCollins imprint in June 2014.

She and Cindy knew me by reputation and thought perhaps I could help them to connect the dots. But she asked that I not write anything until she got clearance from her client.

It was a breathless conversation. Was I hooked and wanted to know more?

You bet.

+++

Armenta gave me the date and time of the court hearing and said I could watch it live on the court's website, which I did.[3]

I hadn't been following the legal side of her case up to this point, and admit that the copyright arguments went beyond me. But I found Armenta impressive. She had confidence, intelligence, and class. The ten judges who showed up for the hearing grilled her extensively, trying to poke holes in her arguments. And except for one brief stumble, where one of the judges found something in Cindy's declaration Armenta had forgotten was there, she did great.

By the time it was over, though, I didn't think she had a prayer of a chance to prevail. Most of the judges openly displayed skepticism of her arguments. Several of them asked what remedy her client would have if they upheld the lower court judgment dismissing her case. That is always a bad sign.

When we spoke briefly the next day, Armenta described the courtroom scene. "Google's lawyer showed up with six people in tow who were live-tweeting in the audience," she said. "Youssef [Nakoula] showed up with the lawyer for Media for Christ. They prayed in the courtroom. And then he handed out business cards and a page from his script, trying to sell the rights!"

---

3   The hearing is archived here: http://www.ca9.uscourts.gov/media/view_video.php?pk_vid=0000006884

I suppose if Nakoula accused the actors of puffing themselves up to think of themselves as Greta Garbos, as he said in his deposition, here he was masquerading as Stephen Spielberg or John Ford.

Welcome to California!

+++

When Armenta called me the next time, two days later, she had Cindy conferenced in. She said she wanted her to "size me up" before they went any further in disclosing the results of their investigation with me.

Armenta swore like a sailor. I wondered how Cindy who was a self-described pastor must be reacting to all the profanity, but she didn't let on that it bothered her. They both thought the fact that Nakoula got out of jail in 2011 and found himself flush with cash the minute he hit the street was suspicious. Cindy now added that she had spoken with Walid Shoebat, who told her that Eyad Salameh, one of Nakoula's partners in the synthetic credit card fraud, was his first cousin. He claimed that Salameh was "a Muslim Palestinian scam artist terrorist."[4] I have seen nothing to substantiate Shoebat's claim that his cousin had terrorist or extremist ties.

Armenta said they wanted to do a book on copyright law and how the White House was assailing free speech. "This is the biggest civil rights case in years," Armenta said. "We've spent $2 million in fees over the past two years, so now it's time to see if we can make it good."

They had found a well-connected free-lance editor in New York and made a deal where they would send him a draft and

---

4   See: Walid Shoebat, "Innocence of Muslims Film was Made by Terrorists," Sept. 22, 2012.

he would turn it around into a finished book within 30 days. He was already talking to publishers. It sounded like they were very close and I wished them well.

Eric Bulock remembers they started bandying about different titles. His favorite was, "Don't be Evil." That happened to be Google's motto, taken from the Code of conduct. They changed it to "Do the Right Thing" in 2015.

"We really felt that Google had leveraged this film to assert their power on the world stage and demonstrate their ability to shape world events," Bulock said. After all, wasn't that vision enshrined in the new book Google CEO Eric Schmidt had just co-authored with former State Department visionary, Jared Cohen?

"The title tells it all," Bulock said. The book is called *The New Digital Age: Reshaping the Future of People, Nations and Business.*

+++

On February 12, 2015, the Islamic State published the seventh edition of *Dabiq,* its glossy magazine, written in English, aimed at recruiting jihadi fighters in the West. Counter-terrorism analysts read *Dabiq* closely, as it gives them precious clues to where ISIS and their allies intend to strike next. It was named after a town in northern Syria where ISIS believes a massive Islamic army will confront and defeat the infidels in an Armageddon-style battle that will spark the End of Times. With a heavy focus on Islamic ideology and purity, *Dabiq* publishes a hit list of apostate Muslim and non-Muslim leaders for the faithful to murder.

Steve Klein didn't realize he had made the ISIS hit list until the FBI showed up at his door.

In an article titled "The Obligation of Killing Those Who Mock the Messenger," the *Dabiq* authors published the photographs of Klein and Middle East scholar Daniel Pipes, and said they should suffer the same fate as Theo Van Gogh, a Dutch filmmaker who was murdered by an Islamist "fighter" for "mocking" the Muslim prophet. Muslims had a "clear-cut obligation to kill those who mock the Messenger," they said, a reference to Mohammad. They cited no fewer than seven hadiths – scriptural stories about Mohammad – that compelled Muslims to kill anyone who mocked him. Klein was a "spiteful Crusader who mocked Rasullah," the Arabic term for the "messenger of God." Pipes was "a wicked Jew who mocked Rasullah".

Klein pointed out that he lives less than 20 miles from San Bernardino, where ISIS affiliated terrorists struck later that year, and that he had identified a top Muslim Brotherhood operative in Riverside County to the local sheriff. "People laugh when I talk about the ISIS threat," he said. "But with a hit out on me from ISIS, we turned my house into an armed camp. There aren't that many husband and wife teams in California with concealed carry permits."

+++

On May 18, 2015, the Ninth Circuit en banc panel handed down its decision, and it was devastating. While the court was not insensitive to the death threats against Cindy Lee Garcia, they ruled very narrowly on whether she could demonstrate she had a copyright interest in the film, and determined that she did not.

Part of their opinion could have been written by the Obama White House. "By all accounts, Cindy Lee Garcia was bamboozled when a movie producer transformed her five-second acting performance into part of a blasphemous video proclamation against the Prophet Muhammad."[5]

Maybe it's just me, but I hadn't realized that U.S. courts were now in the business of determining blasphemy. But that's what the Ninth Circuit had just done. They essentially acknowledged the right of the Islamists to stifle speech in the United States if they felt it was insulting to their Prophet, while at the same time they condemned Cindy for seeking an injunction that amounted to "a classic prior restraint of speech... the most serious and the least tolerable infringement on First Amendment rights."

Have your cake and eat it, too.

Sometimes judges can be humorous without intending to be so.

In his dissent, Judge Paul Watford criticized his peers for crafting "new rules of copyright law," and said that instead they should have rejected Cindy's case on the much more narrow basis of "irreparable harm."

He went on to explain:

> Garcia bore the burden of showing that "irreparable injury is likely in the absence of" the requested injunction [that would have taken down the film]. The only form of injury Garcia has alleged that could qualify as irreparable is the risk of death she faces as a result of the fatwa issued against her. Unlike the majority, I'm willing to assume that the risk of death qualifies as irreparable injury in this context. But... she had to show that removing the film from YouTube would likely eliminate (or at least materially reduce) the risk of death posed by issuance of the fatwa."

---

[5] Opinion, United States Court of Appeals for the Ninth Circuit, Opinion in *Garcia v. Google et al*, 12-57302, May 18, 2015. Docket 197-1

He then provided a "reality check" to those of his colleagues who seemed to think that Muslims would be willing to forgive or forget her blasphemous performance. "The sad but unfortunate truth is that the threat posed to Garcia by issuance of the fatwa will remain whether *Innocence of Muslims* is available on YouTube or not. Garcia is subject to the fatwa because of her in role in making the film, not because the film is available on YouTube."

And that was precisely Nakoula's point in making his film about the "religion of peace." Islam was, from its founding documents, based on violence, intolerance, misogyny, and rigid sectarianism. It divided the world into us and them, the *dar al harb* ("House of War") and the *dar al Islam* ("House of Islam"). If you were a non-Muslim living in the House of War, it was the duty of good Muslims everywhere to subjugate you and bring you into the Dar al Islam, through conversion, the jizya (head tax), or by murdering you, if you refused those alternatives.

In light of the court's decision, Armenta told Cindy there was no point in pursuing the case any further. She began settlement negotiations with Nakoula and with Google's attorneys that led to them mutually agreeing to dismiss the case on June 26, 2015.

It was over, at least for Armenta and the legal team.

+++

I lost touch with Cindy and with Armenta after the appeals court hearing, and was busy on other projects when the decision came down.

That meant that the video was back up on YouTube. I must have missed the outrage bursting across the Muslim world. Where were the protests? The fiery Friday day prayer sermons calling for riots? Why weren't there new fatwas and calls for the arrest of Nakoula and everyone involved in the movie?

Had the movie somehow changed since September 12, 2012 when it first went viral? Had its message about Islam and its Prophet been toned down?

Obviously not. The only thing that had changed was this: Obama and his administration, where John Kerry had replaced Hillary Clinton and Susan Rice was now in the White House, had stopped pumping the movie. They uttered not a word about the Ninth Circuit court decision or the movie.

Without Obama and Hillary to draw worldwide attention to the "blasphemy" and "hate speech" of the movie, it was just a tree falling in a forest with no one around to hear.

That didn't mean the Muslim speech police had gone to sleep. In Garland, Texas, just two weeks before the ruling was handed down, two Muslim gunmen were killed by police when they tried to shoot their way into a Mohammad cartoon contest hosted by activists Pamela Geller and Robert Spencer that featured Dutch lawmaker, Geert Wilders – a man who had been placed under 24-hour police protect ever since he produced a short movie called *Fitna* in 2008 that explained Koranic verses on jihad.

Cindy got back in touch with me in mid-September 2015, and offered to send me all the documents she and Armenta had obtained through discovery. Her book deal had fallen through and she was looking for someone to write her story. From what they had been telling me about "the money trail" and the ties back to Middle Eastern terrorists, I was interested.

Armenta agreed to cooperate as well. The case had cost her $2 million and with the loss in the appeals court, it was time to move on. But she wanted the story to get out.

We had been talking on and off for over a year. She now sent me all the court documents in electronic format, including the bank documents, and I spent weeks going through them.

I spoke to a senior staff member on the Benghazi committee who confirmed they had received the documents Cindy had sent, but he doubted that they would follow up on it. I also spoke with the person at Judicial Watch she had sent the banking documents to, who turned them into a spreadsheet showing the money flows. He didn't think they would follow up, either. Hmm.

In January 2016, I traveled to California to meet with Cindy face to face. She brought all of her documents in the trunk of a rented car and drove down from Bakersfield to meet me in Burbank. I spread out the five battered filing boxes in the lobby of the hotel and spent an entire afternoon trying to organize the contents, to see exactly what she had. Besides the neat binders of court transcripts and filings prepared by Armenta, there were two boxes filled with loose sheets of computer printouts from the Internet in no order whatsoever. Cindy called them her research.

Cindy came from a simple background, steeped in love of God and love of country, and got thrust into a situation nothing in her life had prepared her for. I knew her case was important. But by itself, it left too many unanswered questions. I understood how easy it was to buy into conspiracy theories, and I gently tried to persuade her to let go of them, with mixed success. I explained to her that I felt her case deserved a thorough, dispassionate investigation that looked beyond what she had suffered, beyond even Nakoula and his fraud, that explored how the movie went viral and why.

That's what I have tried to do in this book.

+++

I first met Pastor Wiley Drake by chance in the spring of 2014, at a small demonstration in front of the Mexican

Embassy in Washington, DC, in support of U.S. Marine Sergeant Andrew Tahmooressi who had been arrested by the Mexican authorities for allegedly sneaking across their border with a loaded gun. (Tahmooressi claimed he had taken a wrong turn at night at the San Ysidro, California port of entry and had never intended to enter Mexico). As we got to talking, he said that the filmmaker of *Innocence of Muslims* was staying at his church, and invited me to come out and interview him.

Although Pastor Drake has an Internet television show where he talks about Islam and about Jesus, he was everything a TV evangelist was not. He wore bargain basement suits and American flag ties, and was as garrulous as the California days were long. His cramped office in the ramshackle church doubled as his TV studio. His tiny bathroom across the hall was used by everyone who visited and by many of the homeless men who lived in the flat-roofed building across the dusty parking lot, and it needed a good scrubbing. But that didn't seem to bother Pastor Drake. He was among the first on the scene when news came over the radio that an Islamist couple was shooting up a Christmas party in San Bernardino in December 2015. Without hesitation, he hopped in his small Toyota and drove the 30 miles northeast to the Valley, all the while coordinating with his lawyer, Steven Davis, a former U.S. Air Force Civil Air Patrol pilot who had worked with the CIA in the 1980s.

Davis and another staffer from the church, Lynda Jones, had been up in Riverside for a Court appearance when they heard the news, and coordinated their arrival with Drake by cell phone. "I was recognized as being a former San Bernardino deputy sheriff so I was put to work in the family holding area in the Hernandez Building in a park one mile north of the shooting site," Davis told me. In his younger years, he had been a civilian SWAT sniper, so he knew the drill as uniformed San Bernardino probation officers armed with AR-15s set up a perimeter. Pastor Drake and several other clergy were put to work counseling family members and first responders.

That's just the type of person he was. When stuff happened, he wanted to be there, counseling, praying, sharing the Lord.

As for Nakoula, he was a familiar character – familiar because of all the time I had spent in Egypt as a young reporter. It's often difficult for Americans who have not travelled or lived in the Middle East to understand the different way of approaching the truth that is common to most cultures in the region. Even Christians – and there was no doubt that Nakoula was a Coptic Christian – see truth in shades of purples and grays, not in black and white. For them, truth is like a mirage in the desert that takes on one appearance when you look at it from afar, and starts looking very different once you get closer to it and put your hands on it. To Cindy, it all just sounded like lies. I have incorporated what I learned from Nakoula over the course of a dozen conversations in this book.

Before I left, we discussed the dubbing session, which he described in some detail. "I gave them the CD with the audio," he said. "It was with my deposition."

I realized at that point that neither Cris nor Cindy had ever mentioned having that CD. It was not with the volumes of material they had sent to me, and Armenta hadn't brought it up in any of the court hearings or briefs. But Cindy had insisted again and again that she never said the words dubbed over her performance, "Your Mohammad is a child molester." Not on her life.

I arranged to meet with Cindy the next morning for breakfast at a café in Venice Beach. On a hunch, I bet the CD was still in the back of her car, attached to the inside back cover of Nakoula's deposition. I wanted to listen to it with her.

+++

I arrived at the Sidewalk Café on the boardwalk in Venice at around 9 AM, and Cindy was nowhere to be found. Neither was the other actor who had agreed to meet with us that morning. A lone couple was sitting inside the restaurant. Since it was just another Friday morning in Paradise, I hung out in the sun where I could keep an eye on things and taped a radio show I do every week.

Cindy finally showed up around an hour late. She had parked out back, so I suggested we go to her car. I told her there was a document I needed to see from Nakoula's deposition, and immediately she began talking about the CD with the dubbing as if she knew what was on my mind.

I found it exactly where I had thought it would be, and kicked myself for not seeing it before. I got into the front passenger's seat, leaving the door open because of the heat, and inserted the CD into my computer. I placed a digital voice recorder on top of the computer where she could see it, to record both the dubbing session and her reaction to it.

The woman's voice on the disk was hesitant at first as someone in the earphones coached her how to say the Arabic names.

Mo, she says.

MO!

Each time she pauses around five seconds for the person in the control room to speak another name into the earphones.

*Aisha...*comes next.

Aisha...

Ai-SHA!

She lays on the emotion, trying loss, regret, even something close to hysteria. Then she clips it so it comes out *Asia.... Asia.*

"That sounded like me right there," Cindy said twice, without looking up.

The same voice next says: *Your Mo is a child molester.*

"Your Mo?" Cindy said.

Your MOHAMMAD is a CHILD MOLESTER!

"I didn't say that. We never used those words," Cindy said quickly.

Mohammad...

Mohammad! the same voice says, seven times.

And your MO is a child molester!

"That wasn't me and that wasn't in our script," Cindy insisted.

After the voice repeats the phrase the third time, she sighs. "Yeah."

"You told me that you said 'child molester.'"

"It was in the script, the original script. Not this," she said. "When I went to this, he was feeding me lines to say and there were a bunch of people with him."

"You recognized yourself in the beginning. It's the same voice all the way through."

"I wasn't saying these things," she insisted. "I didn't say Mohammad."

And your Messenger is a child molester!

And your MESSENGER is a CHILD MOLESTER!

"Is that you?" I asked.

"He was telling me what to say."

The voice repeated the phrase.

"One of them sounded like me. And another part of it sounded like me. But the first part wasn't my voice."

I'm the only one who will be doing the fainting around here.

"That was in the original script," Cindy said.

"So is that your voice?"

"That's what I said in the script."

"Is that your voice?"

"'I'm the only one who will be doing the fainting around here,'" she tried out the phrase. The voice repeated the same words in the background. "That's my voice that you hear right now."

"There's only one voice in there."

I suggested that we listen to the whole dubbing session again from the beginning.

Mo.

MO!

"That's me," she said right off the bat this time.

"I don't hear two voices."

"I don't remember saying Mohammad."

"Did you know who Mohammad was?"

"No."

"That's probably why you don't remember saying it."

Your Mo is a child molester!

This time her face dropped in recognition of what she was hearing.

"Oh Jesus, Oh God," she said in frustration and anger.

We kept listening to it for another fifteen minutes or so. I heard only one voice, being coached to say lines she didn't understand, concentrating on saying them with different emotions. Cindy recognized herself many times, not just once. There were no perceptible breaks in the audio, nor did another voice seem to take over. It was the same sound quality from start to finish – and very different from the sound recorded on the set.

Let me be clear: Cindy did not say those words on the set. But Cindy still believes she *never* said those words, period, and that somehow the CD of the dubbing session was a trick. I believe she pushed it out of her memory because she could not bring herself to believe she had said words she later convinced herself were hateful and wrong.

"There's no crime in being ignorant, Cindy," I said.

"Yes, I was ignorant," she said. "But I'm not any more to who these people are. When I learned the things that Mohammad did, and I read verses out of the Koran, I wanted to know why they cut people's heads off. That makes me angry."

+++

Near the beginning of Nakoula's original film script, the modern-day Egyptian pharmacist, Dr. Matthew, is standing at a whiteboard, giving a lesson to his daughter.

"Man + X = Islamic terrorist," he says. "Islamic terrorist - X = Man."

The girl ponders this for awhile, seemingly confused. "What is X?" she says finally.[6]

"X" of course is the hateful ideology written into the Koran after Warraqa, the alleged author of the peaceful verses, died. It is the ideology that Muslim preachers of hate spew from their pulpits across the Islamic world every day. It is the ideology broadcast around the world in Arabic-language programs on al Jazeera television. It is the ideology that motivates the Muslim Brotherhood in Egypt, Gaza, Tunisia, Jordan, and the Sudan, and that drives Al Qaeda in Libya and Syria and beyond. It is the ideology secretly worshipped by the Muslim Brotherhood front groups that have sprung up in every major urban area in the United States over the past thirty years, masquerading – at least in English, for the dupes who refuse to believe what they are saying in Arabic – as a religion of peace. The same ideology spawned ISIS and the Taliban, and has plunged Iran, homeland to a great civilization that once freed the Jewish captives from Babylon and codified human rights, into thirty-seven years of darkness under the guise of an "Islamic Republic."

---

[6]   *Desert Warrior*, by Unknown. Feb. 25, 2011 version. Available here: http://www.vice.com/read/here-is-what-we-believe-to-be-the-final-2011-screenplay-for-innocence-of-muslims

Nakoula's goal from the start had been to expose "X," to dramatize how it all began in the sands of Arabia more than 1,400 years ago. While his effort was cartoonish, caricatural, even grotesque, it was not false. It was Monty Python meets the Koran, without the laughs.

His mentor, the well-known Coptic Bishop Zacharias Boutros Henein, published a commentary when the firestorm over *Innocence of Muslims* erupted. While he did not condone the movie, he wrote, the "offenses depicted in the movie are extracted from the Islamic books. No one appreciates such provocative scenes, they are offensive and unnecessary, yet the real problem is that they are consistent with the story of Mohammad as revealed in the authoritative Islamic literature. The movie is alarming because the life it depicts is so removed from our expectations of religious figures. Examining the lives of historical public figures in itself is not a crime."[7]

Is it blasphemy to speak about another religion in a way members of that religion find distasteful? Does anyone reading this book want to live in a country where their words will be dissected not just by political thought police, but by blasphemy inspectors as well?

"Wake up!" the Egyptian pharmacist and his children scream at the end of Nakoula's film.

"Wake up!
"Wake up!
"Wake up!"
"Wake up all of you!"[8]

---

[7]   Fr. Zakaria Statement concerning his relationship to the making of Mohamed movie," Sept. 2012. Available at http://www.fatherzakaria. net.

[8]   *Desert Warrior*, 2011 version, op cit.

AFTERWORD
IRAN'S INVOLVEMENT IN BENGHAZI

As I was writing this book, I continued to pursue my investigation of Iran's involvement in the Benghazi attacks, a story I first brought to light in my 2014 book, *Dark Forces: The Truth About Benghazi.*

While I had multiple sources at the time, key sources had requested that I protect their identities, including two defectors from Iranian intelligence who unmasked the individual commanders from the Islamic Revolutionary Guards Corps-Quds Force I named in the book. They were the ones on the ground in Benghazi responsible for recruiting, training, equipping, and directing the terrorists who carried out the September 11, 2012 attacks that killed Ambassador Chris Stevens, communications officer Sean Smith, and U.S. Navy Seals Ty Woods and Glen Doherty.

Another source who was then on active duty in an intelligence billet requested that I identify him in vague terms. He has since retired and has now allowed me to reveal that he was a Brigadier General with U.S. Special Operations Command who headed a dedicated intelligence unit in support of overseas deployed troops at the time of the Benghazi attacks. His position required that he maintain active "liaison" relations with fellow intelligence officers from allied countries from NATO, Israel, and a dozen Arab countries.

Even more significant was the partial release by the Defense Intelligence Agency of a highly classified memorandum in response to a tasking order from the Director of the Defense Intelligence Agency, General, Michael T. Flynn, in March 2016.

In the immediate aftermath of the September 11, 2012 attacks, General Flynn wanted to find out what various defense intelligence entities (not just the DIA) knew about Iran's involvement in the attack. So General Flynn asked his intelligence commanders to provide "an assessment of the tactics employed in- al Qaida's reaction to- and the level of Iran's Islamic Revolutionary Guard Corps Quds force (IRGC-QF) involvement in the U.S. Mission in Benghazi attack on 11 September."

The redacted nine-page memorandum in response to General Flynn's tasking order was obtained by the public interest group Judicial Watch in response to a Freedom of Information Act request. They gave it to me for further analysis.[1]

It was stamped "Top Secret/NOFORN," meaning that it contained some of the most classified intelligence information available to U.S. policy-makers. It was also stamped "SCI CONTROL," which means that the contents included "Sensitive Compartmented Information" that came from human sources, defectors, highly-classified communications intercepts, or other "special access" programs.

The SCI stamp is often referred to as "above TOP SECRET" clearance material.

---

[1]   I have posted it here: http://kentimmerman.com/IOMdocs/ 2012_09_21-DIA-Iran-Benghazi.pdf

General Flynn confirmed the existence of his tasking order and the response memo obtained by Judicial Watch in a phone interview and a subsequent email exchange. "I wasn't surprised" by the contents of the memo, General Flynn told me. The information on the Iranian Quds Force presence in Benghazi, and their involvement in the September 11 attacks, was "very predictable behavior based on previous experiences."

+++

The release of this memo, and General Flynn's confirmation of its authenticity, is a hugely significant event, since it changes the whole narrative of what the government has told us about Benghazi.

First, as I have hammered home in this book, President Obama and Secretary of State Hillary Clinton wanted Americans to believe that angry protesters stormed the diplomatic facility in Benghazi after watching an "inflammatory movie" over the Internet. While it took some weeks for the media and Congress to expose that deception, we now know without a doubt that it was simply not true.

Next, we were supposed to believe that an "organized attack" by unknown and unnamed terrorists led to the deaths of four Americans that night, but that our intelligence community just couldn't put their finger on who they were.

The name of a local jihadi group called Ansar al Sharia was kicked about, and possibly others. In the nearly four years since the attacks, just one suspected participant has been arrested and brought to the United States for trial. Several others "disappeared" in Libya and were presumably assassinated by U.S. Special Operations forces or local allies.

But even this version had been sterilized, rendered "politically correct," to suit the agenda of the Obama administration. Who can forget Mrs. Clinton running down the usual suspects during a Congressional hearing in January 2013, before throwing up her hands and saying, "What difference, at this point, does it make?" who killed four Americans that night.

Sources on the Benghazi Select Committee said they interviewed General Flynn about DIA's post-attack analysis and other matters for more than four hours.

"If this document lays out the details of Iran's involvement, then effectively it could turn Benghazi into a state-sponsored terrorist attack," former CIA Director Jim Woolsey told me. "That would significantly change the perception of what we have believed up until now about Benghazi."

If Congress or the American public had known that Iran was involved – not just involved, but was *instrumental* in carrying out the attacks – how might they have reacted when the president and his new Secretary of State, John Kerry, first broached the deeply flawed Iran nuclear deal, officially known as the Joint Comprehensive Plan of Action (JCPOA) one year after Benghazi?

Do you think for an instant the president would have been able to convince Congress to forego its powers to "advise and consent" on the Treaty he had negotiated? Do you think that even this president would have been able to promote a huge giveaway deal with Iran if Americans had known that Iran was behind one of the most spectacular terrorist attacks against the United States since 9/11?

The U.S. military has crossed swords with Iran's Quds Force in Iraq, Syria, Lebanon, Libya, Afghanistan, and Yemen. In the 1980s, the Quds Force trained Hezbollah in Lebanon to carry out the attacks against the U.S. Embassy and the U.S. Marines in Beirut, killing 241 Marines and 63 diplomats and intelligence officers. They kidnapped the CIA Station Chief, William Buckley, and tortured him to death, and took countless hostages in Lebanon. Since 2006, they have been shipping Explosively Formed Penetrators to local terrorist proxies in Afghanistan and Iraq that have been used to kill hundreds of U.S. servicemen. Information on these confrontations has surfaced in lawsuits against Iran brought by terror victims and, over the past decade, in Congressional testimony by senior U.S. military and intelligence officials, including former Central Intelligence Agency director, General David Petraeus.

In Yemen, the Quds Force used a similar tactic to what the DIA identified as their *modus operandus* in Benghazi: infiltrating a para-military operations team into a hostile environment under cover of the humanitarian aide workers for the Red Crescent Society, the Muslim equivalent of the Red Cross.

General Flynn confirmed to me that he was aware that Iran had used the Red Crescent society for intelligence operations in other theaters as well as Libya. "The Red Crescent Society? Oh yeah, you bet we were following them," he said.[2]

+++

Most Americans have never heard of the Red Crescent Society. It is actually governed by the same international board that governs the Red Cross, but it works solely in Muslim countries. It has also been unmasked repeatedly as a front for terrorist organizations, most egregiously in the Gaza Strip, where Hamas guerilla fighters regularly use brightly marked Red Crescent ambulances, meant to carry the wounded, to ferry terrorist fighters and munitions.

Iran's Quds Force has exploited the benefits of Red Crescent cover for intelligence work and terrorist operations

---

[2]   See Kenneth R. Timmerman, "The Iranian Connection to the Benghazi attacks," *Washington Times*, March 21, 2016.

repeatedly.

Here's what happened in Benghazi.

A seven-man Red Crescent team from Iran arrived in Benghazi, Libya on July 30, 2012, ostensibly to provide humanitarian aide to the post-Qaddafi revolutionary regime.

The secret CIA Annex operating in Benghazi had been tipped off about their arrival and dispatched a team of local "watchers" to track their movements, according to Dylan Davies, a British security contractor in charge of the local guards protecting the diplomatic facility in Benghazi.

As the Red Crescent team moved about Benghazi that after noon, the CIA Chief of Base in Benghazi received a steady stream of reports. "Everyone knew the Iranians were in Benghazi," a former CIA security officer told me. "Especially once the Red Cross [Red Crescent] team from Iran was 'kidnapped' by Ansar al-Sharia, we knew about them and were tracking them."

Here was the problem: the Iranians had learned, through their own spies, that the CIA was onto them. So they devised a masterful deception operation to throw the U.S. spies off track.

When the Iranians returned to the Tibesti Hotel at 1 AM on July 31 after a late night Ramadan dinner feast, they were ambushed by a half-dozen Toyota pickups, known as "technicals," with .50-caliber machine guns mounted on the beds. The militiamen "kidnapped" the Iranians and took them to an undisclosed location. The kidnapping was reported in the Libyan press as the result of a "sectarian" feud between local Sunni militiamen and the Iranian Shiite medical team.

But General Flynn and the DIA knew that was not true.

"The kidnapping of the Red Crescent team in Benghazi was a false flag operation," the now retired U.S. special operations intelligence support officer said. "They were actually Quds Force operatives. The kidnapping was arranged to make it look like they were being taken hostage, when actually they were being taken off the street so they could covertly direct the attack on the U.S. compound."

The goal of the Iranians in attacking the two U.S. facilities in Benghazi was to "shut down the aid to pro-Western rebels in Syria coming from Libya and to punish the United States for meddling in what they saw as their sphere of influence," he said.

Several foreign intelligence agencies with "liaison" relationships with the United States had operatives on the ground in Benghazi that night, including Turkey, Jordan, Israel, Qatar, Saudi Arabia, Great Britain, and France.

"We know from liaison relationships that the Iranian Quds Force team in Benghazi was helping to prepare the attack on the diplomatic facility," the flag officer added.

"The Iranians did the training. They organized the militia. It was a military attack, not your typical terrorist attack. The mortar fire was very accurate. They taught the militia how to zero in the mortars. They set up sophisticated surveillance of the consulate – and they did it all while they were 'hostages,'" he said.

All of this information was reported "up the food chain" by the CIA Chief of Base in Benghazi, who was a former U.S. Army officer. "He was later told, don't talk about the Iranian connection, with threat of sanction," the flag officer said.

General Flynn said that the information reported back to him about the Quds Force involvement in the Benghazi attacks was widely distributed. But only consumers down the food chain "reacted appropriately," whereas those up the chain did not.

Those who refused to acknowledge the information on Iran's involvement in the Benghazi attacks included the Chairman of the Joint Chiefs of Staff General Martin Dempsey, Secretary of Defense Leon Panetta, Secretary of State Hillary

Clinton, President Obama, and the Congressional intelligence committees.

I first learned about the Red Crescent operational team in Benghazi from two defectors from Iranian intelligence I had been known for years. I reported their information in *Dark Forces: the Truth About What Happened in Benghazi*.[3]

They claimed that a courier carrying between $8 million to $10 million in 500-Euro notes arrived three weeks before the attack, and that a senior Quds Force operative, Ibrahim Mohammad Joudaki, distributed the money to Ansar al-Sharia leaders controlled by Iran. One of my sources provided a bank transfer document showing a $2.5 million payment to an Iranian front company in Benghazi a year before the Benghazi attacks. The money came from an Iranian Revolutionary Guards money-laundering network that was subsequently blacklisted by the U.S. Treasury Department.

The Iranian defectors also identified a senior Hezbollah operative, Khalil Harb, as playing a key role. "As an Arab [from Lebanon], he could interface directly with the local militias," one of the defectors said. "He handled the logistics" of the operation. The U.S. Treasury also black-listed Harb after the Benghazi attacks, but focused on his terrorist activities in Yemen, not Libya.[4]

Multiple intelligence and operations officers as at U.S.-Africa Command (AFRICOM) in Stuttgart have acknowledged in interviews that Africom had an "ongoing awareness" of the Iranian Quds Force presence in Benghazi and elsewhere in Eastern Libya. Among them is Lieutenant Colonel Andrew Wood, the chief of the 18-man Site Security Team assigned to guard Ambassador Chris Stevens at the U.S. Embassy in Tripoli.

---

[3]   http://kentimmerman.com/darkforces.htm
[4]   See: http://www.treasury.gov/press-center/press-releases/Pages/jl2147.aspx

After seeing a PowerPoint graphic from Africom headquarters that showed Iranian influence flowing into Libya, Colonel Wood sent an email back to his commander, Rear Admiral Brian Losey, asking for additional support. "Sir, Ansar al-Sharia has had their funding approved," he wrote.

Colonel Wood said in an interview he understood that the Iranians Quds Force operatives who had deployed to Libya to train Ansar al-Sharia, the group later identified as involved in the Benghazi attacks, had "gotten authorization to bring their dependents" to Benghazi. That information, which he learned at a June 2012 security briefing at the U.S. Embassy in Tripoli, triggered his email to Admiral Losey for additional support.[5]

+++

I called the effort to pin the blame for Benghazi on a YouTube video Hillary Clinton's "original spin." With this new information documenting Iran's involvement in the attacks, the media sideshow created by Mrs. Clinton and President Obama around the video becomes even more sinister.

---

[5] A 2014 AFRICOM Command Brief that was recently declassified includes a flow chart similar to what Colonel Wood described of foreign influence in Africa. It shows one line of "weapons and fighters" flowing from Iran into Somalia and Kenya, and a separate supply line flowing from Iran into Egypt. AFRICOM has not released the earlier command brief for 2012 that Colonel Wood described with the flow line of fighters and weapons from Iran into Libya.

ACKNOWLEDGEMENTS

I am grateful to the encouragement of Anthony Ziccardi at Post Hill Press as I embarked on this project. Without his help, and the enterprising crew at Post Hill Press led by managing editor Hannah Yancey, readers would not have had this information in time to make a difference for the 2016 elections.

This book would not have been possible without the dedicated cooperation of many of the participants in the *Innocence of Muslims* debacle, to whom I owe a debt of gratitude. After a year of intermittent exchanges, I spent another six months non-stop with Cindy Lee Garcia on the phone, via email and in person, going over the events that so dramatically changed her life.

Her lawyer, Cris Armenta, was extremely generous with her time and has a wicked sense of humor in addition to being a very classy litigator. Thanks also to assistant Heather Rowland who extracted documents buried deep in the files, and to Eric Bulock of DMCA Solutions, Inc., who helped track down buried YouTube torrents and Internet archives and was always ready to answer my questions.

Filmmaker Nakoula Basseley Nakoula decided to trust me when so many other journalists had betrayed him in the past. Without his help, this would have been a one-sided story that would have left far too many questions unanswered. My appreciation also to Pastor Wiley Drake for his ministry and his unwavering dedication to our country and to our freedoms, and for introducing me to his extraordinary chief of security-cum-lawyer extraordinaire, Colonel Steve Davis. I look forward to close quarters firearms training the next time I'm out your way. Thanks also to Steve Klein, Gaylord Flynn, Jeff Robinson, Morris Sadek, and Nabil Bissada for sharing your stories to help round out this picture.

I never would have gotten started down the path of doing this book without the persistent prodding of Paul Webb, a "simple reader" who took the initiative of contacting me after reading *Dark Forces* in 2014, and who urged me to do a more thorough investigation of how *Innocence of Muslims* was made and went viral. While I do not share his conclusion that the film was made by the U.S. government, I have laid out evidence in this book supporting the conclusion that the movie never would have caused the damage attributed to it without the relentless promotion of the Obama administration.

Judicial Watch has played a pivotal role in forcing the State Department and other government agencies to release crucial documents about Benghazi and deserves the thanks of all Americans. JW's Sean Dunagan helped to analyze the banking documents I describe in this book, and turned to me for analysis when Judicial Watch acquired the DIA document on Iran's involvement in Benghazi described in the *Afterword*.

A hearty thanks to all those who continue to seek the truth about the Benghazi attacks: Roger Aronoff and Charles Woods, father of fallen U.S. Navy Seal Ty Woods, and the Citizens Commission on Benghazi; Rep. Trey Gowdy and the members of the Benghazi Select Committee; Col. Dennis Haney, Col. Dick Brauer, Captain Larry Bailey, Colonel Ken Benway, and LTG Jerry Boykin and Special Operations Speaks. Rest assured, the truth will out.

And a special thanks to those individuals who supported this project via GoFundMe.com. In this Obama economy, I appreciate the sacrifices you made and your dedication to getting this story out.

ABOUT THE AUTHOR

Ken Timmerman is a nationally recognized investigative reporter and war correspondent who was nominated for the Nobel Peace prize in 2006. He is the *New York Times* bestselling author of 10 books on national security issues, as well as the critical biography, *Shakedown: Exposing the Real Jesse Jackson*. His work is regularly featured at the *Daily Caller*, *FrontPage* magazine, and other conservative online websites. He has written for *Reader's Digest*, the *American Spectator*, *USA Today*, the *Washington Times*, *Time*, *Newsweek*, the *Wall Street Journal*, and the *New York Times,* and lectures on Iran at the Pentagon's Joint Counter-Intelligence Training Academy, JCITA.

Famed Nazi-hunter Simon Wiesenthal said of Ken, "I have spent my life tracking the murderer's of yesterday. Mr. Timmerman is tracking the murderers of tomorrow."

To schedule appearances, please email Ken directly: kentimmerman@comcast.net